iPad®

in Education

FOR

DUMMIES®

iPad®
in Education
FOR
DUMMIES®

by Sam Gliksman

WILEY

John Wiley & Sons, Inc.

iPad® in Education For Dummies®

004.165
G49I
2013

Published by
John Wiley & Sons, Inc.
111 River Street
Hoboken, NJ 07030-5774
www.wiley.com

Copyright © 2013 by John Wiley & Sons, Inc., Hoboken, New Jersey

Published by John Wiley & Sons, Inc., Hoboken, New Jersey

Published simultaneously in Canada

For general information on our other products and services, please contact our Customer Care Department within the U.S. at 877-762-2974, outside the U.S. at 317-572-3993, or fax 317-572-4002.

For technical support, please visit www.wiley.com/techsupport.

Wiley publishes in a variety of print and electronic formats and by print-on-demand. Some material included with standard print versions of this book may not be included in e-books or in print-on-demand. If this book refers to media such as a CD or DVD that is not included in the version you purchased, you may download this material at http://booksupport.wiley.com. For more information about Wiley products, visit www.wiley.com.

Library of Congress Control Number: 2012954762

ISBN: 978-1-118-37538-9 (pbk); ISBN 978-1-118-41727-0 (ebk); ISBN 978-1-118-42075-1 (ebk); ISBN 978-1-118-43544-1 (ebk)

Manufactured in the United States of America

10 9 8 7 6 5 4 3 2 1

WILEY

Praise for iPad in Education For Dummies

With this important contribution, there are no more excuses for iPad carts to be unused or misused in schools around the world. Sam Gliksman has made a worthy contribution to our students by writing a guide that will quickly become every teacher's new best friend. Written in clear, easy-to-follow steps, the author walks educators through setting up iPads for student use, highlights key apps that will transform your students' learning into a highly experiential and participatory journey, explains how to use iPads for multimedia content delivery, and so much more. The perfect blend of "tech how-to" and pedagogy!

Michelle Pacansky-Brock, Author of Best Practices for Teaching with Emerging Technologies

Sam Gliksman achieves something often missing in "How To" books: He combines a powerful educational vision with down-home practicality. It allows the reader to understand both "Why?" and "How?" For those who believe that education is the essential infrastructure for a successful society, this book serves as the essential explanation of that infrastructure tool, the Apple iPad, which now serves as a primary pathway for education in the 21st century.

Dr. Bruce Powell, Head of School, New Community Jewish High School, West Hills, CA

From large-scale institutional deployment to classroom-level and individual usage, this book is bursting with useful tips, techniques, strategies, and reminders. You're learning from the best: Gliksman's longtime expertise with iPads in schools makes this an extremely valuable resource for any educator using iPads with his or her students.

Scott McLeod, Associate Professor and Founding Director, CASTLE, University of Kentucky

Who better to write the every-teacher book on iPads in the classroom than the person who coined the term *iPads in Education*, which by no coincidence is also the name of his popular iPad social networking site. Sam Gliksman took what could have been a "tap here, tap there" topic and created a professional development book that explains how to effectively integrate one-to-one tablet technology in the classroom. Gliksman excels at explaining both simple and advanced topics without talking down to the beginner or making the advanced user feel bored. This is not just a "tips" book. Be prepared to have your iPad handy when reading as you will find yourself saying over and over, "I didn't know about that feature or app." The book provides a thoughtful list of topics, which can be read in any order, making it ideal for continuing education workshops with individual teachers and their diverse learning goals. Reading and interacting with *iPad in Education For Dummies* is the next best thing to inviting Mr. Gliksman to your school for a week of processional development.

David Wicks, Assistant Professor, Director of Instructional Technology, Seattle Pacific University

About the Author

Sam Gliksman has been a leading educator specializing in technology applications for more than two decades. He has worked in educational and commercial enterprises, having founded and managed a leading software company for many years. He is currently the Director of Educational Technology at a prestigious Los Angeles High School while also acting as an independent educational technology consultant to a number of K–12 schools and organizations.

Sam is recognized as a prominent expert on technology and educational reform and has been very active in promoting the use of mobile technology in education. As a consultant, he works with small and large schools as well as school districts and foreign governments, most recently having been invited to meet and personally consult with the Prime Minister of Greece.

Sam founded and blogs for the extremely popular "iPads in Education" website (http://ipadeducators.ning.com) that has an active membership of many thousands of educators worldwide. A dynamic speaker, he lectures at national and international conferences as well as giving insightful educational workshops about the use of technology and its potential for reforming education. Dedication

So much of whatever I have accomplished would never have been possible without the help and support of my wife and soulmate, Debbie. This book is dedicated to her and my three wonderful children who I adore — Lianna, Yoni, and Daniel. I'm so very proud of all of you.

Author's Acknowledgments

Special thanks to everyone at Wiley: Kyle for asking me to write the book and keeping me (almost) on schedule; Nicole for being an amazingly patient and supportive editor; and Debbye and Dennis for their constructive comments. Thanks also to everyone else at Wiley who I may not know by name but who helped get this book published.

Thanks to Randy, Julie, Leah, Lisa, and all the other wonderful educators for contributing their creative lesson plans for using iPads in class.

Thanks to Deb for proofreading my writing, correcting my ramblings, and helping to identify my "Australianisms". A huge thanks to our dear friend Nurit for dropping everything to come help on the very last, crazy night.

Finally, thanks to the very special family with which I have been blessed, both here in the United States and back in Australia. You've always been supportive, and this book would never have been written without your love and encouragement.

Publisher's Acknowledgments

We're proud of this book; please send us your comments at http://dummies.custhelp.com. For other comments, please contact our Customer Care Department within the U.S. at 877-762-2974, outside the U.S. at 317-572-3993, or fax 317-572-4002.

Some of the people who helped bring this book to market include the following:

Acquisitions, Editorial

Sr. Project Editor: Nicole Sholly

Acquisitions Editor: Kyle Looper

Copy Editor: Debbye Butler

Technical Editors: Dennis Cohen, Michael Wells

Editorial Manager: Kevin Kirschner

Editorial Assistant: Leslie Saxman

Sr. Editorial Assistant: Cherie Case

Cover Photo: © Yunus Arakon/iStockphoto.com. Image of iPad photographed by Wiley Creative Services.

Cartoons: Rich Tennant (www.the5thwave.com)

Composition Services

Project Coordinator: Katie Crocker

Layout and Graphics: Jennifer Creasey, Christin Swinford

Proofreaders: Jessica Kramer, Kathy Simpson

Indexer: BIM Indexing & Proofreading Services

Publishing and Editorial for Technology Dummies

    Richard Swadley, Vice President and Executive Group Publisher

    Andy Cummings, Vice President and Publisher

    Mary Bednarek, Executive Acquisitions Director

    Mary C. Corder, Editorial Director

Publishing for Consumer Dummies

    Kathleen Nebenhaus, Vice President and Executive Publisher

Composition Services

    Debbie Stailey, Director of Composition Services

Contents at a Glance

Table of Contents

Introduction

Back in 2010, the first iPad was sold at the Apple flagship store in New York City. Its release was heralded with heady anticipation and excitement. Apple had done it again! Although it was not the first tablet computer to hit the market, it quickly became the one to define it. Within a couple of short years, iPad sales into schools have soared above MacBook sales by a margin of 2:1. That demand comes partly from the overall popularity of iPads, but it also stems from the recognition that technology has the potential to revitalize our educational systems.

The iPad and its mini counterpart are light and easy to carry; intuitive to use; and, best of all, relatively inexpensive. However, be careful about putting the iPad cart before the horse. If we expect the iPad to be an agent of change, it's important that technology use serves our greater educational vision and doesn't become an objective in itself. The only time "computer" should come before "education" is in the dictionary.

Mobile technology can be used to re-envision education. That's the goal of this book. Its pages include loads of "how to" information, but along the way I try to address the question of "why" we use technology in class as well. Rather than using iPads to deliver and drill content, we should strive to empower students to create, investigate, and innovate. In doing so, we encourage students to develop the skills they'll require to become lifelong learners who can thrive in our exponentially changing world.

Feeling a little overwhelmed? Don't be. You've already made the first important step by buying this informative and easy-to-read book. Just stick with me, and I will guide you through the wonderful and exhilarating world of iPad use in education.

About iPads in Education For Dummies

You've seen what kids look like when they handle an iPad. With little hesitation, they jump right in, and within minutes they start drawing, reading, or finding some other activity that motivates and engages them. It's their canvas, and given the freedom to explore and express themselves, students can be wonderfully creative and imaginative with technology.

Albert Einstein once wrote, "It is a miracle that curiosity survives formal education. If we are to develop our students' sense of curiosity, we must be mindful to carve out time to allow our students to inquire and explore."

This book examines ways you can use iPads to unlock some of those possibilities in educational settings.

Here are some of the things you can do with this book:

- Learn how to use iPads to address 21st-century skills and literacies
- Discover techniques to manage a classroom of iPads
- Learn how to find and purchase apps for yourself or in volume
- Learn how to use the built-in multimedia tools for digital storytelling and creative expression
- Explore ways the iPad can be used to explore, investigate, and create
- Learn how technology can be used to empower and engage students
- Discover ways other teachers are using iPads innovatively in their classrooms

Conventions Used in This Book

I use a few specific conventions in this text for ease of comprehension. When I tell you to type something (in a box or a field, for example), I put it in **bold.** When I refer to text that you see onscreen, I put it in a typeface that `looks like this`. Terms in *italics* are defined as they relate to using the iPad in the classroom. And when I provide a URL, it looks like this:

`www.dummies.com/go/ipadineducationfdupdates`

What You Don't Have to Read

You don't have to read this book sequentially, and you don't even have to read all the sections in any particular chapter. You can skip sidebars and just read the material that helps you complete the task at hand.

You'll find chapters devoted to specific themes ranging from digital storytelling to sciences. Feel free to jump around and read whatever sections have the most relevance for you.

Foolish Assumptions

You know what happens when you assume . . . but as an author, I have to make certain assumptions about you, my readers, in order to target the book to your needs:

- You either own or are considering buying an iPad. The principles discussed in the book apply whether you have the original iPad or the latest iPad or iPad mini. You will, however, need an iPad 2 or higher to take advantage of the advice and directions regarding multimedia use.
- You are not a "techie." This is a book about education written for teachers, administrators, parents, and anyone else who has an interest in education.
- You have access to a wireless Internet connection.
- You know technology can be used effectively as an educational tool, but you just aren't sure how . . . and the thought of a classroom full of children with iPads scares you just a teensy bit.
- You're looking for new and exciting ways to engage and motivate your students.

How This Book Is Organized

iPad in Education For Dummies is split into seven parts. I know your teacher always told you to read a book from start to finish, but this is one book you don't have to read sequentially. You don't have to read all the sections in any particular order. It won't even ruin the plot if you read it back to front. There's no surprise ending (although I guarantee you won't want to miss the Appendix). You can use the Table of Contents and the index to skip to the information you need and quickly get an answer. Really, I promise you won't get a detention.

In this section, I briefly describe what you'll find in each part.

Part I: Meeting the Educational iPad

Part I covers the basics of iPad use and how it fits into a 21st-century educational landscape. You'll get acquainted with the basic functions on your shiny new iPad, and learn how to tap and swipe and pinch your way around it. I also cover some of the options for managing a classroom full of iPads.

Part II: Finding and Using Apps

In Part II, I show you how to use the apps that come preloaded on your iPad. You take a look at them with educationally tinted glasses. You'll discover how to take photos and shoot video; buy, read, and annotate e-books; and find and organize information, among other things. I help you navigate through the veritable ocean of additional apps in the App Store to find, evaluate, and purchase the ones that meet your needs.

Part III: Finding and Organizing Educational Content

Remember how your mom taught you the importance of keeping your room clean and sharing? (Your mom was right — as usual!) Part III shows you how to use your iPad to find and organize content on the Internet, and how to use social networking tools to share content with others. You can get rid of those piles of clippings and printouts when you discover how to organize all your content neatly and efficiently right on your iPad and to upload and share it across different platforms.

Part IV: Exploring Applications for Digital Reading and Writing

Part IV takes a peek at how the e-book revolution is changing the way we read. Whether it's the emergence of highly produced book apps, e-books that you can order through the Apple iBookstore, or apps for Amazon's Kindle (and other e-readers), I show you how to find and order whatever you like reading and have it in your hands within seconds.

I also explain how to create, edit, and annotate your own documents — whether your preference is to type on the virtual keyboard, use a physical keyboard, or break out a stylus and hand-write the "old-fashioned" way. You can even record classes and coordinate the sound to play back in sync with your notes. For the more enterprising among you, I take you on a stroll through some options for creating your own digital e-book.

I take a look at how iPads can be used as a tool for inquiry, data collection, and analysis in math and science, and review some model lessons from teachers.

Last, I discuss how to use assistive technologies to help students with physical challenges such as vision and hearing impairments.

Part V: Expressing Yourself with Media

Get out your director's chair and megaphone. Part V is all about harnessing your creativity for digital storytelling. From creating storyboards to narrating and producing iMovies, puppet shows, and animations — you'll do it all. I also show you how to produce podcasts and screencasts, and release your inner artist with some terrific tools for all ages. And I promise you won't have any brushes to clean afterward, either!

Part VI: The iPad Classroom

Printing, photocopying, presenting, using your whiteboard . . . you know there's a better way, and I show you some exciting alternatives you can start using immediately! Create a digital whiteboard, and share it with others. Record snippets of your lessons for later review. You have a range of options. Try them out!

Part VII: The Part of Tens

I save the best for last. Part VII begins with a chapter of essential apps for any educator. You won't want to miss it.

Any iPad implementation requires some fundamental building blocks. I give you ten key elements that are required for any successful iPad program.

Appendix

The Appendix takes you into a few actual classrooms where I have invited some creative educators to contribute their most innovative lesson plans using iPads.

Icons Used in This Book

What's a *For Dummies* book without icons pointing you in the direction of really great information that's sure to help you along your way? In this section, I briefly describe each icon I use in this book.

The Tip icon points out helpful information that is likely to make your job easier.

 This icon marks a general interesting and useful fact — something that you might want to remember for later use.

The Warning icon highlights lurking danger. When you see this icon, pay attention, and proceed with caution.

When you see this icon, you know that there's techie stuff nearby. If you aren't feeling very techie, you can skip this info.

Where to Go from Here

This book can be read in any order you choose. Each chapter stands on its own and can help you tackle specific tasks. For example, if you have just started thinking about using the iPad in your classroom but don't know where to begin, head to Part I. Your first stop might be to read the Table of Contents and use it repeatedly to find the sections of this book that you need at various times.

Occasionally, John Wiley & Sons, Inc., has updates to its technology books. If this book has technical updates, they will be posted at www.dummies.com/go/ipadineducationfdupdates.

Part I

Meeting the Educational iPad

The 5th Wave   By Rich Tennant

©RICHTENNANT

"I build bookshelves and Bernice buys an iPad."

In this part . . .

Part I covers the basics of iPad use and how iPads fit into a 21st-century classroom. I show you the basic functions of the iPad, including how to tap and swipe and pinch your way around it. I also discuss some of the options for managing a classroom full of iPads.

1

Education in the 21st Century

In This Chapter

▶ Re-evaluating educational objectives for a world of constant change

▶ Examining how iPads meet the needs of a 21st-century education

▶ Reviewing what this book is — and is not

*I*t's nine and a half inches long and only one third of an inch thick. At less than a pound and a half', it can go anywhere with you. It boasts a crystal-clear display, has a microphone and two cameras, and is a great little device for taking photos and video. Whether you prefer to prop it up on a table or lay it in your lap, just tap a button, and you'll instantly connect with people and information anywhere on the planet. Yes, the iPad is the face of modern technology . . . and given the opportunity, technology such as the iPad has the potential to revitalize our educational systems.

Investigating New Educational Models

We've come a long way in such a short time. Many of us grew up in an age of relative stability. Personal computing was still in its infancy, and we'd never heard of anything called the Internet. If you wanted to communicate with your cousin in another country, you'd pull out a pen and paper, write a letter, slap on a stamp, and walk to the nearest mailbox. Imagine that! Welcome to the 21st century, where we find ourselves launched into the beginnings of a new era characterized by extreme, exponential change. The fuel that's feeding that change is technology. Computers have evolved from massive machines that weighed several tons and required several people to operate them to sleek, super-powerful, tiny devices that perform incredibly complex tasks and move information between remote locations at lightning speed. Fifty years ago, people were amazed at being able to deliver a heavily abbreviated message overseas in a telegram that might arrive at its destination a day later. Nowadays, kids complain that e-mail takes too long! The mobile devices we carry around in our pockets today are thousands of times more powerful than those enormous computers were just a few decades ago.

Of course, change isn't a new concept, but it's the amazing speed at which society is changing that takes your breath away. Inventions such as the telephone and radio took generations to become common household items, yet after just a few short years, iPods, iPhones, and iPads have sold several hundred million units. A service such as Facebook didn't even exist ten years ago; now it has a user base approaching a billion. We just reached seven billion people on planet Earth, and there are more than five billion cellphone subscriptions.

Re-evaluating educational objectives in a changing world

Technology has changed almost every facet of our daily life — at work, home, and leisure. Given the right opportunity, it can also transform our educational systems; however, our school systems have largely struggled to keep pace. Take a stroll around many schools today, and they look largely the same as they did when you went to school. The problem is twofold:

- **Lacking technology:** Students lead technology-filled lives outside school, yet many of them have only minimal access to personal technology for learning within school itself.

- **Using technology for a 20th-century education:** Simply adding a dose of technology to the standard educational mix may not be enough if that technology is used to reinforce outdated objectives and practices.

The incredibly rapid changes occurring all around us are having a significant impact on the skills students need when they graduate school. Old models of content delivery and *frontal teaching* (lecturing from the front of the classroom) aren't addressing the evolving needs of a society where information is available freely and instantly, and constantly changing. The technology revolution that encompasses us has changed all our educational paradigms. We need to consider iPad use within the framework of educational objectives that address the needs of our rapidly changing society:

- **Replacing rote memorization with real skills:** Skills such as critical thinking, communication, and creativity increasingly have greater value than the rote memorization of content. After all, the vast majority of content can be easily accessed within seconds on most mobile devices. We've even created a verb to describe it. What do you do when you want to know something? You "Google" it!

- **Navigating the information jungle:** Historically, an important function of education was to provide students with access to textbook content and teacher expertise. Today, content and expertise are abundantly available online. There's so much information available that new educational priorities are needed to help students navigate the vast volumes of content. Information literacy skills help students access, organize, filter, evaluate, and use the enormous amount of information available online.

- **Working in groups (because there's no "I" in teamwork):** We live in an emerging global society, and the development of collaborative skills — the ability to work effectively in teams — outweighs traditional demands that students sit still, listen, and work only on their own.

- **Incorporating multimedia literacy:** Text remains an important medium for conveying information, but multimedia is becoming the language of new generations, and its use should be encouraged in schools.

- **Saying goodbye to the 30-pound backpack:** At higher grade levels, most courses are still delivered and structured around the use of a single textbook — often, one that was printed several years ago. That's a stark contrast to a world where news and information are always up to date and available from a wide variety of sources and perspectives.

- **Reaching beyond the school walls:** School is still the central hub for learning, but technology now enables us to be constantly connected. The old model of learning within the physical confines of a classroom or school campus is being completely redefined. In the age of the Internet, learning can occur anywhere and is available on demand.

- **Staying flexible:** Instruction and curriculum need to constantly adapt to new information, technologies, and interests.

- **Differentiated instruction and assessment:** Some students are great auditory processors. Explain something once to them, and they get it. Others need to sit and read. Many students lean to more visual modes of learning. Technology offers options for differentiated instruction and alternative forms of assessment, which frees us from a "one size fits all" teaching model. (And in reality, that model never worked anyway!)

- **Limiting frontal teaching:** New technologies placed in the hands of students empower them to research, explore, and create. Use of technology can and should move us from frontal, content delivery models of education to more student-centered, discovery-based, and interactive learning practices.

- **Knowing that learning never ends:** We're all students who must continually learn and adapt to constant change. School is only part of our educational journey. Our objective should be to develop students who are independent, lifelong learners who can continue to thrive in a society of continual and rapid change.

Implementing iPads for 21st-century learning

As Ringo Starr reminded us, "It Don't Come Easy." Adding expensive technology to school environments requires significant budgeting, planning, and infrastructure development and training. With all the investment of money, time, and effort, it's even more important to focus the use of technology on critical 21st-century learning goals. The iPad is well equipped to meet these educational challenges:

- **Learning on the go:** An iPad weighs less than a pound and a half, and is well suited to the goal of "anytime, anywhere" education. You can take it with you wherever you go. Store it easily in a bag or backpack, or just carry it on your person. Plus, with up to ten hours of battery life, you won't have to deal with cords and electrical outlets. Charge your iPad overnight, and it will be ready and available all day long.

- **Kicking back and relaxing:** Use your iPad any way that feels comfortable. There aren't any annoying upright screens forming a barrier between teachers and students. It's easily passed around when used in a group setting. Turn it on easily while sitting, standing, or even when lying down (although don't say I didn't warn you that keeping your iPad next to your bed will make it extremely difficult to get up on time in the mornings)!

- **Turning on, tuning in:** The iPad turns on with the simple tap of a button. You don't wait long for it to start, and you don't have to log in to use it. It's instantly accessible and can be integrated effortlessly into any activity inside the classroom or outside. Access any website, look up any information, jot down notes and appointments — all within seconds.

- **Touching and swiping is as easy as A-B-C:** Have you ever seen a small child using an iPad? It's quite incredible how easily children take to the multitouch interface. After all, we grow up manipulating the world around us by directly touching objects: We pick them up, move them, open and use them. A computer that uses direct touching of its interface is a natural extension of that process.

- **Accessing the library at your fingertips:** You can purchase, download, and read e-books (see Figure 1-1) right from within iBooks and other book-reading apps on your iPad. Change the display to meet your taste or reading preference. Highlight or underline text, make notes, look up a word definition, and search for anything in the book . . . even use the VoiceOver feature to have the book read to you. Apple's iBookstore now also includes digital textbooks with interactive and constantly updated content from major publishers.

Figure 1-1: Download and read books using the iBooks app on your iPad.

- **Empowering students:** Put it all together, and iPads have the potential to empower students. iPads enable students to research and analyze information, connect to people, develop and collaborate on solutions to problems, and express knowledge in a variety of media . . . in short, technology empowers students to develop independent learning skills that are essential for success in today's society.

- **Including everyone through assistive technologies:** With features such as VoiceOver reading and the capability to change interface colors, fonts, and size of text, the iPad offers a custom and differentiated learning environment that can bend to the needs of individual learning styles. In addition, several apps are specifically designed for people with special learning needs, such as those with limited vision or motor skills.

- **Focusing on student-centered learning to garner out-of-the-box results:** It's important for educators to understand the potential power of technology use, but you don't need to become an expert. There's a good chance you already have 20 of those tech-savvy students sitting in your classroom. Way too much of our traditional educational models is scripted and controlled. The power of using iPads in education is revealed when they're put in the hands of students and we loosen the educational reins. Technology is the language of their daily life, and the magic of using technology in education is when students are given opportunities to use it innovatively to produce creative results that we never predicted.

Moving from Text to Multimedia

You more than likely grew up using reading and writing for most of your learning in school. The invention of the printing press and the mass production of paper completely altered the way we communicate and learn. In fact, the printing press is thought of as one of the most revolutionary inventions of the second millennium!

Do anything long enough, and it becomes difficult to imagine that there are other ways to accomplish the same objectives. If you look at schooling at any time during the 20th century, you'll notice that education was built on the consumption and production of text. You learned by reading, and you expressed your knowledge by writing about it. Remember those big, heavy textbooks you were expected to read? Many students still have them and drag that 30-pound backpack to school every day just like we did. And most of the work submitted in school is still written the way it was in our day, old-timer.

However, if you stop and take a long look outside the gates of school, you'll see a brand-new world of communication and learning . . . and it doesn't look anything at all like the one in which we grew up.

The world of the 21st century is awash in colorful, vibrant, and interactive media. Important messages are most often expressed in videos and images. When many of us want to learn something, we often look for video tutorials on sites such as YouTube.

Multimedia has quickly become the language of modern communication. Your iPad has a sparkling display with built-in audio and video tools (iPad 2 or higher; see Figure 1-2) for the creation and use of all forms of multimedia. Use it to take and edit video or photos; record podcasts and class lectures; and create animated presentations, multimedia stories, and more. With embedded cameras, a microphone, and a wide range of multimedia apps and tools, the iPad is a little multimedia powerhouse that will become as indispensable to our students as our pens and notebooks used to be back in the day.

Touchscreen

Application button

Front camera

Back camera

Home button

Figure 1-2: The iPad 2 and higher has an integrated microphone and camera.

Asking Why You Want iPads

In his book *Start with Why,* author Simon Sinek claims that we all know *what* we do. You often define yourself by what you do — "I'm a teacher," for example. You usually also know how you should do whatever you do. People usually develop a routine to make their tasks easier. Very few people or organizations constantly discuss and debate *why* they do something. Only by reflecting on the question of *why* are we able to develop and articulate a meaningful vision for what we should be doing . . . and that certainly applies to education. Let me explain.

We all have a vision of ideal education, and it's highly likely that we'll disagree on many of its components. There is, however, one common thread that most of us would agree upon. As strange as it may sound, we aren't teaching children to become good students in school. Yes, you read that correctly. After all, school is simply a transitional stage of their lives. Our objective is to educate and prepare them for life *outside* school. Ideally, we'd like to give them the necessary skills to become happy, productive adults and solid citizens.

When you live in an era of change, asking why helps evaluate whether you are preparing your students appropriately for their lives outside school. It's a natural tendency for humans to fall into routines and to focus on what we do and how we do it without regard for whether it's still relevant. Many people continue following the same educational routines and processes without asking whether they are really preparing our children for their lives in an ever-changing society full of technology.

Simply purchasing and using technology to address the question of how we teach won't advance education. If we buy technology as a means of reinforcing the same old educational processes, we may be totally missing the point. Here are some examples:

- Continuing to use lecturing as a primary pedagogical process but using technology to project the documents and presentations instead of delivering material orally or in printed formats

- Continuing content-based educational practices by having students read a chapter and answer the questions at the end, but allowing them to use technology to submit typed responses

- Continuing to stress memorization of facts but using tools such as flashcard apps to help drill the information

Asking why and looking outside the school walls may lead us to different visions and new directions. Why focus only on text for exchanging information when the world now communicates with a variety of multimedia, and fluency in media literacy is a valuable skill in the workplace? Why continue using the same old textbooks when we can access updated information on any topic within seconds using the Internet or e-books? Why focus on a static content delivery-and-memorization approach to learning when that pool of content is increasing at unprecedented speed, and it's more important for students to be skilled in finding, analyzing, and using information as they need it? Are we preparing students for tests, or are we preparing them for life? We have to ask ourselves, "Why?"

Using technology effectively in education requires much more than just having technical skills. Instead, through the use of technology, we have the ability to sculpt new educational visions that address the real needs of children entering a new world. It's a fundamental reason why I am writing this book.

Sharing iPads in Schools

iPads are designed as inherently personal devices. There are no user logins or custom desktops for different users, as there might be on a laptop or desktop. Can you start to sense the problem here? Many schools share iPads between classes and students in much the same way they share laptop carts. Laptops can accommodate different user logins and therefore protect individual student data. iPads aren't laptops and can't be used the same way.

Most iPad apps cache your login information. In other words, once you've logged in, they automatically remember your login information and open your data when the app is opened again. The little love letter or risqué rap lyrics that Joey wrote will pop right up on the screen for the next user who opens the app.

A 1:1 environment is where every student gets his own dedicated iPad — and it's unquestionably the preferred model for school use. You'll have to overcome quite a few obstacles if you expect to share iPads between students. iPads just aren't built to be shared. Having said that, there are some considerations that make it a little easier and safer to share them:

- **Little kids, little problems; big kids, big problems.** Sharing iPads at lower grade levels is far easier. There's less data produced, and the data tends to be less sensitive. In the upper grades, students may be writing papers and keeping notes that need to be kept private.

- **Stay faithful to your iPad.** Number your iPads, and keep a list or spreadsheet to make sure students use the same iPad every time. At least that way, students' data should be available, and they're sharing that particular iPad only with a small handful of other students. Also, anything that goes wrong will be easier to track. You can always sticker the outside of the iPad with a number, but another approach is to create a large visible graphic with the respective number and make it the wallpaper for each device's home page.

- **You *don't* got mail.** Forget setting up incoming e-mail in the iPad Mail app unless you're prepared to let students see each other's e-mail. Changing e-mail accounts in Mail requires going to Settings; that can get messy and time-consuming (although some schools do it that way).

- **Access e-mail through the web browser.** Many e-mail services, such as Google and Microsoft Exchange, have a web interface that you can access through Safari. Just make sure to log out when you're done.

- **Log out, log out, log out.** Few apps prompt you to log out when you close them, but many have an option to log out on their Settings menus. Encourage students to always log out (or to sign out, as shown in Figure 1-3) before closing an app or website that requires a login.

Encourage students to use logout options.

Figure 1-3: Many iPad apps such as Pocket have options to log in and out.

✏ **Appreciate the silver lining to your cloud account.** Consider saving data to a cloud-based service such as Dropbox. There are simple ways to move content from the iPad to a cloud storage account. On a shared iPad, one practical approach is to use e-mail. For example, some web services, such as Evernote, accept files that are e-mailed to a unique e-mail address the service sets up for your account. You'll still have to delete the files from the iPad, however, if you want to keep the information private.

What This Book Is and Is Not

The objective of this book is to help you successfully integrate the use of iPads into an educational setting.

✏ Although my main objective isn't to teach you mad iPad skills that turn you into the go-to technology expert, you'll pick up a lot of helpful knowledge about iPad use along the way.

✏ It isn't a technical book for the school's "tech guy." He has enough headaches already.

- It isn't a directory of app recommendations. There are several hundred thousand apps on the market (and a few more probably came out as you were reading this sentence!). Learning new apps is fun, but the book's focus is firmly on educational objectives. I demonstrate a variety of apps and web tools to help move you in that direction.

- The book will be helpful for teachers, school administrators, parents, and anyone else concerned with education.

- You will learn how to use iPads effectively as an educational tool that engages students and energizes learning across age levels and academic disciplines.

- At its core, this actually isn't a book about "using iPads in education." Instead, it's a book about "educating using iPads." That isn't just a small semantic difference. It's an important distinction in priorities that stresses the fact that using technology is never the goal.

  Technology is a tool that serves the greater objective of preparing students for their lives outside school.

- Last, if you've ever spent 2 minutes with an iPad, you know that this is a book about having fun!

2

Getting Acquainted with iPad Technology

In This Chapter

▶ Becoming familiar with the physical layout of the iPad

▶ Distinguishing the iPad from other computers

▶ Preparing the other elements that are essential to iPad use

▶ Finding and purchasing apps

▶ Learning basic iPad skills

▶ Accessorizing your iPad experience

The initial days of the very first personal computers were only about 35 years ago. The first commercially available "portable" computer, such as the IBM 5100, sold for a whopping $10,000 to $20,000 and contained around 16KB to 64KB of memory. To put that in perspective, the average personal computer today contains several hundred thousand times the memory and sells for around 5 percent of the cost! Phenomena such as the Internet are revolutionizing how we connect and communicate. Mobile technologies have advanced to the point where portable devices are now smaller and more powerful than we could have imagined back in the early days of computing. Now we're witnessing the emergence of widespread mobile tablet computing, with its unique touch interface. Tablets have skyrocketed into prominence over the last couple of years and are changing the face of popular computing. The clear leader in that field is an amazing and powerful little device that is taking the world by storm — the iPad.

Mobile, tablet computers are substantially different from the desktop and laptop computers you've been using for many years. In this chapter, I explain what sets the iPad's physical hardware apart from traditional computers, and I also demonstrate the different ways you use its software. I walk you through many of the core functions, and look at how to find and purchase software "apps." Of course, throughout the process I make sure to keep my educationally tinted glasses focused on the incredible opportunities that exist for using the iPad as an educational device.

Touring the iPad's Physical Layout

Let's take a quick walk-through of the physical exterior of the iPad. Apple has done a wonderful job designing everything in a small and sleek footprint, and you don't have very many controls to learn.

Looking along the edges

Let's start at the very top of the iPad, where you find the headphone jack, microphone, and Sleep/Wake button (see Figure 2-1):

- **Headphone jack:** Plug your headphones or earbuds into the 3.5mm headphone jack.

- **Microphone:** Pay attention to the location of the microphone, and position it correctly when recording.

- **Sleep/Wake button:** Your iPad can be in any one of three states: powered on, powered off, and sleep mode. Press this button once, and it puts your iPad to sleep. Press it again, and your iPad wakes instantly. (Wouldn't it be great if you could wake your kids up that easily?) Turn it off by pressing and holding the button down for a few seconds and then sliding the onscreen slider to confirm that you want to shut it down. Pressing and holding will also start your iPad.

Putting your iPad into sleep mode rather than turning it off completely will use up a touch more of the battery but keeps it available for immediate use whenever you need it. If you're using a Smart Cover (or an alternative), the iPad automatically goes into sleep mode when you close the cover and wakes up when you open it. If only that worked with my kids. You can also set your iPad to go to sleep after a period of inactivity in Settings, under the General menu and Auto-Lock.

With the iPad screen facing you, look along the right edge, and you'll find the Volume control and the Mute switch/Rotate lock (see Figure 2-2):

- **Volume control:** The Volume control is a single button. Press the upper part to turn the volume up, and press the lower part to turn the volume down. As an aside, the same button can also be used as a camera shutter button on the iPad 2 or higher.

- **Mute switch:** Slide the Mute switch to the down position, and it turns off any unexpected sounds such as notification noises from apps. Note that this doesn't affect the sound coming from sources such as music and video. If you are running a recent version of the iOS operating system, you have the option of using this button as a Screen Orientation Lock instead of a Mute switch. The iPad will switch orientation by default when you move it from portrait to landscape and back. To change the button's function, tap Settings, and go to the General section in the margin. Scan down to see the two options for using the side switch.

Headphone jack   Microphone   On/Off, Sleep/Wake

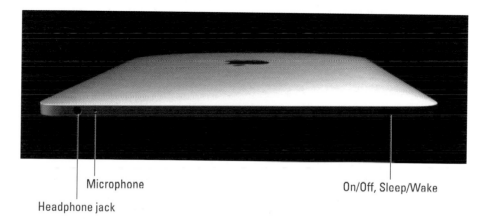

Microphone   On/Off, Sleep/Wake

Headphone jack

Figure 2-1: The top side of an iPad 2 (top) and original iPad (bottom).

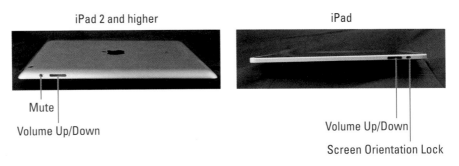

Figure 2-2: The right side of the iPad.

Take a look at the bottom of your iPad to see the built-in speaker and the 30-pin dock connector (see Figure 2-3):

- ✓ **Speaker:** It's the little speaker that could. It's not overly powerful and mono, not stereo, but still fine for personal listening.

- ✓ **Dock connector:** This port is used most often to charge your iPad. It does have other important functions as well, such as connecting your iPad to a computer for synchronizing content, connecting to a Camera Connection Kit to transfer images, and connecting to AV connectors for screen projection.

Figure 2-3: The bottom of the iPad and iPad 2.

Looking at the front and back

Time now to take a closer look at that dazzling display:

- ✔ **Screen:** It starts with the beautifully clear display — amazingly crisp if you have a third-generation iPad. This is where it all happens and where you find icons for all your apps.

- ✔ **Home button:** Directly below the screen you find the indispensable Home button. Think of it like Hansel and Gretel's bread-crumb trail — wherever you are, just press the Home button to take you back.

- ✔ **Front and rear cameras:** If you have an iPad 2 or higher, you have one camera in the front and another in the back. Just toggle between them as needed. Take it from me, though, there's nothing quite so startling as preparing to take a picture, only to have your face suddenly fill the screen because you're using the wrong camera!

It's Not Your Father's Computer

For many years, people who were going to make a presentation at a different location had only one option: Pack up the desktop computer and lug it along. Today, you can just drop your iPad into your bag, and off you go. With its sparkling display, built-in media tools, and Internet connectivity, it has most everything you need. Let's see what makes it tick.

Exploring how iPads differ from laptops

Don't waste your time looking for the keyboard and mouse. The most fundamental difference between an iPad and a traditional computer is that the iPad uses the same input device you've been using to manipulate objects since the day you were born. The iPad's "touch" interface is based upon manipulating objects on the screen with your fingers. Drag them, drop them, size them (the objects, not your fingers!) . . . everything is based on gestures you make with your fingers. The touch interface is what makes iPads such a natural fit for children. We grow up learning about the physical world around us by touching objects. The iPad interface is a simple extension of that process.

You've probably developed certain work habits on computers that will need to change a little when you start using your iPad. Some of the most fundamental changes include the following:

✔ **See me, feel me . . . touch me.** It has a very simple and intuitive touch interface. There's no physical keyboard or mouse. Everything you need to move or type is right there onscreen — under your fingertips. Using an app is as simple as tapping the icon onscreen with your finger. When you need to type anything, the iPad automatically slides a virtual keyboard up on your screen.

✔ **Don't look for folders.** iPads don't use the folder and file storage structure that computers use. Files are associated with apps and accessed through them.

✔ **No drives, no ports.** iPads don't have a USB port or a CD or DVD drive. The most common ways to transfer content on and off your iPad are cabling it to a computer or synchronizing your content wirelessly. Add a dose of cloud storage to the mix, and your content is available on any device in any location, giving you universal access to all your information. Magic.

✔ **Stay focused!** iPads keep only one app open on the screen at a time. You can, however, keep several apps open and then switch between them as needed; refer to the "Switching between apps" section later in this chapter.

✔ **Network cables? Phooey.** IP4, IP6, TCPIP, DHCP . . . all those technical acronyms are enough to give anyone a headache. The iPad doesn't have an Ethernet port, which is really just a fancy way of saying you can't plug in a network or Internet cable. Set up a simple connection to your wireless network, and the iPad connects to the Internet automatically and effortlessly. The only acronym you need is SBAL — Sit Back and Relax!

✔ **What you see is what you get.** The iPad doesn't have an open architecture. You can't open it and mess with components. The bad news is that you can't add more hard drive space or memory. The good news? You can't mess it up by trying.

✔ **Save the trees.** You can't cable your iPad to a printer. Chapter 20 provides some options for printing, but there are also many possibilities for paperless, digital communications.

✔ **It just plain works!** I've worked with computers for two decades. One of the biggest differences between an iPad and a traditional computer that I've noticed is probably also the most important: Turn the iPad on, and it just works. The iPad is intuitive to use, and you just don't run into many technical issues. You can spend your time being productive and having fun instead of connecting cables and calling for technical support.

Apps versus software

You may be accustomed to purchasing and installing computer software yourself. You know what I mean: Purchase a CD or download it from the publisher's website and then run through some installation procedure that often requires you to configure options, file locations, and more. Not so on the iPad. Software programs for any iOS device such as your iPad are called *apps* — short for applications. Apps need to be approved by Apple, and then they are listed for purchase and download directly through the Apple Store (see Figure 2-4). Tap the button to buy an app, and within seconds, the icon appears on your screen. No setup screens, no file locations, and very little way to mess it up. For most of us, that's got to be a great thing.

You need an iTunes account to purchase apps . . . don't go away. I discuss that in the next few pages.

Figure 2-4: Tap the price button to purchase an app in the App Store.

Finding the keyboard

Your iPad has a virtual keyboard (see Figure 2-5) that appears onscreen when needed. It intelligently detects when you tap in an editing field and just automatically slides up, ready and waiting for you to type.

One of the advantages of the virtual keyboard is that you actually get access to several keyboards that change according to the context in which it's being used. For example, when you're browsing the Internet in Safari, your keyboard will include a special .com key. When you're typing an e-mail address, the keyboard automatically adds an @ key.

Figure 2-5: The iPad has a virtual keyboard that displays onscreen as needed.

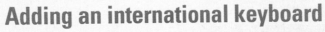

Adding an international keyboard

One of the advantages of using a virtual keyboard is that you can switch keyboards with a couple of taps. Adding a foreign-language keyboard is a fairly simple process:

1. **Tap the Settings icon on your iPad home screen.**

2. **Select and tap the General option; then scroll down and tap the Keyboard option.**

3. **Tap International Keyboards.**

4. **On the next screen, tap Add New Keyboard.**

5. **Select your language of choice.**

Your international keyboard is now installed, and you can display it as needed. Whenever you want to switch languages for typing, simply tap the Globe icon in the bottom left of your keyboard, select your language, and start typing.

Storing and moving files

You have many options to create content on iPads. You'll be creating and editing documents, photos, presentations, video, and more. However, there's no way to directly access and move files and folders on an iPad in the same way you can on a laptop or desktop. Although there are some wireless utilities to work around it, there's no USB port to plug a flash drive into your iPad.

You'll want to move content off your iPad for synchronization with other computers and devices and also for backup purposes. This issue of "workflow" — moving content on and off iPads — is even more critical in a classroom setting, where teachers have to deliver content and students need to share and collaborate on content that gets returned to the teacher.

Don't run off to get your headache medication just yet. What happens on the iPad doesn't have to stay on the iPad. You have lots of options for moving files — so many, in fact, that I devote a section of Chapter 3 to discussing them.

Planning for the Essential Extras

The iPad is an amazing device that will open up rich opportunities for you to create and use media, read books, listen to music, connect through the Internet, and much more. You do, however, need to create the right environment to get the most out of your iPad. Two of the most important factors are the strength of your wireless Internet connection and your ability to find and purchase apps — especially in a school environment.

Connecting wirelessly

One of the major strengths of the iPad lies in its capability to connect you to information, people, events, media, books, and more. Having an iPad that can't get a connection out to the Internet is almost like having a car without any gas. Unless you have an iPad that supports a connection with a data plan through your cell network, you'll be connecting using Wi-Fi. Of course, not all connections are created equal. There are two considerations when planning the setup of your Wi-Fi network:

✔ **The speed of your incoming connection:** Internet connectivity is becoming faster and cheaper. Depending on the area in which you live, you may or may not have many options for fast Internet service. The amount of bandwidth you need depends on the following:

- *The number of people using the wireless connection — especially concurrent users.*

- *The type of activity occurring wirelessly.* For example, e-mailing and texting won't require much bandwidth, but watching high-resolution streaming video will gobble it up quickly.

✔ **The distribution of the wireless signal:** You've signed a tremendous deal to get oodles of fast Internet connectivity for your home, school, or office. Don't get too smug yet. You're only halfway done. Your Internet service provider (ISP) will bring its connection into a central, wired point on your property. If you expect to get a wireless signal, you need to distribute that Internet signal throughout the required areas. If you're setting up a home Wi-Fi network, a fairly inexpensive router (less than $100) will probably do the trick. The larger the area, the more important it becomes to invest in a solid system for distributing your wireless signal. This is extremely important when considering the strength of your wireless system on a school campus.

No other factor will kill enthusiasm for the budding use of technology on campus than the inability to get it working when it's needed. There will be areas to save on your technology budgets. This is not one of them.

Tuning your iTunes account

There are many methods for handling the purchasing and downloading of apps, books, music, and other content for your iPad. Let's start with the easy way. In order to get personal access to content in the iTunes or App Store, you must have your own Apple ID (see Figure 2-6). If you don't already have one, you have two easy ways to open an account, the first from your computer and the second from your iPad.

On a computer:

1. **Go to** `http://www.apple.com/itunes/download/` **to download and install iTunes on your computer.**

2. **Open iTunes on your computer.**

3. **From the Store menu, choose Create Account, and follow the prompts.**

You'll need to provide personal details along with a valid method of payment, such as a credit card. The billing information will be used if and when you purchase apps and content.

4. When asked, verify your e-mail address, and log in.

You're set to go.

On an iPad:

1. Tap the Settings icon on your home screen.

2. Tap the Store menu item in the left column.

3. Tap Create a New Account, and follow the prompts.

4. When asked, verify your e-mail address, and log in.

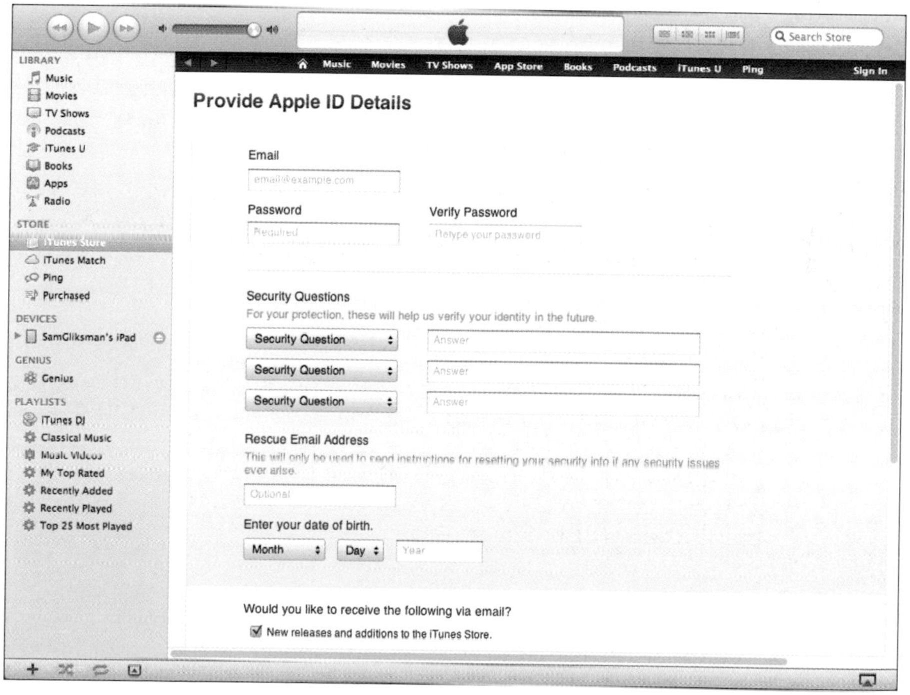

Figure 2-6: You need to create an iTunes account to download apps.

Once you've created and verified your Apple ID and billing information, you'll be able to start using it to acquire apps, music, books, and more.

As a general rule, the school will manage any and all accounts used in the process of buying apps for students. Some schools elect to allow students to manage their own iPads. As a result, students would use their own Apple IDs to buy and download apps. Note that there is a minimum age of 13 to use the iTunes service.

Using Apple's Volume Purchase Program

Apple's VPP is what most schools use to purchase larger quantities of apps and books at a discount. After apps and books are purchased centrally, they can be distributed to school employees and students using vouchers. The key components of the VPP are as follows:

- **Select a program manager.** A designated person at the school — usually an administrator or someone in the financial office — enrolls to become a Program Manager.

- **Select program facilitators.** The Program Manager can select several Program Facilitators. All Program Facilitators receive a unique Apple ID they can use to purchase apps and books for the school using Volume Vouchers.

- **Purchase volume vouchers.** Volume vouchers are physical cards your school buys from Apple. The cards are distributed to the program facilitators and used to purchase apps and books in the Volume Purchase Program Education Store. The Education Store can be found at `https://volume.itunes.apple.com/us/store`.

- **Acquire the codes.** Once the purchase is complete, the program facilitator is given a set of codes that are used to download apps and books onto individual iPads.

- **Receive discounts.** Publishers determine the amount of discount given for when their apps are purchased in larger volumes. The common standard is a 50 percent discount when quantities of 20 or more are purchased.

If it all sounds a little complicated, that's probably why, like me, you're very happy you don't work in the school's financial office. For a detailed explanation of the VPP and how to use it within your school, visit `www.apple.com/education/volume-purchase-program/`.

One additional option that is worth considering is purchasing iTunes Gift Cards in set, smaller amounts and giving them to teachers to buy and try individual apps for their classes. If an app looks promising, a teacher can recommend that the school use Its VPP to purchase that app in larger quantities.

As long as you're using a modest amount of iPads, the tools provided by Apple should be sufficient to manage your iPads. A few companies offer Mobile Device Management (MDM) software solutions for the larger-scale deployment of iPads in schools and organizations. MDM products provide a central administration point where devices can be configured wirelessly. If you're managing hundreds or thousands of iPads, researching and purchasing an MDM solution will be well worth the investment of time and money. I look at management alternatives in Chapter 3.

Communicating through e-mail

When the first iPad was released, many argued that it was just a fancy device for the consumption of media. Along came the release of the iPad 2, with its built-in cameras and apps, and all of a sudden, the iPad was a more-than-capable device for production and creative expression. One characteristic was largely overlooked in the debate over whether the iPad was capable of both consumption and production: The iPad is a wonderful device for connecting and communicating with others in a wide variety of methods. One of the most prominent communication features is the iPad's superlative Mail app (see Figure 2-7).

Figure 2-7: Accounts with popular e-mail providers are simple to set up on the iPad manually.

I'm not going to run through all the options for setting up and managing your e-mail. Most are fairly straightforward. If you work at a school, you may be lucky enough to have a tech person set up e-mail on your iPad for you.

If you have to set up your e-mail account, the simplest option is to have your e-mail accounts, calendars, and contacts placed on your iPad as part of the overall iTunes synchronization process. If you have Mac Mail, Microsoft Outlook, Gmail, or Yahoo! Mail set up on your computer, you can synchronize your e-mail directly with your iPad. The other option is simply to set it manually. You can do that by going to Settings and tapping the Mail, Contact, Calendars menu option in the left column.

E-mail is not only a great communication medium, but also an enormously useful tool in the iPad classroom. Most apps that enable you to create content also contain an option to e-mail that content directly to a recipient. That makes e-mail one of your options for moving content, whether e-mailing a file to yourself (so that you can continue working on it later), delivering something to a student, or receiving assignments from students. Chapter 4 delves more deeply into e-mail.

Operating an iPad

Tablet computers such as the iPad have taken a refreshing new look at how people and machines should interact. The emphasis has been placed on keeping everything compact and mobile, and using the sense of touch to directly manipulate objects and operate the iPad. There are no external components, such as a mouse, keyboard, USB, or CD drive. Just pick up your iPad, and take it anywhere. That's all you need — and I know you're going to love using it. My only word of caution is that you keep close tabs on it. Your family and workmates will constantly find reasons to borrow it, or as my youngest son would say, "Just to look something up for a second." Uh-huh . . .

The iPad actually uses a common operating system with the iPhone and iPod touch. It's called, naturally, iOS. If you can use an iPhone, you're well on the way to using an iPad; the devices use similar iOS features. If you've never used an iOS device before, just settle back, grab a cup of tea or coffee or other beverage of choice, and browse through the following pages. I assure you the iPad will be the easiest and least technical device you've ever had to learn. Now let's get started.

You can connect to the Internet through a wireless network, or if you purchased the model that supports Wi-Fi and 3G or 4G, you can connect directly through your cellular service provider by subscribing to a monthly data plan. For the purposes of this book, I assume you're using a Wi-Fi–only model. That's because this is the predominant model being used in education.

Turning on

You've set up an Apple ID, your wireless network is up and running, and you're all set to go . . . except for one simple thing. Where's the On button? Press the Sleep/Wake button on the upper-right corner of the iPad. Hold it down for a few seconds, and your iPad will power up. Turn it off the same way; hold the Sleep/Wake button down for a few seconds until a large slide control appears at the top of your screen. Slide the red arrow across to turn off the iPad.

If you've used an iPhone, you also know that you can lock your iPad without actually powering it off completely. Locking your iPad is a convenient way of protecting it. You can even create a passcode to prevent anyone from accessing your data. The iPad will lock automatically after a few seconds (you can set the time in Settings), or you can just tap the Sleep/Wake button quickly. Tap the Sleep/Wake button or the Home button to turn it back on.

Staying in charge

Your iPad comes with a USB power adapter. Plug in the adapter to charge your iPad. Charging it from empty to 100 percent can take a few hours. This is the fastest method for charging, but you also may be able to charge your iPad by plugging it into the USB port of your computer. You should note, however, that it requires a high-power USB port.

Pumping up the volume

You can adjust the volume on your iPad in several ways. The most accessible way is to use the volume control on the right side of the physical frame, pressing the upper portion to increase volume and lower part to decrease it. Many apps also have sound controls built into them, and you can change the volume from there as well. Last, system sounds such as calendar alerts and new e-mails can be controlled by using the iPad's native Settings app. Look for Sounds under the General category in the left menu.

Using the built-in cameras

The camera functionality on the iPad varies from model to model. If you have an original iPad, you were a trailblazer . . . but not in a photographic sense. Unfortunately, that iPad doesn't have a camera. If you have an iPad 2 or higher, you have both a front- and rear-facing camera (see Figure 2-8). The difference in image quality is substantial, however, with the third-generation iPad boasting a 5-megapixel (rear-facing) iSight camera with autofocus and HD video recording.

Accessibility to a built-in camera has allowed for the simple integration of media into a variety of educational activities. Chapter 4 more fully explains how to take photos with the Camera app.

Touchscreen

Application button

Front camera

Back camera

Home button

Figure 2-8: The iPad 2 and third-generation iPad have front and rear cameras.

Getting Comfortable

You won't need years of computer science training to master the iPad, but you will need a basic familiarity with some of the core functions. Ironically, the younger you are, the less training you'll need.

The following sections take you on a quick tour of some of the basic functions. I suggest taking a look at the general *iPads For Dummies* series of books for more detailed discussions of the core iPad features and apps.

Navigating the home screen

Tap the large round Home button at the bottom of your iPad, and it will take you to the home screen (see Figure 2-9). Each icon on the home screen represents a different app, and your iPad comes stocked with around 17 to 20 apps, depending on your version. Apps included with your iPad include Settings, App Store, Mail, Calendar, Contacts, iTunes, Maps, Photos, and more.

Figure 2-9: Each icon on your home screen represents an app.

Swipe the home page to the right with your finger, and it takes you to another screen of apps. As you start to purchase and download more apps, you'll notice they are automatically arranged into more screens.

The Dock is the row of apps at the bottom of the screen that can hold up to six icons. When you swipe from one screen to the next, the Dock remains. It's a good idea to keep your most commonly used apps in the Dock so that you can tap and start them from any screen.

Putting your apps in order

You can move app icons to any screen and location. Simply press any icon and hold your finger on it until you notice the icons begin to jiggle. Now you can press and drag any icon to move it. If you want to move it to another screen, press and swipe it out to the very edge of the screen; the next screen will appear. You can also move apps down into the Dock area at the bottom of the screen. Move your popular apps down into the Dock so that they'll be available on all screens.

You can even organize your icons into folders by following these steps:

1. **Press and hold your finger on an icon until all the icons start jiggling.**

2. **Press an icon and drag it over the top of another icon that you want grouped with it in a folder.**

    A new folder is automatically created with a folder name that's based on the nature of the apps in the folder.

3. **(Optional) Rename the folder and continue dragging other icons into it.**

Removing apps from a folder is done in a similar manner. Press and hold any folder until it jiggles and then drag any icon out of it. Now, if only organizing my desk were that simple.

You can arrange and delete icons (and also home screens) when you're cabled to a computer with iTunes. If you have a lot of housecleaning to do, it's probably a more efficient method.

Pressing and holding icons isn't just for moving them. When they start to jiggle, you'll notice that a little X appears in the top-right corner of most app icons (with the exception of the native iPad apps that cannot be deleted). Tap the X to remove that app from your iPad. Don't worry — it's just removed from your iPad. You can restore it next time you sync your devices or by going to the App Store and downloading it again.

Learning multitouch gestures

Computers have largely been using external input devices such as keyboards and mice since the popularization of the first personal computers. In retrospect, it seems so much more natural to directly touch and manipulate objects with your fingers than to use an external device . . . and although the iPad isn't the first computer to use a touch interface, it probably is the simplest and most advanced.

Some of the gestures vary between iPads and operating systems. The basic gestures, however, are common to all and include

- ✓ **Tap** basically selects something. Tap with your finger to open and activate items such as apps and menu selections.

- ✓ **Flick** is a quick and easy way to scroll up and down pages and lists. Stop the scrolling by tapping the page or list. You can also flick left or right on an item in a list to delete it.

- ✓ **Two-finger stretching** zooms into a page or image. If you've never done this before, it's sure to elicit a "wow" the first time you try it. Just pick any two fingers, place them on the screen, and move them apart. Pinch them closer together, and the screen zooms back out. You'll never have to search for one of those little magnifying-glass icons again. By the way, double-tapping with your finger often has the same effect.

- ✓ **Drag** is when you tap and hold your finger on the screen and then move it in any direction. You'll often drag to move an object or to move around in a web page or other page.

Apple introduced some cool new gestures when it released the iOS 5 operating system. You'll have to make sure Multitasking Gestures are enabled in the General category within the Settings app. If you want to impress your friends and work colleagues, try some of the following, and bask in the glow of admiration!

- ✓ Swipe up with four or five fingers to reveal the multitasking bar.

- ✓ If you're in an app, swipe to the left or right with four or five fingers to switch to the next/previous open app.

- ✓ Pinch with four or five fingers inside any app to return to the home screen.

Creating and editing text

I don't mean to freak you out, but your iPad is pretty smart and often can sense what you need. Don't you wish you had more people in your life who could do that? Let's say you want to send an e-mail. The second you open a new e-mail message and tap in a field that requires text, your virtual keyboard automatically pops up on the screen, ready for you to type.

One of the features that helps many users type more fluently on the iPad is Auto-Correct. Yes, there's no doubt that it does lead to the occasional hysterical error, but overall, it helps correct many common errors that occur when you accidentally tap the wrong keys. Turn Auto-Correct on or off with the following steps:

1. **Tap the Settings icon on your home screen.**

2. **Tap General.**

3. Scroll down and tap Keyboard.

4. On the Keyboard screen, turn Auto-Correct on or off.

Here are some other tips that will enhance your iPad keyboarding skills:

✓ **Special characters:** Hold down many of the keys for a list of alternative characters. For example, hold down the dollar key, and you'll get a pop-up list of characters for other currencies. If you hold down keys such as I or N, you'll get a list of foreign-language equivalents of those characters.

✓ **Periods:** Double-tap the spacebar at the end of a sentence, and it automatically adds a period at the end of the sentence.

✓ **Quick keys:** You can swipe some keys for easy insertion of other characters. For example, swipe the comma key, and it adds an apostrophe. Swipe the period key, and you get double quotation marks.

✓ **Split keyboard:** Have you ever noticed that your kids are masters at typing text messages with their thumbs? If that's your thing, you'll love this tip. First, make sure that you've turned on the Split Keyboard option in Settings (tap General; then tap Keyboard). Now return to any app that uses the keyboard. If you have iOS 5 or higher, press and hold the keyboard key in the bottom right of your keyboard. It gives you the option to Undock your keyboard and move it anywhere onscreen. A second option splits the keyboard into two parts, as shown in Figure 2-10. In portrait mode, splitting the keyboard makes it easy to type with your thumbs, but I don't recommend it for those of us over the age of 30!

✓ **All caps**: Double-tap the Shift key to type something in ALL CAPS. (Enable this option in Settings: Tap General, tap Keyboard, and then toggle Enable Caps Lock to On.)

Using copy and paste can be a valuable timesaver when you're typing a lot of text. Tap and hold any text in an e-mail, document, or web page. A magnifying bubble appears (see Figure 2-11), enabling you to move to text that you want to copy. Lift your finger, and a little pop-up menu offers you options to Copy or Select All. The highlighted text has handles in two corners, as shown in Figure 2-12, that you can drag outward to expand your selection. Tap Copy when you're done.

The copied text is now in the iPad's clipboard and can be pasted into any app that has a text field. Simply tap wherever you want and select Paste from the pop-up menu. And if you feel a little more ambitious, here are a couple of cool shortcuts:

✓ Double-tap any word to select it.

✓ Tap text four times quickly to select the entire paragraph.

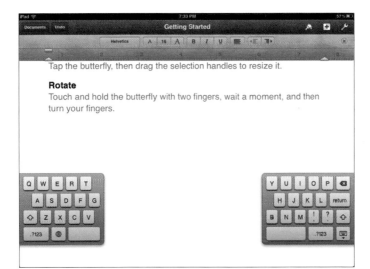

Figure 2-10: iOS 5 and higher allows you to move and split the virtual keyboard.

Figure 2-11: Tap and hold to reveal the magnifying bubble.

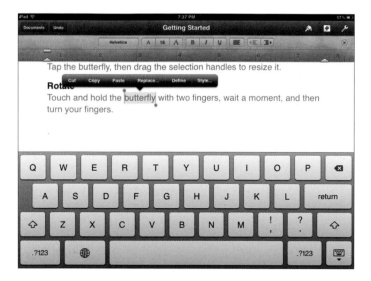

Figure 2-12: Tap, hold, and drag the handles to select text.

Putting Auto-Correct to work for you

Auto-Correct can be a great way of creating shortcuts for words and phrases that you often need to type. Let's say that you work for New Horizons for Global Economic Change. The facility has a great cafeteria, and you're always asking people to meet you there for lunch. Their vegetable lasagna has this amazing tomato . . . sorry, I digress. You send several people an e-mail and have to type **New Horizons for Global Economic Change** every time. That's quite a challenge. One slipup and Auto-Correct will have them searching the New Horizons for Glorious Economical Cheese. Here's a slick and easy little solution. Use Auto-Correct to create typing shortcuts. Here's how:

1. **Tap to open the Settings app.**

2. **Tap General in the left menu and then tap Keyboard from the menu of options in the main window.**

At the bottom of the main window, you see the section for Shortcuts.

3. **Tap to Add New Shortcut.**

You have two choices:

- **Phrase:** Type the longhand version of the text you want to appear. That's **New Horizons for Global Economic Change.**

- **Shortcut:** Type a short series of letters that the iPad will then expand and auto-correct for you. For example, you might type **NHGEC**. Now every time you type **NHGEC,** Auto-Correct will jump in, and presto — it automatically expands the text into New Horizons for Global Economic Change. Now don't forget to try the lasagna.

Switching between apps

Although you can't have more than one app open on your screen at the same time, the iPad does allow you to keep several apps open and then switch among them as needed.

Here's how you can quickly switch among open apps:

1. **Double-tap the Home button on the bottom of your iPad.**

   You see a row of icons showing the list of currently open apps, as shown in Figure 2-13.

2. **Swipe to the left or right with your finger if the app you're looking for isn't there.**

   There may be more than one row of open apps.

3. **Tap the icon of the app you want, and it will open, usually at whatever state you left it.**

Figure 2-13: Double-tap the Home button to switch between open apps.

You can also swipe left or right with four or five fingers from within any app to slide between open apps. (Refer to the earlier section "Learning multitouch gestures.")

Using iPhone apps

When you search the App Store, you'll find that apps can be designed for use on the iPhone/iPod touch or iPad. In many cases, the app developer will have a version for both, and in other cases there are hybrid apps that adapt their display to the device being used. The main distinction between them is the size they occupy onscreen. iPhone apps are designed for the smaller iPhone screen, but most will work equally well on your iPad (unless they require iPhone-specific features such as dialing a number).

When you're using an iPhone app on the iPad, the app defaults to running in its original size. You'll see a little 2x button in the lower-right corner of your screen. Tap it, and the app will expand to fill the entire screen. You'll notice immediately that the image isn't as crisp, but I find it especially useful when the app has a keyboard and I need larger keys for typing.

Some apps are hybrids and work across iOS devices. They automatically detect the device and adjust their screen display accordingly. You'll find them listed in the App Store with a small + sign in the corner of the icon.

Searching your iPad

If you go to your home screen and swipe to the left, you'll find yourself on the Spotlight Search page, as shown in Figure 2-14. This is your one-stop shop for finding anything in your iPad. Things you can search for include

- ✔ **Apps:** As you get more and more apps that fill multiple screens, this often becomes the easiest way to find an app quickly.
- ✔ **Mail messages:** Searches only the From, To, CC, BCC, and Subject fields (not message content).
- ✔ **Media:** This includes music, podcasts, videos, and more.
- ✔ **And more:** Including contact, events, reminders, messages, and notes.

Type your search term in the field at the top of the page. You can type any part of the item that you're searching, and the results will narrow down as you continue typing the term. The results are categorized by type. Tap the item you want, and it opens in the appropriate app.

Figure 2-14: Spotlight Search categorizes your search results by type.

Accessorizing Your iPad

I've yet to meet anyone who hasn't loved using an iPad. Having said that, a number of accessories can make it even more functional and keep it physically safe and secure. Purchasing accessories is really a matter of taste, but here's a list of some that you may want to consider:

- **Physical keyboard:** Everyone has his own favorite type of keyboard. With a little time and practice, most people become quite fluent typing on the iPad's virtual keyboard, but it may take time to become comfortable using it. You do have options. A number of external, physical keyboards can be used with your iPad.

    - *Wireless keyboards:* Apple offers its own wireless keyboard that uses Bluetooth and just needs to be placed somewhere near the iPad. The company also offers a separate stand that can prop up your iPad for easier viewing while you type.

    - *Combination case with keyboard:* Some companies, such as Logitech, Belkin, and Zagg, offer iPad covers and cases with built-in keyboards. The case generally opens and props the iPad up on a stand in front of an attached keyboard.

- **Screen cleaners:** It won't take very long at all for your screen to be covered with annoying smudges that you want to clean. A spray glass cleaner may do a great job on windows and tabletops, but don't even think of using it on your iPad! Stay away from using any cleaning fluids, abrasive cloths, towels, and paper towels, too. They may damage the screen. Apple recommends using only a soft, lint-free cloth.

- **Cases:** The iPad is actually pretty sturdy, but it still makes sense to protect it with a case. Your choices number in the hundreds, and I've seen some bulky options that look and weigh like military flak jackets and flimsy little covers that would barely protect against a breeze. When selecting a case, keep the following in mind:

  - Make sure your case still gives you access to the buttons and ports. It's very annoying when you have to peel back or take off a case to do something as simple as accessing the volume control.

  - Consider a case that has options for propping up the iPad when opened. Some even have separate stands for vertical and horizontal use. It's often very convenient when you want to stand your iPad up on a table or desk.

  - Drooping an iPad on its corner will often cause the worst damage. Select a case that protects the corner edges.

- **Earbuds:** When you're blasting that AC/DC music, you'll be doing everyone a favor if you pull out and use a set of earbuds. Generally, any earbuds that work with an iPhone or iPod will work with your iPad as well. Rather than sharing, especially if you're using iPads in a classroom, consider having children bring their own for sanitary reasons. Their parents likely will prefer that, too. Also, some models include a built-in mic that can come in very handy.

- **Belkin Rockstar:** In class, you may often need to have several students listen to audio on an iPad at the same time. The Belkin Rockstar will be your savior. It connects to your iPad and offers five adapters for students to plug in their own earbuds. Be warned, though: It's a "splitter," which means that the volume is shared among the different earbuds and will therefore have lower volume for each.

- **Stylus:** I'll leave it to you to decide the value of using a stylus to write on your iPad. Certainly, many apps accommodate handwriting with a stylus although some people adapt to using one better than others do. (Consider me in the latter group . . .)

- **Screen protector:** An invisible screen protector can be an inexpensive way of preventing scratches and keeping the screen clean.

- **Adapters:** Your iPad is very compact and mobile. As a result, it doesn't have ports for attaching peripheral devices. However, wherever there's demand there's a product, and you'll find adapters for most of the uses you'll encounter, such as connecting cameras and external displays.

3

Managing the iPad Classroom

*I*f you're lucky, you have an IT professional who has been trained in device management and takes care of it for you. If so, you can happily skip to the next chapter, knowing that, at least in this instance, ignorance is bliss. Unfortunately, it's more likely that you're at a school that's dealing with a patchwork of misunderstood solutions — some of which work and some of which don't, with others that are so confusing, nobody understands what to do. If that's the case, welcome! This chapter is for you.

This chapter provides an overview of the issues that affect device management:

✔ Models of management that address different-size deployments and the degree of centralized management that is required

✔ Options for device configuration, app distribution, and updates

✔ Information workflow, which involves how you are distributing information, collecting work from students, and allowing for sharing and collaborative processes with iPads

I'd like to promise you that device management is simple and headache free. It isn't, but I hope that with a little guidance it won't end up being quite as painful as you may fear.

Setting Up and Configuring Devices

The truck rolls up and drops several large boxes of iPads at your door. You need to get them ready for class use, but you don't have any training or experience setting up mobile devices. Take a deep breath while I map out some options. Your first step is to define the size of your deployment; doing so enables you to know what deployment path to take. After that, you have three stages to complete: preparation, supervision, and assignment (an optional stage). I discuss all these issues in this section.

Defining the size of your deployment

I recommend that you start by defining the size of your deployment and developing a strategy for the deployment. Are you setting up a few iPads for teachers to try out, maybe anywhere from 20 up to 150 or so for a few classes to use — or a few hundred for an entire organization? Deployments fit neatly into the following three categories.

Personal, with iTunes

This personal deployment is thankfully the easiest and closest to the model being used by millions of iPad users around the world. Just set them up one by one with an Apple ID and an iTunes account. You can either share a school account or allow some users to manage their own. Buy the apps, or tap the Purchased option in iTunes and download apps that have already been bought and made available to each device. Synchronization and app upgrades are relatively easy. You can attach the device to a computer with iTunes and elect to have updates done wirelessly. Use iCloud, and documents and data can also be synchronized among your various devices.

It's painless, quick, and gets you rolling quickly . . . even leaving you with a smile on your face!

Large, with MDM solutions

I now jump to the other end of the spectrum. Large-scale deployments are for entire organizations, schools, and school districts. The numbers can range from 150 iPads up to many thousands. To clarify what may be obvious, if you aren't an IT professional, run screaming . . . now.

You stayed. For large-scale deployments, you need a system that enables centralized control over the management of large numbers of devices. Those solutions fall under the category of what is generally called Mobile Device Management, or MDM solutions.

MDM software gives IT departments the capability to enroll devices in a centrally managed environment, wirelessly configure and update their settings, and even remotely wipe or lock managed devices. Several third-party MDM solutions are available for managing iOS devices. They communicate using the Apple Push Notification service to wake up enrolled devices and check in with the MDM server to retrieve pending actions or queries. If you Google *MDM management of iOS devices,* you'll get a comprehensive list of options that you can evaluate. Just make sure you give it to the right IT professional.

Small to midsize, with Apple Configurator

The small to midsize deployment is characterized by anywhere from 10 to 150 iPads, and it could be for a small school, a pilot program, or individual classes. Apple has made important strides in enabling the management of smaller deployments without the need for dedicated IT involvement. It does still require a fair amount of reading and training, but it's definitely possible to manage your small deployment of a class set of iPads.

Your best option is using a free tool from Apple called Apple Configurator (see Figure 3-1). Use Configurator to set up new devices, install apps, and manage individual settings. It's a perfect solution for classrooms or smaller deployments, especially because settings, apps, and policies change so rapidly. You can use Apple Configurator to assign devices to specific users and personalize them with data and documents.

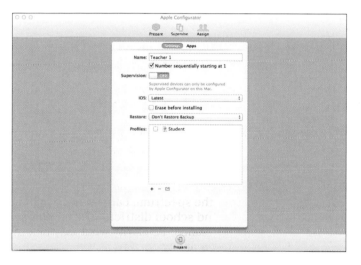

Figure 3-1: Manage devices, profile settings, and data on devices with Apple Configurator.

Apple Configurator works on your laptop or desktop and can be downloaded from the Mac App Store. It uses three simple workflows to prepare new iOS devices for distribution, supervise device configurations, and assign those devices to users.

Preparing devices

Device management has three stages: prepare, supervise, and assign. Each stage has a corresponding pane (shown along the top in Figure 3-2) in Apple Configurator.

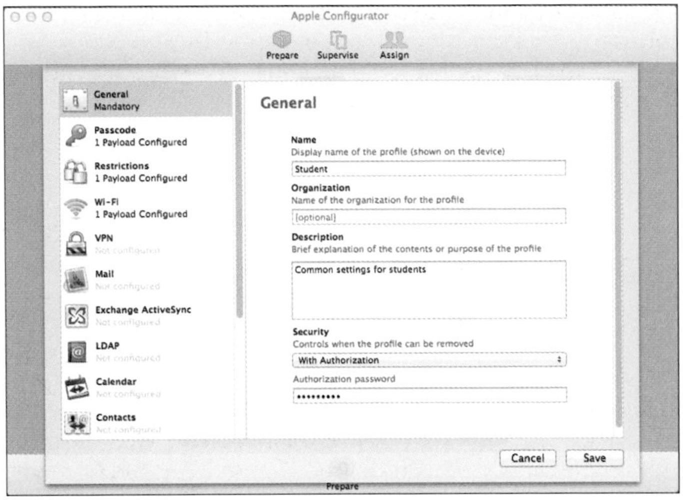

Figure 3-2: Set profiles in Apple Configurator with settings for groups of users or devices.

The first stage prepares a set of iOS devices. The most common practices are as follows:

- **Create a master iPad.** A *master iPad* has all the apps and settings you want to deploy. You use Configurator to back up this iPad and restore the backup to other devices. You can apply only one backup to any specific device.

- **Create a series of configuration profiles, which are then deployed to devices and users.** A *profile* is essentially a template that consists of a combination of settings that applies to a specific group of users, such as students, teachers, or administrators, or to devices, such as library iPads, Science iPads, computer lab, and so on. Unlike with backups, you can apply as many configuration profiles to devices as you'd like. For example, you may want to apply the library profile with the student profile.

Profiles can be used to set restrictions such as disabling app downloads and in-app purchases; disabling apps such as FaceTime and iTunes; and disabling the capability to change e-mail accounts, multiplayer gaming, and many additional options. Profiles determine and set e-mail accounts, wireless network connections, policy for passcode length, Safari preferences, common user contacts and calendars, and more. Also, you may create different profiles according to user. For example, you may want your teachers to have YouTube access and access to a wireless network that isn't filtered. That can be easily accomplished by creating and applying a different user profile for teacher iPads.

Additional options include the installation of a specific version of iOS and, more important, whether to supervise devices. If you elect to configure a device as supervised, it means you can't supervise it or sync it with any other computer running Apple Configurator or iTunes.

Supervising devices

The second stage is supervision; you access the settings for this stage under the Supervise tab in Configurator's main toolbar. Typically, you would have your computer connected to a set of iPads in a cart or powered USB hub at this stage. When you connect supervised devices, they are erased, and you specify which configurations to restore.

You may supervise devices with an identical configuration that needs to be controlled and configured by Apple Configurator on an ongoing basis. Supervised devices can't be synced with iTunes or Apple Configurator on a different computer.

The first two columns list your devices — those currently connected through a USB connection and other supervised devices that aren't connected. The iPads are listed in groups, and you can add and organize devices into groups as needed.

A group is essentially a combination of settings and apps as defined by the third panel on the right. You would probably have a separate set of settings and apps for your science faculty than you might for the history faculty or for the students in third grade.

Select the device you want to configure, or click All to configure all devices in the current group. Make any changes in the Settings and Apps panes and then click the Apply button. You can also make changes to devices that are not currently connected, but those changes will not take effect until the next time the device is connected.

To add apps to a device or group, I recommend using the Volume Purchasing program. In Apple Configurator, click Prepare or Supervise, click Apps, and then click the Add App button at the bottom of the window. When you click the Apps tab in the Supervise pane, Configurator will display your purchased apps or prompt you for their location. As discussed in Chapter 2, Apple's Volume Purchasing Program (VPP) enables schools to purchase apps in larger quantities at a discount. A spreadsheet is created with redemption codes for each purchased install. Add the paid app to Apple Configurator and then import the VPP codes for it by clicking the indicator next to the app with the numeral 0 in it. Select the Import Redemption Codes option and the spreadsheet containing the codes purchased for the app.

Assigning devices

This optional third stage enables you to assign any supervised device to a user you've defined within Apple Configurator. Supervised devices that have been assigned to users can be personalized with documents and data. User data is backed up and restored each time a device is checked in or out so that users can access their data no matter which device they use. The Assign pane in Apple Configurator lists users and the devices each user has checked out. You can use the Assign pane to check out and check in devices, create users and user groups, and install and retrieve documents.

Management Tips

Managing iOS devices is still a work in progress, and it's likely to undergo several important revisions in the near future. In the meantime, maybe a couple of tips from the field will help make the task a little easier for you.

Using restrictions on student iPads

Whether you manage devices and profiles centrally or by individual device, you'll want to put some thought into how to set the restrictions on iPad use. Of course, the restrictions will be different depending on the users and what they should be doing with the iPad. If you're assigning restrictions directly on the iPad itself, go to the Settings menu, and tap General on the left. Tap Restrictions, and you'll get the pane shown in Figure 3-3. You'll be required to set a passcode that can be used later to change or delete restrictions.

Here's a quick look at some of the most important restrictions:

- Disallow apps such as Safari (in case you want to use a different, filtered browser), FaceTime, and the iTunes Store.
- Disable the camera and FaceTime.
- Install and/or delete apps.
- Disable multiplayer games in Game Center.

You can choose to prevent changes to the following settings and accounts:

- Location Services (a good idea if students are posting any data to the web that contains geolocation data, such as photos)
- Mail, Contacts, Calendars, iCloud, and/or Twitter accounts

In addition, you can choose to prevent access to specific content types, such as music and podcasts, movies, TV shows, and more.

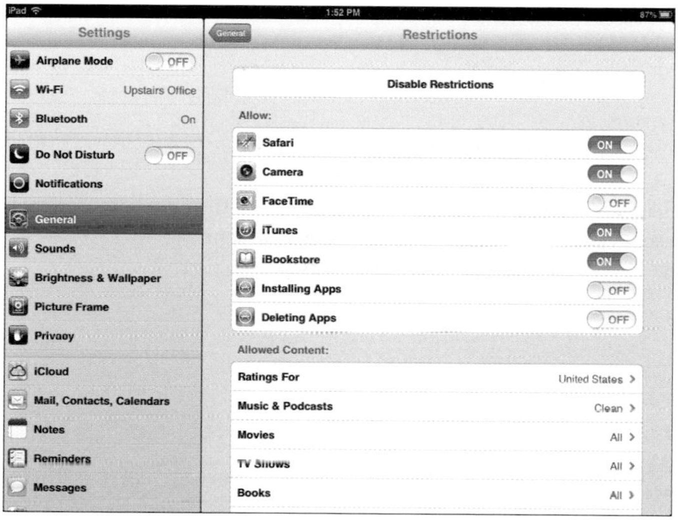

Figure 3-3: Set restrictions on iPad use on the iPad itself or in a profile management tool.

Tracking devices with Find My iPad

Activating Find My iPad can be a valuable tool for tracking down lost iPads on campus or off. You need an iCloud account to use it; then you can log in to iCloud on any browser, and it will show you the location of your iPad on a map if and when it's powered on.

Go to Settings on your iPad, tap iCloud, and enable Find My iPad. Then, if you misplace the iPad, sign in to www.icloud.com from any web browser on a Mac or PC to display the approximate location of your iPad on a map. Find My iPad will allow you to play a beep, display a message, lock your iPad remotely, or even wipe your data off it.

Managing that syncing feeling

Everything changes so quickly, doesn't it? I took a look at my iPad this morning and noticed that almost 90 apps required updates! Fortunately, you have two options for syncing content such as apps, books, music, and photos:

✔ **Tethered syncing:** You can sync by connecting an iPad to a computer with iTunes or connecting a cart of iPads to that computer, assuming that the cart supports syncing. Use iTunes on your computer to identify the devices and content to sync.

✔ **Wireless syncing:** I recommend relying on wireless syncing only for smaller deployments because it will devour your bandwidth. However, if that's your situation, it's simple to set up, and it will save lots of time.

Here's how to set up wireless syncing:

1. **Connect your computer to a wireless network, and open iTunes.**

2. **Tap to open Settings and then select General.**

3. **Tap the iTunes Wi-Fi option in the right panel.**

   You'll see a list of all computers available on the Wi-Fi network.

4. **Select one, and tap the Sync Now button.**

If you don't have iOS 6 installed, one of the best reasons to install it is that app updates no longer require an iTunes password. It makes sense, doesn't it? If you already validated the purchase of an app, why should you have to sign in every time the app requires an update? The huge advantage from an educational standpoint is that teachers can simply and immediately update classroom iPads as needed.

Identifying iPads

Each iPad has a specific name. If you open Settings and tap General and then About, the name is the first item that appears in the pane on the right. However, when you need to quickly identify an iPad to hand out to a student, that takes too many steps. Sure, you can put a sticker on them (the iPads, not the kids!), but stickers fall off.

Some schools identify iPads by creating an image with a number on it and setting it as the wallpaper. That way, as soon as you turn the iPad on, the number shows up on the screen. A nice idea. Why not take this idea a step further and use a little introductory lesson that is also educational? Why not use the opportunity to have the students tell you something about themselves or their interests? Have them find an image that represents something meaningful to them — a fun task that can be done at home with a parent or relative.

Use an app such as Skitch (a free art app) to combine the image with text containing a fact or some identifiable information about the image. It might be something about the student's favorite car, hero, or pet (as shown in Figure 3-4). Set the image as the iPad wallpaper or Lock screen. The students will be extremely motivated and identify more with their particular iPads.

Managing content with e-mail

I talk a little more about classroom data workflows later in this chapter. iPads don't have a standard login or file system, so it can be a challenge moving content off the iPad for submissions to teachers or backup. One tool that's available in almost every iPad is e-mail, and it can always be used to move content quickly and easily — whether you actually e-mail it to a teacher or to a cloud storage service.

TIP

Self-management of iPads

Managing tens and hundreds of iPads can be a difficult process with any tool. Some schools have decided to let older students manage the devices themselves. They are responsible for downloading and updating apps, updating operating systems, and more. Theoretically, you could still set the devices up with some limited restrictions if needed and then just hand them over to the students. Granted, it's a leap for many administrators, but it relieves schools of the headache of centralized management while also nurturing student independence and responsibility. It's worthy of discussion.

To enable e-mail, however, you need to ensure that each iPad has an e-mail account configured. Most schools prefer to restrict that account to outgoing mail. I strongly recommend that each iPad have an outgoing e-mail account available for use. A second option to consider is to create a custom e-mail signature that identifies the iPad (for example, "Sent from Norwood MS, 7th grade iPad #17").

Figure 3-4: Have students set the wallpaper for their iPads to help identify them.

Classroom Workflow Options

When you think of managing iPads in schools, the focus is generally on how to set up and use the device itself. What we forget is that school is essentially about communication and the exchange of information. Enabling simple and effective exchange of information is critical to the process of education. That type of information exchange is typically called a *workflow*.

Defining workflows

When you go to an architect, you don't just ask him to design a house. You begin by discussing your needs and desires. What sort of house do you want? The same logic applies to the design of information workflows. Here I define some workflows for a 21st-century classroom, and then I dive into some solutions that accommodate our requirements.

- ✓ **Delivering information:** Content delivery was the staple of education in the 20th century, and even though we strive for a more student-centered approach to learning, there are still times when teachers need to deliver content. This is best served by a web-based service; teachers can drop the information in a folder, and students can easily pick it up.

- ✓ **Submitting information:** Students need to be able to easily submit work to teachers. One important distinction today is that information is multifaceted. It's no longer just text. Information may be images, videos, or links to the web, and our workflow often has to deal with files that can be quite large.

- ✓ **Communicating anywhere, anytime:** Key elements of 21st-century learning are access and communication. Students need to be able to work in class and edit and share that work outside class. Using secure cloud storage can enable anywhere, anytime access.

- ✓ **Annotating, marking up, and returning documents:** Receiving constructive feedback is critical to learning. Many teachers require workflows that enable them to mark up and annotate documents, create a digital copies, and then return those copies to students in a secure location.

- ✓ **Providing continuous student narrative:** A blog is an ongoing narrative owned and edited by a single student. What distinguishes it from a regular journal is that it can be shared privately with a single person such as a teacher, shared within a group, or shared with the general public.

- ✓ **Enabling collaborative work:** Students often need a secure location to share information and work together on projects securely.

Now I move on and show you some ways to structure solutions for these workflows.

Creating workflow solutions

The options here are many and detailed. Select workflow solutions that aren't too complex for your needs, don't break your budget, and work efficiently with your population of students and iPads. For example, sharing a cloud folder with each student is fine if you have to manage only a handful of accounts, but it might become cumbersome if there's no organizational management, and you're dealing with a hundred students. Another factor that will influence workflow is whether you're in a 1:1 environment where each student has his or her own iPad or the iPads are being shared. A shared environment requires a workflow that doesn't expose one student's account to another.

The bottom line is that there's no single solution for every situation. Try a few things out, and see what works best for you. In this section, I outline workflows using Dropbox and Evernote.

Using Dropbox file sharing

Dropbox is one of the many cloud-based solutions for file storage and sharing. It's popular because of its features; its price; and the fact that it works across devices, platforms, and over the web.

Open a free account at www.dropbox.com. You can easily store files in a Dropbox folder from any device and set sharing permissions for the folder. Depending on the intended usage, you can keep the folder private, share it with individual Dropbox users, or make it completely public. Dropbox enables you to do the following:

- **Distributing information:** Pushing information out to students is a piece of cake. Just create a folder and share it via a link that students have on their iPads. They tap the link, and anything you've placed in the folder is immediately available. Students don't even need an account.

- **Submitting work:** Students can submit their work without having an account if they have access to e-mail. Check out http://sendtodrop box.com. Sign up, and an e-mail address is linked to your Dropbox so that anyone can e-mail content that is automatically filed in your Dropbox.

- **Annotating and returning work:** If you want to collect and return content, you should have each student sign up for a Dropbox account. Then you can create and share Dropbox folders with individual students. They can simply save assignments and content in the shared folders. You also have the option of using an annotation app (see Chapter 9) to mark up the content, create a copy, and then save it back into the shared folder for the student.

- **Accessing your Dropbox account:** Access your Dropbox account over the web, or download the Dropbox app on your iPad for even simpler access. In addition, part of the appeal of Dropbox is that it's available from within a wide variety of iPad apps. Uploading and accessing your Dropbox files from those apps is fairly simple, as shown in Figure 3-5.

If you're in the United States and want your students to sign up and use any web account or service, the Children's Online Privacy Protection Act (COPPA) requires that they need to be at least 13 years old or have permission from a parent or guardian. I strongly recommend that you have a Responsible

Use Policy signed by the children and their parents and that you include a section that explicitly grants permission to sign up for web accounts that are intended strictly for educational purposes.

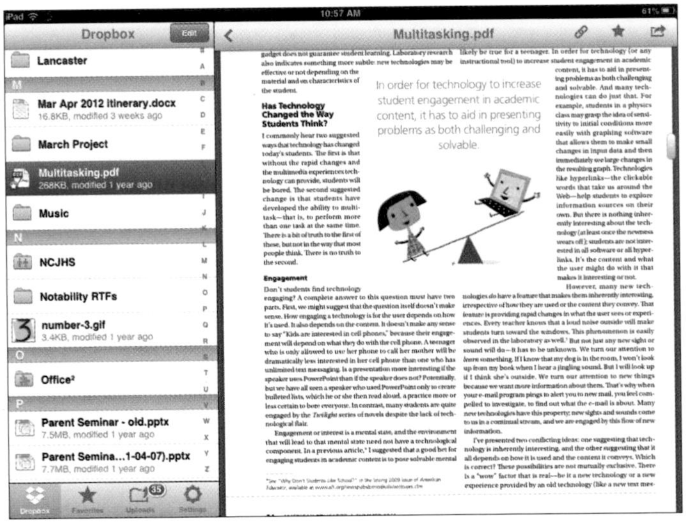

Figure 3-5: Sharing and accessing files from any device is simple with a Dropbox account.

Managing workflows with Evernote

I mention Evernote throughout the book. It's such a versatile app that it can be used for a wide variety of objectives, including managing your classroom workflows. It's versatile enough to handle almost anything you require.

Each Evernote account has notebooks that you can create and customize. Each notebook contains notes. Those notes can contain almost anything digital, including text that you type, attached documents, images, sounds, videos, and even linked web pages. The secret to using Evernote as a workflow solution is that each notebook has sharing options ranging from private to shared with individuals and shared publicly with a link.

Go to www.evernote.com to open your account. Like Dropbox, Evernote fits many of your workflow needs. Students can get free accounts, and Evernote works across devices and web browsers, has tiered sharing options, and also allows e-mail submissions:

- ✔ **Opening an Evernote account:** You can sign up for free accounts or pay an annual fee for a premium account. I recommend that you get a premium account for teachers and free accounts for students. Please note that you must have an e-mail account to sign up.

✔ **Distributing information:** Simple as pie. You have one teacher account with a notebook that you share with a public URL that students can access from their iPads. Anything you place in that notebook is available to people with access. No student accounts are needed. I love it when things are simple.

✔ **Submitting work:** This can also be achieved without student accounts. Every Evernote account has an associated e-mail address. Log in to the web interface at www.evernote.com, tap your name in the top-right corner, and select Settings from the drop-down menu. You'll find your Evernote e-mail account listed on that Settings page. Add the address to Contacts on each student iPad, and give it a descriptive name (for example, Sam: Evernote Submit). Then students can e-mail work from any app to that e-mail address, and it goes right into your Evernote notebook. Make sure students write their names in the subject line of the e-mail as standard procedure.

Using the magical @ symbol: But wait; it gets better. Create a notebook for the submissions, and students can e-mail their work directly to that notebook. For example, if I create a notebook for homework, students would send the e-mail with the subject line John Doe @Homework. The @ symbol automatically tells Evernote to file the submission in the specified notebook.

✔ **Enabling collaborative group work:** Log into your account at www.evernote.com. Create a notebook, and change the sharing options to give each member of the group access. When you add members, you can specify the level of permission to give them — anything from View Only to Modify and even Invite Others.

Members can create and share within that notebook however they please. By the way, you also have access because you created it, so you can check in at any time and review work or give feedback. It's ideal for the 1:1 iPad classroom!

✔ **Sharing work in progress (see Figure 3-6):** Share individual notebooks with students on a 1:1 basis (you both have Modify permissions), and you can check on work in progress. Use this structure for students keeping a blog or any other work in progress. Teachers can check student work and add comments or annotations.

Reviewing a few parting tips

Management tools and techniques will evolve rapidly with the increased use of iPads in schools. Here are a few tips that work for me:

✔ **Moving large photos and videos with PhotoSync:** Photo and video files tend to get pretty large in the multimedia iPad classroom, too large sometimes to e-mail. Try using PhotoSync instead.

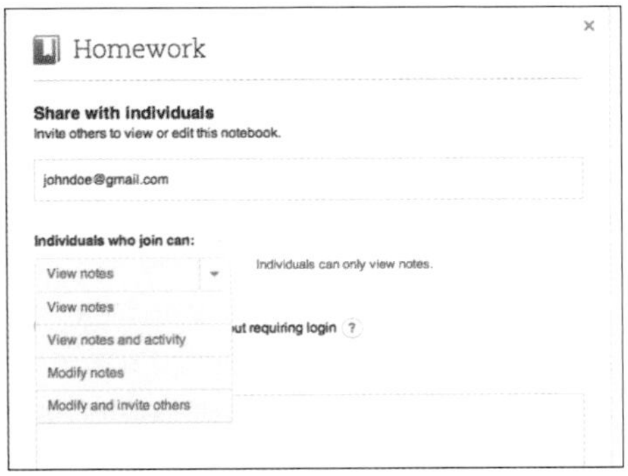

Figure 3-6: Sharing Evernote notebooks.

PhotoSync wirelessly transfers your photos/videos from or to your computer and other iOS devices. Simply install the app on your iPad and download the software on your computer. PhotoSync will also transfer files to a host of web services, including Dropbox, Picasa/Google+, Facebook, SmugMug, Flickr, Box, Google Drive, and more. Select your files, select the target, and transfer them all at once. And it's all wireless!

✔ **Using Printopia in lower grades:** Solutions such as Evernote, Dropbox, and others are great if your students are around fourth grade or higher. A simple solution for collecting student work is to create virtual printers with Printopia. Create a folder on your desktop, define the folder as a virtual printer destination in Printopia, and have the students print their work to it. Refer to Chapter 20 for more detailed information.

✔ **Using WebDAV with Otixo in iWorks:** WebDAV is a method that enables you to edit and manage files stored on remote servers. If you use iWorks — Pages, Numbers and Keynote — on the iPad, you'll discover that iTunes and WebDAV servers are the preferred options for moving content from them. You may be lucky enough to have an IT department that can set up a WebDAV server and create folders for storage. If that isn't true for your situation, consider Otixo.

Otixo is a cloud-based file manager that connects to any of your other cloud services, such as Dropbox, Google Drive, Box, and more. What's great is that it has a WebDAV server that enables you to edit and save files to any of your cloud services. Open an account with Otixo and link it to your other cloud accounts, such as Dropbox, and all of a sudden you're saving and opening your Dropbox files in Pages. Neat.

Part II
Finding and Using Apps

The 5th Wave   By Rich Tennant

"What I'm doing should clear your sinuses, take away your headache, and charge your iPad."

In this part . . .

*W*ith educationally tinted glasses, this part starts with a tour of the apps that come preloaded on your iPad. You discover how to take photos and shoot video; buy, read, and annotate e-books; and find and organize information, among other things. I help you navigate through the veritable ocean of additional apps in the App Store to find, evaluate, and purchase the ones that meet your needs.

4

Tap Dancing with Your iPad's Apps

*Y*ou've just brought home that shiny, sleek new iPad from the store. It's crammed full of apps that let you start surfing the Internet, take photos and video, e-mail, video-chat, watch movies, read books, and more. It's there waiting for you . . . as soon as you master a few basics about using your iPad's apps. It's all really very easy. It's just that we start at such a huge disadvantage. After all, we're adults.

Children pull the device out of the box, power it up, and start using it instantly. They're so tech-savvy, it's almost as if they were using technology in utero. Adults? In the best-case scenario, you look for a user manual. Worst case, you close the box and go find a book to distract you from the need to learn another electronic device. No problem. Just make sure it's this book, and you'll be an expert app user in no time!

The iPad is a tool with almost limitless possibilities once you master some of its core apps. This chapter walks you through using most of the apps that came with your iPad and shows you some of the amazing things you can do with them. It discusses how to use e-mail, access the Internet, use the camera, read e-books, and more. Put on your seat belt, and let's get going.

Making Mail a Communication Tool

One of the least heralded characteristics of iPads is that they really are terrific communication devices. The wonderful Mail app is a perfect example.

Many of us have more than one e-mail account. You may have one for work, one for home, and possibly another account for the cousin who constantly sends you jokes you don't want to read. One of the many convenient features of your iPad's Mail app is its capability to collect and display messages from different e-mail accounts in one simple location. You don't have to log into different websites to check your personal, work, and school e-mails because all your messages are organized in one easy-to-access location. You'll never have to worry about which e-mail you've forgotten to check, and you don't have to waste time reentering your username and password again and again. The iPad's Mail app will keep you connected to your e-mail and make it simple for you to track and reply to all your digital correspondence . . . even with your annoying cousin.

Opening Mail accounts

The first step to using the Mail app is to sign in to your e-mail account(s):

1. **Tap the Mail icon on your iPad home screen.**

   The Mail icon often can be found on the application Dock at the bottom of your home screen.

2. **Choose your e-mail provider.**

   Mail works with popular e-mail providers, including Google Gmail, Microsoft Exchange, Yahoo! Mail, Hotmail, and AOL (see Figure 4-1). They are listed as default options for mail setup. If your e-mail belongs to one of those services, tap and select it. If you don't see your e-mail provider listed here, tap Other and then tap Add Mail Account; enter specific details about your mail provider.

3. **Follow the prompts on your iPad.**

   The Mail app will ask for information such as a username and password during the initial setup.

If you ever need to change details about an existing account, go to your home screen, tap Settings, and then tap Mail, Contacts, Calendars. Select the account you want to edit, and modify the information.

The best part about Mail is the capability to have all your e-mails in one place! (See Figure 4-2.) You can only do that if you add in all your e-mail accounts. To add another account, head back to your home screen. Tap Settings, then tap Mail, Contacts, Calendars, tap Add Account, and follow the onscreen instructions. You'll never miss an e-mail about a staff meeting, an e-vite to your niece's birthday party, or an electronic half-off coupon again!

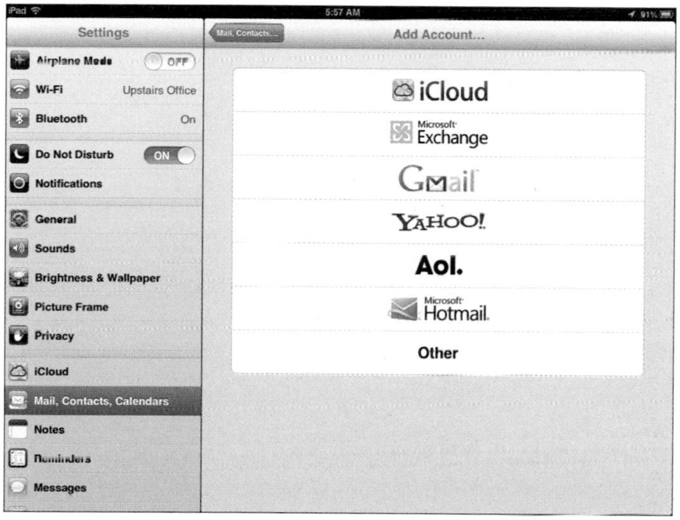

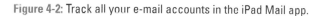

Figure 4-1: Follow the prompts to set up your e-mail accounts.

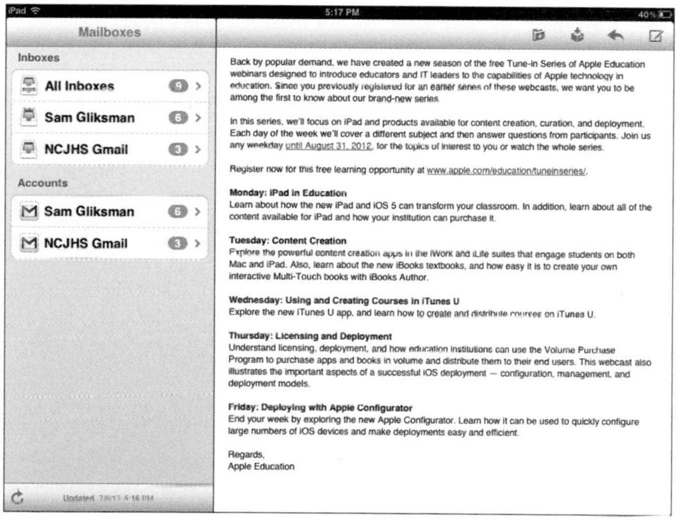

Figure 4-2: Track all your e-mail accounts in the iPad Mail app.

Your iPad settings give you control over quite a few of the Mail defaults, such as how many messages to show and how to display them. The options are listed under the Mail, Contacts, Calendar menu category in Settings. You'll notice that there's also a choice entitled Fetch New Data. That enables you to set the method and frequency your iPad uses when getting your e-mail. The more often you fetch your e-mail, the more battery you'll use. If you want to prolong your battery life, fetch your e-mail less frequently.

Browsing mail

Once you have set up your mail accounts, simply tap the Mail icon on your iPad home screen to open the Mail app and check your e-mail. If you're holding your iPad in landscape orientation, you'll see the following:

- ✔ Your accounts are listed on the left. The Mail app has one section for Inboxes and another for all the folders you have in your account. Tap any option in the left pane to start browsing mail.

- ✔ When you tap the option, it opens the appropriate folder and lists the mail in it. Scroll through the list and tap any mail to browse it in the pane on the right. Messages may be grouped in threads (that option can be changed in Settings) so that the original e-mail and its replies are kept together in a list.

- ✔ If an e-mail contains images, the images will appear in the body of the message. Tap and hold any image, and you can save it to your Camera Roll. You can also tap any document attachments such as PDF, iWork, or Word files to open and view them.

- ✔ If you added more than one e-mail account, you'll have the option of tapping the All Inboxes choice on the menus, where you can browse all the messages from all your accounts in one integrated list.

If you hold your iPad vertically, the navigation pane automatically disappears so that you have more space to read your e-mail. Tap the button with the account or folder name in the top-left corner of the screen, and the navigation pane will slide back in.

Creating and sending an e-mail

Creating and sending e-mail is a piece of cake. The top-right corner of your screen includes the Compose icon (refer to Figure 4-2). Tap it to start a new e-mail. The virtual keyboard will slide up when you tap in any text field. Enter the recipient in the To field, and fill in the Subject. Tap anywhere in the body to start typing your message. When you're done, tap Send in the top-right corner, and your message is on its way!

Everyone asks the same question about e-mail at some point. The answer is "No, you can't get your message back once you've sent it." The moral is simple: Read your e-mail carefully before tapping that Send button.

Using contacts

Digital address books have been around for quite a few years, and they make tracking and using your contact information simple. Your iPad has a Contacts app as well, and it integrates directly with Mail. You can add contacts in several ways:

✔ Tap the Contacts icon on your iPad; then press the + icon to enter data about a new contact directly into the app.

✔ Tap the name of any person who sent you an e-mail in the From field of the e-mail. A pop-up window will display the sender's details and options to Create New Contact or Add to Existing Contact. Tap either option to add the sender's e-mail address to your Contacts list.

✔ Synchronize your Contacts list with an existing list as part of your iPad synchronization. Refer to Chapter 3 for more information.

When you compose a new e-mail, you'll notice a + sign on the right of the To field. Tap it to bring up your contact list, and select a recipient.

You may also notice that your iPad Mail app has an excellent memory. It keeps a history of people whom you have e-mailed and will pop up a list of suggested names from the history list when you start typing in the recipient field. Now, if it could only remember where you put your keys . . .

Deleting e-mail

Swipe across any e-mail in your mail list, and Mail will prompt you to delete it. You can also tap the Trash icon on the toolbar above any open e-mail to delete it. Of course, there's always that time you delete an e-mail and then realize you could use that coupon for another power drill after all.

Mail generally moves deleted e-mail to a trash or archive folder. Tap your account in the menu on the left and look for the folder with your deleted messages. Don't fret — your e-mail is just as you last saw it and can be accessed there. Your only problem might be explaining that sixth power drill to your wife.

Taking an Educational Internet Safari

What if you're standing in front of the class teaching history and you can't remember the date of Henry VIII's fifth marriage? Talk about egg on your face! Seriously, having quick and easy access to the Internet is an invaluable learning tool. With Safari, iPad's web browser, the Internet is always just a simple tap away.

Browsing and tabs

Safari was given a major upgrade when Apple released iOS 5, and one of the most prominent new features is the capability to keep multiple pages open in tabs within the browser, as shown in Figure 4-3. This list gives you the basics of working with tabs:

✔ **Opening a new tab:** You'll see each page displayed in a row of tabs along the top of your browser window, and you can open a new tab at any time by tapping the + icon at the right of the row.

✔ **Switching tabs:** Tap any tab to switch focus to that page.

✔ **Closing tabs:** Tap the little x on the tab to close it.

You can keep up to nine pages open in tabs. Safari will remember your open tabs and reopen them when you next browse the Internet.

Figure 4-3: Safari in iOS 5 and higher uses tabbed browsing for keeping multiple pages open.

Safari was given a major facelift when Apple released its iOS 5 operating system in October 2011 and then again with the release of iOS 6 in 2012. Features such as browser tabs for multiple pages, Reader, Reading List, and more are all significant upgrades to the prior version. I focus on the iOS 6 version of Safari in these discussions, and I strongly recommend that you upgrade to it if you haven't already.

Googling

I have to confess that I'm a sentimentalist at heart. I still treasure the smell and feel of those old encyclopedias I had as a kid, and it's hard to believe that brands such as Britannica are no longer published. On the other hand, I absolutely love the fact that I can type a few words in a web browser and access information anywhere in the world instantly — and the most popular key to searching that vast knowledge base is Google.

It has become so popular that the word *Google* is used as a verb, and we now refer to searching as *Googling*. Jump-start your Google searches by using one of these two shortcuts:

- **Safari's built-in Google search:** This is a great tool to use if, while you are using Safari, you realize there is information you want to look up. In the top-right corner of your Safari screen, you will see an oval text field with the word *Google* in gray. Tap in the field and type in whatever it is that you want to know, and your wish is Google's command! (Note that you can also use Settings to change the default search engine used by Safari to either Yahoo! or Bing.)

- **iPad's built-in search engine:** From your home screen, you can tap your Home button one more time and go to the iPad search screen. Type your query into the box at the top of the screen and then tap Search Web. This opens a new tab in Safari with your Google search results.

You can set your default web search provider on the iPad. To make sure that Google is your default search engine, go to your home screen and tap Settings. Then tap Safari on the left navigation pane. The first option allows you to select which search engine to use.

Getting rid of clutter with Reader

It seems like websites are getting more and more cluttered — between the advertisements, stock tickers, and pop-ups, it's hard to identify the actual content you're trying to read. If you're using iOS 5 or higher, Safari has added a solution with its Reader function, shown in Figure 4-4.

When you browse through most websites, a Reader icon appears in the right side of the address bar. Just tap the Reader, icon and Safari will display only the article. All the clutter is gone! If only I could do that to my desk . . .

Using bookmarks

Bookmarking is a must with Safari. Save websites you frequently visit to avoid having to remember and type their addresses manually. The following highlights how to bookmark in Safari:

- **Add a bookmark:** When you are visiting a page you want to bookmark, tap the curved arrow directly to the left of the address bar. This will bring up a menu of options. Tap Add Bookmark, edit the name if you like, and tap Save. Your bookmark has been added!

- **View your bookmarks:** Tapping the Bookmark icon at the top left of your Safari browser will display your list of saved websites. Select any site in the list by tapping it, and it will open in your Safari browser.

> ✔ **Edit your bookmarks:** You can add, delete, and organize your saved websites. Tap the Bookmarks icon and then tap Edit in the top-right corner to delete bookmarks, move items in the list, create folders, and more.

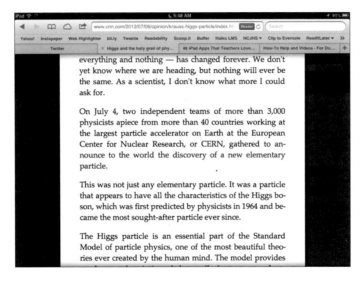

Figure 4-4: Safari's Reader function removes clutter and makes it easier to read articles.

Bookmarks include a folder called Bookmarks Bar. Everything in that folder is displayed on a toolbar at the top of the Safari browser window. Save sites to the Bookmarks Bar folder for quick and easy access.

Safari in iOS 6 has added several new Share options that you can access from a number of apps, including your Safari web browser. When you tap the curved arrow to the left of the address bar in Safari, you can now send the web page directly to the Message app, your Facebook page, and more.

Making a Reading List

"So much to do, so little time." Sound familiar? It's certainly the case that there never seems to be enough time for everything you want to read on the Internet. Safari now includes a Reading List function that helps you keep track of all those I'm-going-to-read-it-as-soon-as-I-have-a-free-moment articles and websites.

If you want to add a web page for later reading, tap the curved arrow to the left of Safari's address bar and select Add to Reading List. When you want to catch up on your reading, tap your Bookmarks icon; the top item on the menu is Reading List. Tap to select it. Your saved pages will appear under the Unread tab. Use Reading List to build your own personalized library of articles.

Adding a website to your home screen

What if you use a website so frequently that simply bookmarking it doesn't give you fast enough access? If you have that need for speed, consider adding the website's link directly to your home screen. It's as easy as 1, 2, 3:

1. **Open the web page in your Safari browser.**

2. **Tap the curved arrow to the left of the address bar to display a menu of options.**

3. **Tap Add to Home Screen to add the website icon directly on your iPad home screen.**

   You can edit the name to make the site easily recognizable; then tap Add. Now when you tap that icon on your iPad, it will automatically open Safari and display that web page.

Adding a website directly to the iPad home screen is a great option to use if you have a classroom website. Add the icon to all student iPads, and with one tap, they're on the class page and working.

Saving images from the web

In the Digital Storytelling chapters later in this book, you see some of the tremendous potential for creating multimedia content on the iPad. You may have frequent occasions in which you'd like to use an image on the web. Tap and hold the image in Safari, and a menu will pop up with options to Save Image or Copy (see Figure 4-5). Tap Save Image, and the image is added to your Camera Roll — and will be available in other apps as well.

Using images from the web provides an excellent time to discuss copyright and fair use. Make sure students are aware of when and how they can legally use images, video, music, and other web content.

Figure 4-5: Tap and hold any image to save it.

Searching the page

Here's a typical scenario: You do a Google search for *Philosophy Quotes Descartes.* You tap one of your Google search results and get a page that lists quotes from every famous person in history who has ever uttered a quotable phrase. That quote you want from Descartes is in there *somewhere,* but it would take you about 20 minutes and a couple of aspirin to find it. Safari has your solution: You can search the page. Just follow these steps:

1. **Open the web page in Safari that you want to search.**

2. **Tap in the Google search field on the top right of your browser, and type your search term.**

   Type whatever word or phrase you're searching in the Google search field. For example, you may type **Descartes**.

3. **Search the page using one of these two options:**

   a. *Using Google Search:* At the top of the search results are Google suggestions. If you tap any of those, Safari runs a new Google search.

   b. *Using On This Page:* If you scroll down to the bottom of the list, you see an On This Page option. Tap that option to see all instances of the search phrase on the current web page.

   Depending on your version of Safari, a Find on Page toolbar (shown in Figure 4-6) may also open above your keyboard when you tap in the Google search field. That allows you to type your search term and automatically have it applied to the current page. Now, wasn't that easy?

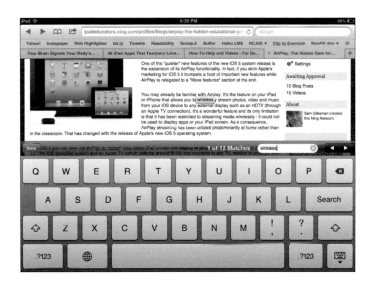

Figure 4-6: Tap in the Google search field to open a Find on Page toolbar in Safari.

Taking and Using Photos and Video as Learning Tools

Modern society is awash in multimedia. Movies, mobile devices, YouTube, video chat, social networking — it's all around us in work and at play. Multimedia is finally starting to make an impression within our educational spaces as well. Projects that used to consist of cardboard posters with glued pictures and articles are often now being created, edited, and delivered as sophisticated video presentations. Your iPad is well equipped with several capable tools to assist in those important multimedia communications.

Taking photos

If you have an iPad 2 or higher, it comes with both front- and rear-facing cameras (see Figure 4-7). Access to the capability to take photos at any time is not only extremely convenient for classroom use, but can also be a great tool for creativity and innovation. The possibilities are limited only by your and your students' imaginations:

- Use it to document student work and create a digital portfolio to share with parents.
- Snap an image of a busy whiteboard to record important information.
- Stage and take photos as part of digital storytelling projects.

✔ Document science experiments with photos.

✔ Take photos of real-world examples of mathematical concepts such as shapes and angles.

✔ Develop students' visual literacy skills by using photography as a communication tool.

Camera button

Camera roll

Switch between front and rear camera

Switch between camera and video

Figure 4-7: The iPad 2 and higher have front and rear cameras for use in the Camera app.

To use the iPad camera:

1. **Go to your iPad home screen, and tap the Camera icon to open the app.**

   Make sure that the Switch Camera/Video icon in the lower-right corner is in Camera mode (refer to Figure 4-7).

2. **Select a camera view by tapping the Switch Camera icon to toggle between the front and rear cameras.**

3. **Aim your iPad so that your desired photo is displayed on the screen.**

   You can also zoom by pinching your fingers together to activate the zoom slide bar. Slide right to zoom in and left to zoom back out.

4. **Tap the Camera icon or press the Volume button on the side of the iPad to snap your image.**

   The photo will be captured and saved in the Camera Roll on your iPad.

Shooting video

The iPad makes the creation of video a realistic and practical option for students. If you have an iPad 2, the rear camera takes video at 720p. The third-generation iPad iSight camera shoots video at 1080p. What does that all mean? If you have an iPad 2, your video quality is reasonable, but if you have a third-generation iPad, it's even better. Either way, it's an excellent option for developing the creation of video as a core tool for learning and communication.

Shooting video is as simple as taking a photo. Here's how:

1. **Go to your iPad home screen, and tap the Camera icon to open the app.**

2. **Using the Switch Camera/Video toggle in the lower-right corner, select Video mode.**

3. **Tap the red Record icon or press the Volume button on the side of the iPad to begin shooting your scene.**

4. **Tap the red Record icon or Volume button again to stop the recording.**

    Your video will be captured and saved in the Camera Roll on your iPad.

Remember that forward-facing-camera option? You know, the camera that made you jump when all of a sudden your own face appeared onscreen! That camera can be most useful in a classroom setting when in video mode. If you teach a foreign language or are working on an oral language learning goal, you can have students record themselves reading a passage or engaging in dialogue. This can be played back for student reflection or submitted to you as a form of assessment. And let's face it: Kids love listening to their own voices!

Importing pictures and videos

You can import photos to an iPad using any of these methods:

- ✔ **iTunes:** Synchronize photos from applications or folders on your computer using iTunes.

- ✔ **iCloud:** If you have an iCloud account with Apple, it synchronizes and pushes your content to all your devices wirelessly.

    From your camera: Apple sells an optional Camera Connection Kit, which you can connect to your iPad to copy photos directly from your camera.

✔ **An e-mail, the web, or a cloud account:** E-mail photos to any list of recipients. With the e-mail open, the recipients can tap and hold the image and select to save it to their Camera Roll. You can also place images on a class home page and have students tap and hold to save them to their iPads. Alternatively, use a cloud storage account such as Dropbox (www.dropbox.com). Upload any list of images to a Dropbox account and then open and save them on your iPad.

✔ **Apps:** My favorite app for transferring photos and video is PhotoSync, shown in Figure 4-8. Open PhotoSync, and select the photos and video you want to transfer. It automatically detects any device on the same Wi-Fi network that has PhotoSync installed — including any laptops or desktops — and allows you to transfer the files wirelessly and effortlessly. PhotoSync can be a terrific solution for collecting photos and large video files from student iPads onto a teacher's laptop.

Figure 4-8: PhotoSync can transfer photos and video wirelessly between devices.

Editing pictures

It happens rarely, but this time you were in just the right place to snap that perfect photo at the exact instant it happened. You open it in your photos app only to find out the photo is too dark. Luckily, if you have the newer release of the Photos app (see Figure 4-9), you have access to some handy editing tools to clean up your image.

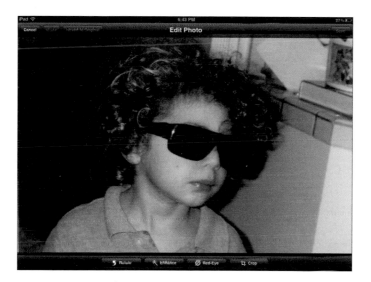

Figure 4-9: The Photos app includes four tools for editing your photos.

Tap the Photos app, and select an image by tapping it. A toolbar with four editing tools appears along the bottom of the image:

- **Rotate:** Each tap of the Rotate icon turns the image 90 degrees counterclockwise.

- **Enhance:** Tap Enhance, and the photo editor analyzes the lighting, color composition, and contrast of your photo and automatically makes adjustments. You'd be surprised how much better you can look after a little enhancement!

- **Red-Eye:** Follow the onscreen prompt, tap an area to remove red-eye, and tap again to Undo.

- **Crop:** Tap the Crop button to

    - *Crop:* Tap and drag the brackets in the corners of your image to crop the desired portion of your photo.

    - *Straighten and zoom:* Tap your picture with two fingers and swivel to rotate the image. To zoom, unpinch two fingers outward.

    - *Constrain:* Tap the Constrain button to set the cropped image to popular proportions such as 4x6 or 5x7.

You think the photo looked better before you started messing with it? No problem. Tap Undo on the top menu bar, and you can step back through your changes. Tap Revert to Original to go all the way back to the original image.

Editing video

You don't have to get a degree in cinematography to edit your videos. You can easily do some simple trimming of your video right in your Photos app. Tap to select the video to perform these video-editing tasks:

✔ **Set the start and end frames:** At the top of the screen, you'll see a bar with video frames. Drag the sliders at each end to the frames where you want your video to start and end.

✔ **Trim:** Tap the yellow Trim button, and then choose to either overwrite the original version of the video or save your edited clip as a new version.

Those last few seconds where your hair looked all messed up? Gone.

Using pictures and video in projects

The iPad puts multimedia at your fingertips and allows it to become an integral part of the learning process. You and your students have myriad ways to use media, and I devote Chapter 13 to the very important topic of *digital storytelling* — the art of creating stories and conveying knowledge through the use of media. Here's just a quick snapshot of some ideas to get you started:

✔ Narrate a slide show of photos to learn a foreign language.

✔ Create videography detailing the life of your favorite U.S. president on Presidents' Day.

✔ Create a regular student news video outlining what students have learned.

✔ Have students write and narrate a story using a slide show of images that best convey its plot and sentiment.

Refer to Part V, "Expressing Yourself with Media," for lots more information and ideas.

Reading and the E-Book Revolution

As much as some of us still enjoy the feel and smell of that well-worn paperback book, there's no denying that the nature of reading is shifting. Everything from cookbooks to the Bible can now be downloaded and read in digital format. Given that digital storage is becoming cheaper and data transfer is becoming faster, within a few years you will probably be able to download libraries of e-books to mobile devices within minutes.

The iPad represents one of the first fully featured mobile computers that also doubles as an excellent reading device. It's extremely simple to purchase and download books that can be read on your iPad and transferred to other devices. You have a selection of many excellent reading apps for the iPad, including Apple's iBooks app. Apple aptly describes iBooks as both a way to buy books and to read them. It connects directly to Apple's iBookstore, where you can purchase and download books. Downloaded books are stored in the iBooks bookshelf on your iPad and opened for reading with a simple tap on their cover. (See Figure 4-10.)

Figure 4-10: Open any book in iBooks by tapping its cover.

Customizing reading settings

Tap the iBooks app icon on your home screen, and you'll see a bookshelf with any books that you have downloaded. Tap any book to open it, and start reading. Now, before you wiggle your way into a comfortable reading spot on the couch, take note of some adjustments you can make in iBooks to enhance your reading experience.

Start by tapping the Options icon on the top menu bar (shown in Figure 4-11), and you'll see these options:

- **Selecting a theme:** Themes change the color scheme to match the needs of different lighting settings. Select Normal, Sepia, or Night.

- **Adjusting brightness:** Set the Brightness slide control to the level that makes it most comfortable for you to read.

- **Choosing font size:** Under the brightness slider, you'll find two buttons with the letter *A*. As you tap the smaller *A* button on the left, the text will get progressively smaller. Tap the larger *A,* and the font size increases.

- **Picking your favorite font:** Tap the Fonts button to change the text font. Experiment and find the one that makes it easiest for you to read.

iBooks will remember your settings each time you use the app.

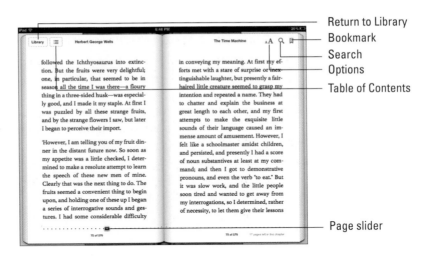

Figure 4-11: iBooks allows you to change reading options and jump to any page.

Changing pages

You can change pages in an iBook in several ways:

- **Tap:** If you want to turn the page to the right, tap or flick your finger in the right margin.

- **Swipe:** To turn the page to the right with a little more flair, place your finger in the right margin and swipe to the left.

- **Jump:** Tap anywhere near the center of the page to brings up the Navigator controls. Drag the slider along the bottom of the page and jump to any page in the book.

- **Table of Contents:** Tap the Table of Contents icon on the top toolbar, and tap to go to a specific chapter or title in the book.

If you activate the VoiceOver feature, the iPad will read the book out loud to you. It's one of the many assistive technologies that have made the iPad so popular with users who have special needs. Chapter 12 covers this topic in detail.

Using bookmarks, highlights, and notes

Don't think for a moment that all you can do with iBooks is *read* books. You can also

- **Set bookmarks:** No need to tear strips of paper to keep your place. iBooks remembers where you left off every time you open it. You can also add a bookmark to any page in the book you want to remember.

Tap the Bookmark icon in the top-right corner of your page, and a red bookmark slides down. Tap it again, and it disappears.

To find your bookmarks, tap the Table of Contents icon, and tap the Bookmarks tab to view the list of bookmarks you added.

✔ **Apply highlights:** I'm not sure about yours, but my memory is like a sieve. I always need to highlight text in a book so that I can browse and review the important sections I've read. Highlighting text in iBooks is similar to selecting text in any editor on the iPad:

- *Tap and hold any word.* It highlights with a shaded box that has grab points in the corners. A pop-up menu offers options that include Highlight, Note, Define, and more.

- *Drag the grab points out to highlight the area of text you want to highlight.*

- *Tap Highlight, and select a highlight color from the pop-up menu of choices.*

✔ **Write notes:** Are you the sort of reader who fills the margins of your favorite books with comments? Fortunately, that's a feature you can also access when using iBooks. Tap and hold to select text on the page, and then tap Note on the pop-up menus. Type your notes in the little Post-it that pops up onscreen, and your note will be saved right where you left it. It's a great way for students to gain a better understanding without defacing school property!

Access your highlights and notes in the same manner as you got your bookmarks. Go to the Table of Contents (see Figure 4-12), and tap the Notes tab at top. Your Table of Contents becomes the central navigation point for everything in the book.

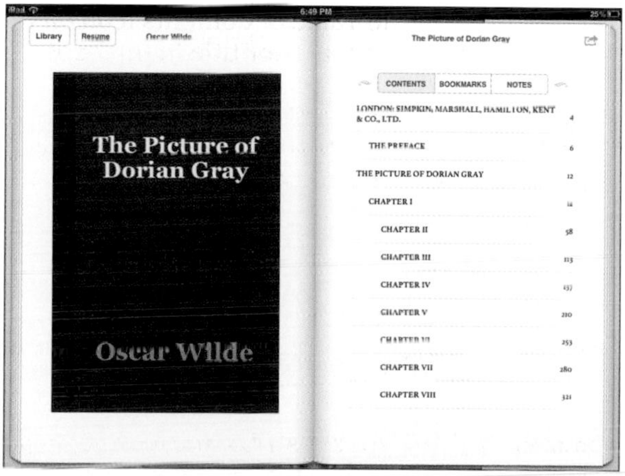

Figure 4-12: Access your Bookmarks, Notes, and Highlights in the Table of Contents.

✓ **Look up word definitions:** One of the nicest features for students using iBooks is the capability to easily access word definitions. Tap and hold to highlight any word, and select Define from the pop-up menus. That's a lot simpler than hauling around that huge and heavy dictionary, don't you think?

Searching

You're trying to find that page in your book that mentioned the name of Roosevelt's dog. You've scoured the table of contents, but it lists only general chapter headings. That's when the Search tool becomes a tangible advantage that you can use in e-books.

To search through the text of a book, tap the magnifying-glass icon on the top menu bar, and type in the word or phrase you want to find. A list of search results is displayed; you can tap any one to jump to that reference in your book. Search even includes options to expand your search to the web (or Wikipedia). By the way, Roosevelt's little dog was named Fala.

Purchasing books

As is the case with many people in my generation, I often find myself with one foot planted in two completely different eras. I'm an avid technologist, yet I grew up as part of the pre-Internet generation. Growing up, I loved perusing the shelves of a bookstore, and I have to confess to feeling some sadness that many bookstores are closing. On the other hand, browsing and purchasing iBooks couldn't be simpler. The iBookstore has several hundred thousand books that I can search and sample. Finding the book I want is quick, and any book I buy is delivered directly to my device, available for me to start reading in a matter of seconds. No driving or parking. No back orders or waiting in lines to pay. Any time, 24/7. It couldn't be more convenient. Just follow these steps:

1. **Tap the Store button in the top-left corner of your iBooks bookshelf to enter the online iBookstore.**

2. **Browse for titles.**

   Navigating in iBookstore is similar to moving around the App Store. Look through the top charts, review featured and new lists of books, browse based on category and genre, or search for a specific title. There's even a section with the list of *New York Times* bestsellers.

3. **Tap any book to read a description and see reviews from other readers.**

4. **(Optional) Tap to download a sample.**

   A sample is downloaded, which you can review to decide whether you want to make the investment of actually buying the book.

5. **To buy a book, tap the price, and confirm that you want to buy the book.**

6. **Complete your purchase by entering your iTunes password.**

   In a few moments, the book will appear in your iBooks bookshelf, ready and waiting for you to flip open the cover and turn the pages — virtually, of course.

There are several wonderful e-reader apps for downloading and reading books on the iPad. Each has its own specific and unique features. Check out Chapter 8 for a review of some of the more popular book reading apps.

If you have an Apple iCloud account, you can sync your iBooks content between devices wirelessly. Start reading a book on your iPad, and when you're in the waiting room at the dentist, you can pull out your iPhone and continue reading right where you left off on the iPad (complete with the note you left in the margin reminding yourself to go to the dentist!). It's really as simple as that. And remember to floss every day, and you'll cut down on those visits to the dentist.

Adding PDF documents

iBooks is also a great way to store and organize your PDF documents. Any time you're viewing a PDF, whether in Safari, in Mail, or in one of the many other apps that can display PDF documents, you'll have an option to open the document in iBooks, as shown in Figure 4-13. It's automatically added to your PDF collection and can be saved and accessed at any time through iBooks.

This can be an effective way to deliver content to students. E-mail a PDF or place it on a classroom website, and have the students open and save it in their iBooks app. Many other apps also allow you to open, save, and annotate PDF documents. I look at those later in the book.

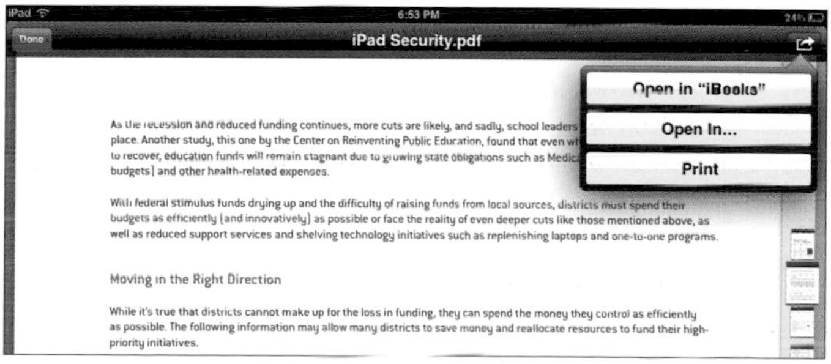

Figure 4-13: PDF attachments and documents can be opened in iBooks.

Organizing collections

When you first open iBooks, you'll notice it has two collections: Books and PDFs. Think of a collection as a bookshelf. It's simply a group of books or content that you can set up to keep them organized.

Tap the Collections button on top of your iBooks bookshelf to add and edit your collections. You can also move books and documents between collections by tapping the Edit button in the top-right corner, selecting the content, and tapping the Move button that pops up on the left of the top toolbar.

Collections were added after the initial release of iBooks. If you don't see them in your version of iBooks, it's time to update it. It's free and simple. Tap the App Store icon on your iPad, and select the Updates option on the bottom toolbar. Find iBooks in the list, and tap the Update button. I recommend updating because the newer versions also support Apple's new iTextbooks.

Introducing iTextbooks

The days of students carrying that 30-pound backpack filled with heavy textbooks may finally be coming to an end. Traditional textbooks are expensive and cumbersome, and come apart with increased usage. Most important, we live in an era that's characterized by very rapid changes and developments in information. Scientific facts are evolving, maps are being rewritten, and political leaders and systems seem to be shifting all around the world.

Can educators and students afford to be using static textbooks that are several years old? Can we continue to lean almost exclusively on traditional text-based information in education when the rest of our world is saturated in multimedia? Digital textbooks offer a significant step forward, and iBooks 2, released in early 2012, now has features to support the use of vivid, media-rich textbooks on iPads. iBooks 2 can display books that contain videos and other interactive features. As with apps, textbook content can also be updated with the simple tap of an Update button.

When you go to the iBookstore, you'll now see a category for Textbooks, as shown in Figure 4-14. Many major publishers have started producing interactive content for use on iPads. In addition, Apple has released free software for Mac computers, called iBooks Author, that enables anyone — publishers or individuals, authors, teachers, or even students — to create and publish their own interactive, multimedia textbooks. I take a closer look at iBooks Author in Chapter 10.

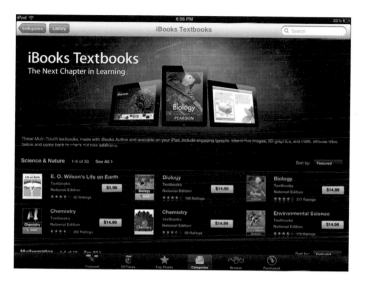

Figure 4-14: The iBookstore now has a Textbooks category.

Getting Organized with Contacts and Calendar

My closet still has around three old briefcases that I used for carrying notepads, papers, organizers, lesson plans, and more. They've been in there collecting dust for several years. Why? Yes, because I don't clean out my closet very often, but that wasn't the answer I was looking for! Most of us now use digital tools to stay organized, and they've become an essential part of our daily lives. Of course, your iPad came with apps to help you get organized as well:

- **Contacts:** Your Contacts app lists the important contact information about the people you know. Add contacts manually or set them up to sync them with your computer or e-mail account.

- **Calendar:** Like Contacts, the Calendar app enables you to add appointments manually or to sync them with an existing calendar.

If you're planning on syncing your contacts or calendar to a mail account, make sure you have that option turned on in Settings. Tap and open Settings from your home screen; then tap Mail, Contacts, Calendars. Check your e-mail account to ensure that the contact and/or calendar option switch is set to On.

Finding Value in Other Apps

You'll find tremendous value in the apps that come with your iPad, whether you're at work, school, or home. I discuss several of them in detail earlier in this chapter. Here is a quick breakdown of a few of the other apps you'll find when you first power up your iPad:

- **FaceTime:** FaceTime allows you to make video calls with other FaceTime users on iPads, iPhones, iPods, and Mac computers. To call someone using FaceTime, you need his phone number or e-mail address. Add that person as a contact and then simply tap his name within the FaceTime app to call.

  FaceTime uses the front-facing camera as its default, but you can also tap and switch to the rear iPad camera during your call and show your surroundings.

- **Messages:** Yet another way to avoid cellular fees is to use Messages as an alternative to text messaging. Because Messages also uses a Wi-Fi connection, you can send unlimited free text and multimedia messages to other Apple product users. And if you have more than one iOS device, Messages keeps the conversation going across all of them.

- **Reminders:** If you're loaded with too many things to do, you'll appreciate Reminders helping you keep track of your tasks. It's simple to add any sort of to-do, with a due date and time, and Reminders will alert you as needed.

- **Photo Booth:** Pose for a photo and add an effect with Photo Booth. Whether you take a photo of a flower with a kaleidoscope effect or a shrunken-head self-portrait, Photo Booth puts some creative fun in your photos.

- **Music:** Who doesn't love listening to music? Hum your way through the day with the iPad's Music app. It can sync with your other devices to ensure that you always have access to all the songs you download through iTunes.

- **Videos:** Download videos from the iTunes Store or transfer them from a computer. Either way, they'll look great on the iPad, and you can watch them with the Videos app. You can even connect your iPad to a TV via cable or Apple TV and turn your iPad into an entertainment hub.

- **App Store:** Whether you want to play games with maladjusted birds or order a pizza delivered to your front door . . . as you've heard, "There's an app for that." The place you'll find those apps is the App Store. There are several hundred thousand apps you can run on your iPad. I discuss how to find and download them in the next chapter. Just be forewarned that I cannot cover every last one of them.

5

Purchasing and Downloading Apps

In This Chapter

▶ Perusing apps in the App Store

▶ Knowing the difference between iPad and iPhone apps

▶ Finding and selecting educational apps

▶ Deciding between free or fee-based apps

*O*ne of the greatest features about personal computers, including iPads, is that they are tools that you can personalize. The simplest way to customize your iPad is by finding and downloading apps that align with your personal objectives. To the accountant, the iPad might provide a way to stay in touch with financial news and data. The businessman might need to access documents and create a mobile office environment. A designer could envision it as the perfect tool for delivering client presentations and portfolios. To the educator . . . well, that's where you come in.

You'll want to load your iPad with apps that fit your educational objectives and teaching style. To put it mildly, there are more than a few to choose among; Apple currently reports that there are already more than 200,000 apps designed specifically for the iPad and another several hundred thousand iPhone apps that you can also use on your iPad. Browsing the list of apps is like standing in an ice-cream store with a tantalizing array of ice cream flavors and toppings. So many delicious flavors, colors, and smells — which ones do you pick?

Several factors will affect your choice of apps. You'll need to consider the cost. Some apps are free, and others cost a few dollars. You may work at a school that can purchase apps in bulk at a reduced rate, or you may be paying full price for them yourself. You'll also clearly need to weigh the features an app offers and how it has been reviewed by experts and other users.

Select the right apps, and your iPad becomes your e-book reader, personal assistant, game player, mobile office, movie theater, and more. The challenge lies in wading through the oceans of apps to find the ones that work best for you (but then, that's why you're reading this book).

Browsing the App Store

The App Store is the key to personalizing your iPad experience. You can access the App Store on either your computer or your iPad. The functionality is fairly similar on both. For the purposes of this book, I use the iPad as the platform for accessing the App Store and focus more on helping you find the best educational apps. If you'd like a more detailed step-by-step tutorial on using the App Store, check out *iPad For Dummies,* 5th Edition, by Edward C. Baig (John Wiley & Sons, Inc.). It's an excellent introductory book, especially helpful for new iPad users.

Tap the App Store icon on your iPad to open it. You'll immediately see a row of six icons on the toolbar at the bottom of the app, as shown in Figure 5-1.

Figure 5-1: The App Store toolbar offers six icons to help you browse and find the perfect app.

Each icon reflects a different way of browsing and finding apps in the store, as described in this list:

✓ **Featured:** Use this section to browse the latest and most popular releases. At the very top, you'll notice three tabs that represent different categories in the Featured section: New, What's Hot, and Release Date. Tap them to see what's included in each.

✔ **Genius:** If you've used iTunes, you're familiar with the Genius feature. It makes recommendations based on items you've already purchased. You may need to approve turning it on because it sends information about your purchases to Apple when you use it. The Genius section can be a great way of finding additional apps once you've purchased the first one.

✔ **Top Charts:** As the name indicates, this lists the most popular apps and breaks them down by whether they are free or paid.

✔ **Categories:** This section breaks apps into categories based on their functionality. Categories include Books, Business, News, Games, and of course Education.

✔ **Purchased:** This tab shows you what you have already purchased. At the top of the screen, note the two tabs that break your purchases into All and Not On This iPad. That's a really helpful way of identifying what you've purchased that isn't on your iPad and then deciding which ones to download. You aren't charged anything additional for downloading apps that you've already purchased.

✔ **Updates:** This highlights existing updates for apps that you have on your iPad. The badge indicates the number of updates that are currently available for download. Tap the Update button next to any app, or tap the Update All button in the top-right corner. As your mother told you, drink your milk, eat your veggies, and keep your apps updated as often as you can if you want your iPad to work smoothly.

Selecting Between iPad and iPhone Apps

As you browse through apps, you'll quickly notice that they are often categorized by device. Some are designed for the iPad and others for the iPhone. Some are hybrids that work on both. You can use either device, but they work differently on your iPad:

✔ **iPhone (iPod touch) apps:** These apps were designed for the smaller screen space of an iPhone, but they can be used on iPads too. What you have to remember is that their native resolution (just a fancy way of saying screen size) will be the same on an iPad, but they will appear to be relatively small on the larger iPad display.

✔ **iPad apps:** The interface on apps designed for the iPad takes full advantage of the complete iPad display area.

✔ **Hybrid apps:** Hybrid apps are denoted by a little + sign on the app icon and will automatically adjust to the resolution of your device. In other words, the same app that works on the smaller iPhone screen will also expand to take advantage of the full iPad display.

✔ **Resolution, pixels, and other mumbo jumbo:** You just want to know which apps to use. Well, here's the scoop on iPhone versus iPad apps. It's like the difference between watching your favorite movie on a 27-inch television in the bedroom versus watching that movie at a theater. To quote an old cliché, size does matter.

Apps designed specifically for the iPad simply look better. It comes down to their screen size as measured in pixels — those little invisible dots that make up the images on your screen. Here's how the resolution breaks down by device:

- iPhone apps have 480x320 pixel resolution.

- Apps designed for iPhone 4 or later have 960x480 pixel resolution.

- iPad 1 and iPad 2 apps have 1024x768 pixel resolution.

- Apps designed for the third-generation iPad have an amazingly crisp resolution of 2048x1536 pixels.

✔ Then, of course you have the hybrid apps that can adjust their display according to the device they detect.

I know. You bought your iPad a while ago, and now you're sitting there with a terrible case of iPad envy. Don't worry. When it becomes available, you'll go out and buy the latest and greatest iPad and have the last laugh . . . well, for a few months, anyway.

Using iPhone apps on your iPad

Some apps are available in both iPhone and iPad versions. In those cases, always select the iPad app, of course. Many publishers will allow you to download the iPhone version free if you have both an iPhone and an iPad and have paid for the iPad-based version.

In some cases, however, the app you really want may have been designed only for the iPhone. As an example, having grown up in Australia, I'm an avid follower of Australian football. Guess what: The app I use to follow games "down under" is available only as an iPhone app, but I can still use it on my iPad. It just displays in its smaller native resolution. See how that looks in Figure 5-2. You can also tap the little 2x button in the bottom corner, and the display doubles in size to fill the iPad screen. Be aware, however, that this doesn't increase the pixel resolution of the app. It's just displaying that resolution over the entire screen. It looks fine in most cases. It's never as sharp as an iPad app, but really, what's a guy to do when you need the football scores from Australia?

Tap to double the image size.

Figure 5-2: Display iPhone apps at their native size or tap the 2x button to enlarge.

Using the App Store on your iPad or computer

You can access the App Store on your iPad or on your computer. In both cases, you need an Internet connection and that all-important iTunes account (see Chapter 2). Apps that are purchased on your computer will be transferred to your iPad the next time you sync them. For a more in-depth discussion of syncing, see Chapter 3.

Have you ever tried walking into a bank where nobody knows you and cashing a check without your ID? You'll get the same cold shoulder in the App Store if you don't have your user ID and password. Make sure that you've signed up for an Apple ID, or you won't be able to download any apps. Refer to Chapter 2 if you need instructions on signing up for an account.

Finding the Golden Nuggets

Some apps are incredibly imaginative, well designed, and productive. Others may not be worth your time and money. With hundreds of thousands of apps to choose among, you'd be well advised to learn how to sort the wheat from the chaff. Here's some advice from someone who has had to battle a fair share of chaff.

Searching for and purchasing Apps

If you have an idea of what you're looking for, get right to the point by using the Search field in the top-right corner of the App Store screen. Search by typing any portion of the app title or an associated keyword and then tap the Search key on the keyboard.

Refine your search by using filters. Enter your search term in the Search field, and tap the Search key on your keyboard. The iOS 6 App Store features three filters — Price, Categories, and Relevance — along the top of the results, as shown in Figure 5-3. The filters help sort your search results. Tap any one, and a menu of choices will drop down. Suppose you're looking for a free app to help you learn algebra. If you type **algebra** in the Search field, you'll get a wide range of apps from puzzles and arcade games to utilities. Instead, apply filters that set the category to Education and the price to Free. The results will be a more meaningful list.

Figure 5-3: Use search filters to narrow down your search results.

Once you've found an app that could potentially serve your purpose, tap the app name or icon to get more information about it. The information page will detail the app's features and include some screen shots to give you a taste of the interface (see Figure 5-4). The description is written by the app's developer. The editors at the App Store try to keep hyperbole to a minimum, so when app descriptions use adjectives such as *fun* or *exciting,* just keep in mind that they likely are somewhat biased. That's when you scroll down to the bottom of the page and scan the user reviews. Reviews will show an average star rating from 1 to 5, along with individual ratings and comments.

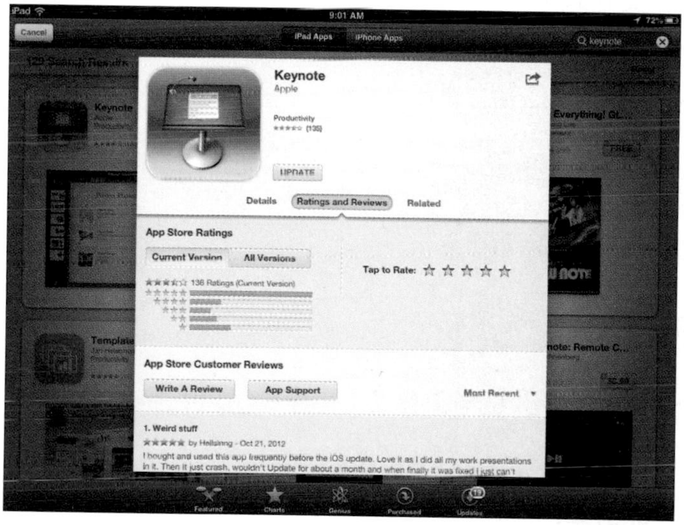

Figure 5-4: User reviews and ratings appear on the app detail page.

Reviews are tied to a specific release of an app. Earlier releases may have been buggy and even crashed, so make sure you check the ratings and reviews of the current release for the latest information. Also, I wouldn't rely solely on the star ratings. Read the reviews of the app, especially if it doesn't have a lot of ratings.

Thousands of educators, bloggers, and technical reviewers are trying out and recommending apps all the time. The better approach to finding apps is often to identify your objective and then see what others are recommending. Some paths to consider might include the following:

✔ **Search Google.** Try a Google search using the app name; you'll often get a host of reviews from magazines, websites, and blogs. Sometimes those blogs may even be from teachers explaining how they use the app in their classes.

✔ **Keep reading.** After searching for and reading some information on blogs and websites that review educational apps, follow the ones you like, and see which apps they recommend.

✔ **Join an online learning community.** iPads in Education (`http://iPadEducators.ning.com`) is a place where you can connect with like-minded people and learn from them.

✔ **Follow educators on social networking sites.** Twitter and Google+ are the obvious choices here. See which apps educators are using in their iPad classrooms and how those educators are using those apps.

✔ **Take an online course or webinar.** Dozens of companies and professional organizations offer online learning opportunities all year long.

✔ **Attend educational conferences.** Conferences are good opportunities to learn about effective practices and network with others.

After you've decided on an app, it's fairly simple to purchase and download it. With your iTunes account information handy, follow these steps:

1. **Tap the Price or Free button.**

   You'll find the Price button under the app icon on the top-left of the details screen. It may also say Free if there's no . . . uh . . . price.

2. **Tap the Install button.**

3. **Enter your account information and then tap the OK button.**

   Your home screen appears, and the app is downloaded to your iPad. The app icon will be placed in the first open slot available. You can rearrange icons on your iPad screen, as I describe in Chapter 2.

There's an app for finding apps

They say there's an app for just about anything you'd want, so why not think about using an app for finding apps? Several apps recommend apps based on your preferences, and some will notify you when particular apps are being offered at a discount. Here's a small selection:

✔ **AppGrooves** (`http://appgrooves.com/`) **recommends apps based on your tastes.** AppGrooves looks at your installed apps and learns about your preferences by asking you to compare and rank them. Based on your selections, it recommends apps that have similar features but have been given higher rankings.

- ✔ **Appsfire Deals (**`http://appsfire.com`**) notifies you of daily specials.** Set your preferences, and Appsfire Deals will notify you of the best rated apps that are either free or on special on any given day.

- ✔ **Moms with Apps (**`http://momswithapps.com`**) recommends kid-friendly apps.** Recommendations are grouped by category.

There is no lack of websites that review and recommend apps. Try a Google search for *iPad app reviews,* and you'll get a list of websites.

Deciding Between Lite and Full Apps

Many iPad apps offer a *lite* version with some of the features stripped out so that you can try the app before buying it. For example, one popular educational app that is used for storyboarding and mind-mapping is Popplet. At this writing, you have the option of downloading Popplet Lite free or purchasing the full version of Popplet for $4.99, as shown in Figure 5-5.

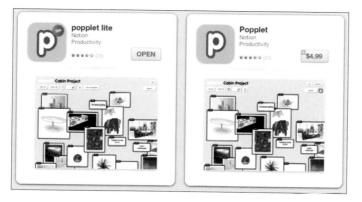

Figure 5-5: Many apps, such as Popplet, offer free lite versions and full paid versions.

Read the product descriptions of both the free and paid versions of the app to identify the benefits of the full version and to see whether it meets your needs and is worth the cost. In the case of Popplet, purchasing the full version allows students to create their projects online and then continue them outside of class on other computers if needed. Students can also share and collaborate on Popplet with others. If you want your students working in groups and outside class, opting for the paid version might be a good idea.

Although $4.99 may not break the bank for one copy, if you want all your students to use it, you may end up purchasing multiple copies. That said, make sure you'll use the additional features.

Apple offers a Volume Purchase program, which can help cut costs in this arena. See Chapter 2 for more information.

Part III
Finding and Organizing Educational Content

In this part . . .

Remember how your mom taught you the importance of keeping your room clean and sharing? Part III shows you how to use your iPad to find and organize content on the Internet and how to use social networking tools to share content with others. You can get rid of those piles of clippings and printouts when you discover how to organize all your content neatly and efficiently right on your iPad and to upload and share it across different platforms.

6

Finding and Organizing Content

In This Chapter

▶ Googling for information on your iPad

▶ Filing web pages for later reading

▶ Tagging, highlighting, and annotating web content

▶ Creating a custom digital news magazine

▶ Using a digital notebook for creating and storing information

W e used to live in a world where information was controlled and released to us by news media, book publishers, and even schools and teachers. The majority of what we learned in school was determined by authorities who set curriculum and selected textbooks. But now, the Internet — a technology most of us hadn't even heard of just 20 years ago — has completely revolutionized information access.

Many argue that it has democratized the methods in which information is published and accessed. Anyone can post information online and or even write and publish e-books. We don't have to wait until the evening news or the morning paper to get the latest world news. It's already been reported the instant it happens — on Twitter, Facebook, blogs, and more, and most of us first hear the news through these social networking channels. Encyclopedias and journals? How useful are they when we can increasingly access facts and opinions over the Internet at any time from a device we carry in our pockets?

How vast is the Internet? We're approaching 1 billion websites. That's a staggering figure considering that there are 7 billion-plus people on the planet. Even more, some estimates have the size of the Internet currently growing at a rate of over 5 percent a month. That means it doubles every 15 months! The bottom line is clear. It's imperative that we become proficient in using tools for finding, organizing, and accessing all the information we come across online. It's also essential that we integrate these tools into our educational processes and that children become fluent in their use.

That's the focus of this chapter. I look at different ways to archive and organize information for later reading. As your archives start growing, you need to have tools that make it easy to sort through your digital archives and find what you need. This chapter examines different tools that aid in that process.

Googling on Your iPad

They say that Google is the ultimate arbiter of most arguments. Whenever you need information, someone inevitably pulls out a mobile device and uses Google to search for the answer. When students are allowed to use mobile devices at school, they're constantly using them to search during class discussions. Google has become such an integral part of our lives that we use it as a verb in our everyday vocabulary. You don't search for an answer to a question any longer; you Google it.

One of the very first apps you should download on your iPad is the free app from Google. Chapter 4 looks at how to use Google as your default search tool in Safari. The Google Search app puts that search capability right on your iPad home screen, along with some very handy additional features. (See Figure 6-1.) Other than Mail, it's probably the app I use most on my iPad. Along with the regular Google search, you can also search using voice or even an image you take with your iPad camera.

Figure 6-1: The Google app uses an integrated browser to display search and results pages.

Tap the Google icon to start the app, and you'll immediately get that familiar-looking Google search page (refer to Figure 6-1). Type your search term, and the Google app presents your search results in its integrated browser, just as it would in a regular web browser. You'll even have the standard Google search options along the top of the results page that allow you to restrict your search to images, videos, news, and more. Tap any of the results, and the browser will display the page. One handy feature is that results are presented on a separate tab right within the app itself. You can simply swipe the tabs left and right to switch between the results page and your Google search, as shown In Figure 6-2. Whenever you need to, tap the Google logo and left arrow in the top-left corner to start a new search.

Figure 6-2: Swipe to switch between your Google search and the integrated browser.

If you're more of a visual person, like me, you can opt to see your results in Instant Previews mode, as shown in Figure 6-3. Tap the double-rectangle icon in the top-right of your search results page; Google will display the results as a series of web page previews instead of the standard text listing. Swipe left and right to move through the results, and tap the icon at any time to return to the text results page.

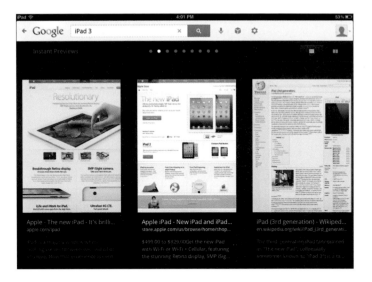

Figure 6-3: Google enables you to browse your search results in Instant Previews mode.

One addition to the latest version of the Google app is the row of icons representing additional options at the bottom of the search page (refer to Figure 6-1). These include

✔ **History:** I have to confess that my memory is like cheesecloth. I regularly need to look back through my search history to find pages I read and have since forgotten. The problem is that your search history shows you the terms that you searched for but normally doesn't show what you did with the search results. Well, this nifty little feature goes a step further, presenting you a visual search history of each search term you used, along with the pages you visited. Simply swipe through the list of graphical page previews to return to any page.

✔ **Apps:** Tap the Apps icon, and you'll be presented with a listing of icons for all the different Google apps.

✔ **Voice:** Having trouble maneuvering those greasy fingers over the virtual keyboard while eating that grilled-cheese sandwich? Don't worry. Google also allows you to search using your voice. Tap the Voice icon, and speak clearly into your iPad microphone. Google does an excellent job of interpreting your search request (especially in light of the fact that your mouth is filled with cheese).

✔ **Goggles:** While still a little rough around the edges, Google Goggles searches by interpreting an image. Tap the Goggles icon, and it takes you directly to the iPad camera. Focus in on an object, and snap your image. Google uses image recognition to think about it for a few seconds and then presents its best guess on the search result. Goggles is best at recognizing objects such as landmarks, books, DVDs, logos, artwork, and bar codes, as shown in Figure 6-4.

Figure 6-4: Google Goggles recognizes objects such as books, logos, and bar codes.

Evaluating Google Search results

We tend to place way too much importance on the ranking of Google search results. I've heard statistics ranging from 50 percent to 80 percent of users clicking one of the first three results on a Google search result page (after the advertised links). Couple that with the fact that students have a tendency to believe everything they read on the Internet, and that can sabotage effective learning. Google uses an algorithm to determine the ranking of its search results. It takes factors such as presumed relevance and popularity into account. Often, the Google algorithm delivers very pertinent results; however, there are times that it doesn't. That may be because of a badly framed search term. It might also be because many website owners play the SEO (search engine optimization) game. They create their websites with content and links that manipulate Google's search engine and push their sites up the rankings for the desired search terms. On occasion, the Google search results can even be downright scary, presenting users websites that try to sell products or display offensive opinions and images by tricking the Google algorithm into thinking results are something that they aren't.

Educators have traditionally adopted the role of information curators, carefully weeding and selecting textbooks and articles for students to read. We now live instead in an age where anyone can post information on the Internet for all to access and read, and Google is often the key used to open the door to that kingdom. It's a fantastic search tool, but you can never rely on any search tool or website to deliver accurate information. Help children navigate the Internet. Teach them how to frame their searches using terms and conditions that deliver the most accurate results. Ensure that they know how to identify owners of a website and to research and evaluate the information presented. Most important, teach them to always use a critical eye when reading anything, whether that be on the Internet or elsewhere.

Saving Web Pages for Later Reading

So much to read and so little time. I find myself needing to read more and more every day and am increasingly left with less time to do it. Fortunately, you have some excellent tools on the iPad that enable you to keep a list of the things you come across and want to read later. I describe a couple in this section.

Reading List

I start with the more recent entry: Apple's own Reading List included in Safari. When you come across any web page that you want to revisit later, simply tap the curved arrow at the left of the address bar and select Add to Reading List from the menu. Your page is saved. Whenever you want to go back and read anything in your Reading List, tap the Bookmarks icon in Safari and then tap the Reading List item at the top of the menu. Simple. It basically creates your list as a separate category in Bookmarks. Reading List also categorizes your saved pages into Read and Unread tabs, which it updates every time you open and read a saved page. In iOS 5, Safari would save only a link to the page, and you'd need a live Internet connection to read it. In iOS 6, Safari saves the page itself to your device, complete with text, images, and layout. You can also opt to sync that list with your other devices using your iCloud account. Add a page on your iPad and then read it later on your iPhone.

As nice as it is to have the Reading List built right into Safari, you can't access it in other browsers For example, if you use the Chrome browser on your iPad, you won't be able to use or access your Reading list. Also, Reading List lacks other features, such as being able to see what your friends are reading.

Reading List is, however, a great place to start saving pages. See Figure 6-5.

Figure 6-5: Adding pages for later reading is simple with Safari's Reading List feature.

Now I look at another option that offers even more features.

Instapaper

Instapaper is one of the most popular of a slew of programs for saving and reading content from the web. For people who need to stay updated on the latest web content, Instapaper belongs in the toolkit of essential apps. If you're trying to empower students to use the Internet to gather, evaluate, and use information, a tool such as Instapaper is indispensable for keeping that content organized and available as needed.

Among its many features, here are some of Instapaper's most striking benefits:

✔ **Any device or platform:** Instapaper is available on most computers and devices. It's an app that works on your Apple iOS devices as well as Android phones. Instapaper is also web-based so you can use it on any computer that has access to the Internet — Apple, Windows, or otherwise.

✔ **Organize:** Create folders for easy filing and organization of your articles.

✔ **Offline reading:** Save articles for offline reading. This is great for those times when you're in a car, plane, or anywhere where you may not have Internet access.

✔ **Easy viewing:** The Instapaper app offers a variety of ways for browsing and reading your content.

✔ **Integration:** Instapaper not only works with Safari, but also integrated into a host of other iPad apps, such as Twitter and popular social news apps such as Flipboard, Zite, and others. When you find a link to any article in those apps, you can simply tap a link within the app to send it to your Instapaper account.

✔ **Favorites:** Tag articles with a "Like" to store them in your Favorites list and share them with others.

✔ **Networking:** As I discuss in the next chapter, you can connect with your friends and share articles with each other.

Instapaper has a variety of methods for saving articles. Follow these steps to install and use it:

1. **Go to the App Store on your iPad, search for the Instapaper app, and download the iPad version.**

2. **Tap the icon to start the app.**

   The app prompts you for your account information.

3. **Either tap to open an account within the app, or go directly to** www.instapaper.com **and open your account there.**

   You'll want an account so that you can log in on any device and access your Instapaper content.

4. **Install the bookmarklet or e-mail contact.**

   Most of us using an iPad also use a laptop or desktop. Once you have your Instapaper account, ensure that you can save pages from any device or computer. Installing a bookmarklet — a button that sits on the browser toolbar — in your browser is the simplest way to save pages on your laptop or desktop. It's a little more complicated on your iPad, but you have some alternatives:

   • *Desktop browser:* Go to www.instapaper.com, and click the Extras link on the top menu bar. Follow the instructions for dragging the Read Later bookmarklet to your browser toolbar.

   • *iOS app:* Open the Instapaper app, and tap the Setting icon to get the menu shown in Figure 6-6. You can install the bookmarklet in Safari by tapping the Install Read Later in Safari option. It starts your browser and steps you through the process, but it does take a few detailed steps in Safari. Your second option is to install the Instapaper e-mail address in your Contacts folder by tapping Add Read Later by Email. A custom e-mail address was created for your account when you opened it, and this allows you to e-mail any page link to your account. I take a look at that in the next step.

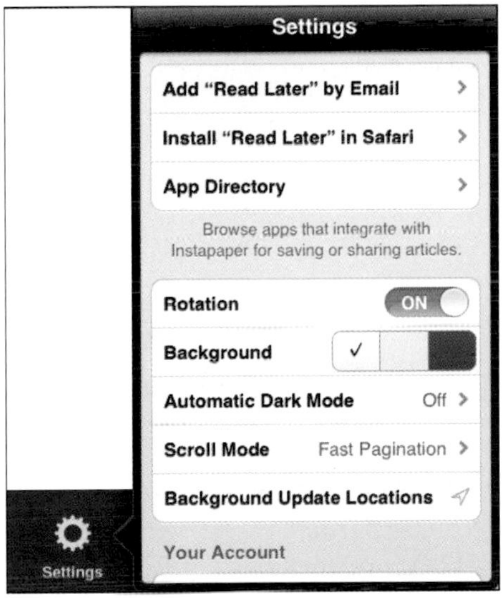

Figure 6-6: Instapaper can add an e-mail account for saving pages or a Safari bookmarklet.

5. Add pages to your Instapaper library.

You have two options:

- *Using the bookmarklet:* If you've installed the bookmarklet on your browser toolbar, simply tap the Read Later button when you're on any page you want to save for later reading, and it's added to your Instapaper library. It couldn't be easier.

- *Using e-mail:* If you have added your Instapaper e-mail address to Contacts as described in Step 4, tap the curved arrow on the top menus in Safari and select Mail Link to This Page. An e-mail message pops up with the URL of the page in the body. Start typing Instapaper in the To field, and Mail recognizes the Instapaper e-mail address and offers it as the default addressee. Send the message, and the page is added to your Instapaper library.

6. Tap to open the Instapaper app, and tap the Read Later icon in the menus on the left, as shown in Figure 6-7.

Your list of articles is displayed, along with the opening text for each.

7. Select any article by tapping it.

The integrated reader presents the article in a clean format after stripping it of ads and distractions.

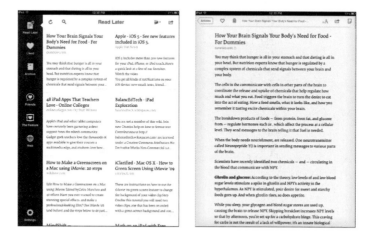

Figure 6-7: Tap any article in your Instapaper library and it opens in a clutter-free reader.

Many additional options are worth exploring. Here's a synopsis of the best ones:

- ✔ **Organize:** Tap the folder icon on the top toolbar to add and edit folders. When reading any article, you can tap the curved arrow on the toolbar and use the Move to Folder menu option to move articles between folders.

- ✔ **Like or Archive:** When reading an article, tap the heart icon on the top toolbar to Like it and add it to your Favorites list. Tap the Trash icon to delete the article or tap the Archive icon to save it into your Archive folder for later reference.

- ✔ **Synchronize:** Tap the curved arrow at the top of the main Instapaper screen to sync to the latest list of articles you've saved on all devices.

- ✔ **Share:** I look at this in more depth in the next chapter, but there are several ways to share content with people you know and browse the articles they recommend.

- ✔ **Search:** This feature requires a paid subscription. Once your library builds, you may want to consider it; it offers a full text search through all the articles in your account.

The social networking features of Instapaper can be a real bonus for educational research. Consider creating an Instapaper account for your class or for groups in your class if they are working on collaborative projects. It's a great way for students to find and share information.

Creating Custom News Feeds

The quantity of available news, articles, and information is escalating at a rapid rate, and no single website or source can possibly keep you updated with all the information you need to access. A host of new apps seek to use the iPad's wonderful interface for reading to combine multiple sources into an integrated magazine format. In this section, I show you a couple of excellent choices.

Flipboard

Flipboard describes itself as the "social magazine." The topic actually belongs in more chapters than just this one, which discusses finding and organizing content. The next chapter focuses on sharing. Flipboard performs both functions very well.

Download the Flipboard app, and select your news and information sources. Flipboard creates a personalized magazine out of everything you've selected. Flipboard combines your list of news websites, blog posts, social networking feeds, images, and more into a beautifully displayed layout of articles that mimics the digital equivalent of flipping through the pages of a magazine. The latest versions even allow you to add video and audio feeds to your multimedia Flipboard magazine. Using Flipboard requires a few short steps:

1. **Tap to open the Flipboard app.**

2. **Create your Flipboard magazine by tapping the Get Started option and tapping some of the content categories.**

3. **Tap the Build Your Flipboard button.**

   Flipboard drops you back into its beautifully designed magazine layout, now filled with content from the various categories you selected.

   You can customize your content even further by creating a Flipboard account.

4. **Tap the Flipboard account option in the bottom right of your display and sign up for your free account by entering your e-mail address and password.**

After you've created your account, you're presented with a listing of the Flipboard Content Guide. Categories include News, Business, Sports, and Tech & Science.

5. **Tap any category to get Flipboard's recommended sources.**

For example, if you tap News, the sources include ABC News, The Economist, The Guardian, and more, as shown in Figure 6-8.

Click Accounts to link to Twitter, Facebook, and others

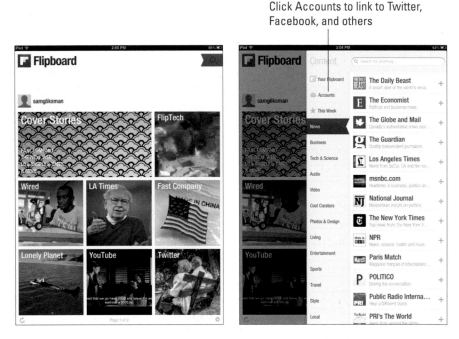

Figure 6-8: Create a Flipboard magazine by selecting sources and linking to web accounts.

Whenever you open Flipboard, you'll get the latest news from your selected sources. Turn any page by flicking it to the left or right. Tap any source to open it, and you'll get all the latest articles presented in a beautifully designed magazine format. Simply tap any article that interests you ,and read further.

Flipboard offers these sharing options:

  ✔ **Link to your web and social networking accounts.** Take your customization to the next level by linking your web accounts to Flipboard. Tap the magnifying glass on the top-right of the main interface and select the Accounts menu option at the top of the Content menu shown in Figure 6-8.

You can link to accounts such as Twitter, Facebook, Google Reader, and more. Select any account, and Flipboard will pull your information feed from that account and include it in your magazine. You can also customize the news feed from accounts. For example, you can elect to include only saved searches from your Twitter feed.

✔ **Share, comment, and save.** When you open an article, you'll notice a row of icons along the bottom-right corner. Use them to share the article on social networking accounts (such as Twitter), add your comments to it, and even save it to that Instapaper account you opened when you read about it a few pages earlier in this chapter.

 Flipboard is great for personal use, staying up with the news and professional development. It also has a place in your classroom. Consider having students build a custom magazine with categories that track news events for class discussion and opinions on the web about specific topics they are studying.

Diigo

Diigo is my favorite tool for cataloging and saving information on the web. You're probably familiar with the process of bookmarking a website. Most browsers come with a simple mechanism for saving bookmarked sites, and I discuss Instapaper earlier in this chapter as a way of saving and organizing bookmarked content for later reading. Diigo also works on desktop computers and mobile devices but takes a very different approach to saving and organizing content.

What differentiates Diigo is that it uses tagging, annotations, and highlighting tools to give you far greater control over how you manage and manipulate the content you save. Learning deepens when you connect new information to your existing knowledge and experience and see ways to apply it. There's that "aha" moment when you read something and the light goes on. Diigo lets you capture those moments with highlights and annotations.

To see if you like Diigo as much as I do, install it and start using it by following these steps:

1. **Go to** www.diigo.com, **and sign up for a free account.**

    Diigo offers a free upgrade to premium accounts for educators. Diigo Educator accounts have additional features such as the capability to create student accounts for an entire class and to automatically set the class up as a Diigo group so students can share bookmarks and annotations. It's a terrific way for students to compile, annotate, and share content.

2. **Install Diigo on your browser toolbar.**

   As with Instapaper and other script-based bookmarklets, installing the Diigo button on your toolbar will differ slightly on desktop and mobile browsers.

   - *Desktop browsers:* On the Diigo home page, tap Tools in the top toolbar. Tap to select Diigolet under the Bookmarklets category, and follow the instructions to drag the Diigo button to your browser toolbar.

   - *iPad (and mobile devices):* Start by downloading the Diigo app. Tap to open the App Store on your iPad home page, and search for Diigo. Download the free app. Once it's installed, tap to open it, and log in with your username and password. Tap the Settings (gear) icon in the lower-left corner, and tap the Install Web Highlighter option. Follow the directions to install the Diigo Web Highlighter on your browser toolbar.

3. **When you find a page that you want to save, tap the Web Highlighter/ Diigo button in your browser, and tap Bookmark.**

   You're prompted to add *tags* that help you find that page later, as shown in Figure 6-9. You can add multiple tags; just separate them with spaces. You can create multiword tags by using a character such as a dash between the words or by enclosing them in quotation marks. As you start typing a tag, Diigo will prompt you with any similar tags you've used in the past.

Figure 6-9: Diigo prompts for you for tags when you save web pages.

4. **When you finish typing your tag, tap Save.**

5. **(Optional) Tap the Web Highlighter button, select any text in the article, and then tap Highlight.**

   (You could also choose Sticky Note; see Step 6.)

Diigo adds a colored overlay, as shown in Figure 6-10. It's as though you used a marker to highlight it. That's a nice tool to help you scan the main points of the article when you come back to it later.

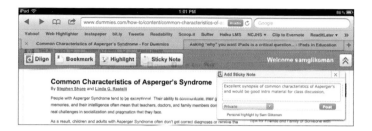

Figure 6-10: Highlight text and add notes to pages that you save with Diigo.

6. **(Optional) Tap the Web Highlighter button and then tap the Sticky Note button.**

   A yellow note opens.

7. **Type your notes in the body, and tap Post when you're done.**

   Diigo leaves a little yellow icon on the page that represents your note and opens it whenever you tap on it.

   Whenever you come back to that page in the future, whether on your iPad or any other computer, Diigo remembers your highlights and notes and presents them to you when you tap the Diigo button.

8. **To search for content in Diigo, open the Diigo app on your iPad or go to** www.diigo.com **in any web browser.**

   I currently prefer using Diigo in a web browser because it offers more options than the iPad app; however, the developers promise more iPad app updates soon.

   Using a desktop browser, you'll see all the tags you've used in the left column, and you see how many times each has been used.

9. **Tap (or click, if you're on a computer) a tag, or type it in the search field next to the My Library Tagged heading on the top left.**

   All the articles that use that tag immediately appear, complete with any highlights and notes that you've added to them. Figure 6-11 shows where I have searched for my *edreform* tag.

Another part of the magic of Diigo is that it's a social bookmarking tool. That means you can follow other Diigo users and what they are saving, and you can also share with them the content that you're tagging. I take a closer look at the wonderful sharing features of Diigo in Chapter 7.

Organizing: Folders or tagging?

What's the difference between tagging content and organizing it in folders? Folders use a linear, top-down tree structure for storing content. It's like keeping papers in a filing cabinet in which you organize in separate drawers, folders, and files. The problem is that our lives are flooded with information these days, and it doesn't always fit neatly into a single category. For example, you just read an excellent article about the Great Depression. Do you file it under a folder for Economics, History, Politics . . . or maybe Prohibition? Probably all of them. That's why tagging is such a great way of archiving articles. It uses the computer's capability to search content quickly and compile results for you. You save content with tags that trigger your association to it, making it that much easier to find. When I search for *prohibition,* Diigo presents a list of all the articles I tagged with that keyword, complete with any highlights and annotations I made on the page.

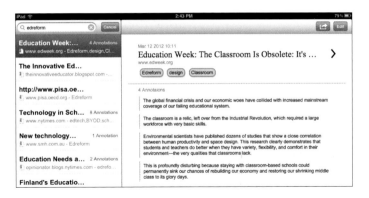

Figure 6-11: Diigo displays content related to a tag, complete with highlights and notes.

Keeping a Digital Evernote Notebook

When you were a kid and prepared your school supplies the week before school started, one of the first things you likely packed was your notebook. Evernote is the digital equivalent of that notebook, with an impressive list of features that lend themselves to a wide variety of creative uses.

As with Instapaper and Diigo, Evernote (shown in Figure 6-12) is a web-based service that can be used across all your devices. Having tools that work on both mobile devices and computers is indispensable when you use your iPad while you're out and about and then need to continue your work on a laptop or desktop. Evernote is a blend of digital notebook and all-purpose filing cabinet. You can use it to create and keep information or to store and organize all types of digital content. In fact, Evernote is so multidimensional that it's difficult to pin down a simple description.

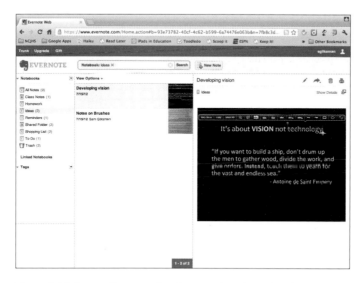

Figure 6-12: Access Evernote in a browser (as shown here) or with the Evernote software or app.

Evernote keeps digital content in notes that you organize in notebooks. The Evernote publishers describe their product as a way to "help you remember everything across all of the devices you use. Stay organized, save your ideas, and improve productivity."

It's easier to describe Evernote by what you can do with it. The following list highlights just a few examples:

- **Take notes.** Type class notes, meeting notes, to-do lists, ideas, and more. Just set up notebooks in Evernote, and create notes as you need them. Take Evernote with you on your mobile device wherever you go, and use it to remember everything. Your notes will be waiting for you on your desktop or laptop when you sign in.

- **Record audio.** Notes don't have to be text. Use the microphone on your iPad or mobile device to record audio in your notes. Record a lecture. Have students record themselves reading or speaking in a foreign language. Record a snippet of a song you want to remember. Record voice reminders.

> ✔ **A picture is worth 1,000 words.** Take and record photos with the iPad camera. Whether it's the cover of a book you want to read or the whiteboard in your class open a new note, tap the camera icon, and snap your pic.

> ✔ **Collect content from the web.** Evernote can be used to archive web pages, images, or any other portion of a web page. Using a tool called Evernote Clipper, you can cut out any portion of a page for archiving.

> ✔ **Archive anything you can e-mail.** You don't need to have Evernote with you to archive your digital content. Every Evernote account has its own unique e-mail address. As long as you can e-mail anything, you can save it to your Evernote account.

> ✔ **Share.** Share folders with others so that you can collaborate and access content together.

Getting started

Some software tools have a well-defined but limited scope of use. Evernote is at the opposite end of that spectrum. As you start using it, you'll begin discovering imaginative new ways to create and store digital content. Sign up for an account by going to www.evernote.com and selecting the Create Account option in the top-right corner of the Evernote home page. As with every web service that synchronizes content across devices, you need an account so that you can access your files from any location and computer (versions are available for both the Mac and Windows computers). You can sign up for a free account or opt for the Premium account, which gives you additional storage and features. In most cases, it makes sense to start with the free account and assess your ongoing needs once you start using the service.

Create notebooks while you're on the Evernote website or when you're using the Evernote software on your laptop or desktop. At this writing, the Evernote app doesn't have a function for creating notebooks. The app enables you to create, read, and synchronize notes, but you need to create your notebooks through the website.

Think of how you intend to use Evernote, and create the notebooks that represent the different categories of use. For example, you may want a notebook for taking notes in class. You may want a separate notebook for a project you're researching. I was looking for a used car recently and set up a notebook for storing car advertisements. Don't worry; you can always come back and edit your notebooks at any time.

To download the Evernote app, tap the App Store icon on your iPad, type **Evernote** in the search field, and download the Evernote app. Once it's downloaded, tap the app icon, and log in when prompted on the opening screen. You're in!

Adding and editing content

There are many ways to add and edit notes in your Evernote notebooks:

✔ **Add a new note within Evernote.** Click the New Note icon on the Evernote account page in your web browser or the downloaded software on your Mac or Windows computer, or tap the app on your iPad or mobile device. They all work the same way.

Type a subject line, and fill out the body with your text, images, or media. You can upload and attach any documents or images, and don't forget that if you're using your iPad, you can take a photo by tapping the camera icon or record sound by tapping the microphone. Select a folder for filing your new note, and add some keywords in the Tags field to enable you to find the note easily. Separate your tags with commas.

Note that anything you add to your Evernote account, no matter where you added it, is automatically stored in your Evernote account and synced to all your devices.

✔ **Save web content with Evernote Web Clipper.** Save content from the web to your Evernote account with the Evernote Web Clipper, as shown in Figure 6-13.

If you're on a laptop or desktop, open your browser, go to http://www.evernote.com/download, and scroll down to the section on Evernote Web Clipper. Select your browser from the list, and follow the download instructions to add a button to your toolbar. Save entire pages or highlight any part of the web page you're viewing, and click a button in your browser's toolbar to save it.

You can install a bookmarklet in your iPad browser and use the Web Clipper there as well, but it's a lot trickier and takes a little fussing to get it working. If you're brave enough to give it a whirl, open your browser, and go to www.support.evernote.com. Type **clipping web pages in iOS** in the search field, and follow the instructions on the page. It's worth the effort.

Figure 6-13: Highlight any web content and use the Web Clipper to save it to a Notebook.

✔ **E-mail content to Evernote.** Every Evernote account is given a unique e-mail address. To find your Evernote e-mail address, tap to start the Evernote app on your iPad and then tap the Settings gear button at the bottom right. Scroll down and tap Evernote e-mail address under Settings. Here are a couple of nifty little tricks that will make e-mailing content really simple.

First, copy the e-mail address, exit the Evernote app, and find your Contacts app. Tap to start and add a new contact. Call it something like Evernote, and paste the e-mail address into the e-mail field. You've created a new contact for your Evernote account.

Most apps on your iPad have functions for e-mailing content, whether it's photos from the Photos app, web pages in Safari, or documents in Pages. When you e-mail the content, start typing **Evernote** in the To field (or any other name you gave the contact), and your Evernote e-mail address will pop up as the default.

Here's the second tip. In the Subject line of the e-mail, add an @ symbol and the name of the notebook you'd like to use for the note. Suppose that you want the content to be filed in the Research notebook. At the end of your Subject line, type **@Research**, and send the e-mail. Magically, when you open Evernote, you'll see a new note in your Research notebook with the content you e-mailed.

Browsing and searching for information

There's a host of ways to search your Evernote content. The more you start saving content, the more you'll want to become proficient in different ways of finding what you need. Of course, we all have to walk before we can run, so here, I show you a few simple ways of searching:

✔ **Browse by notebook.** Tap Notebooks on the top menu bar of the iPad app, and each notebook is presented as a stack of notes. Tap any stack to browse the notes in that notebook.

✔ **Browse by tags.** If you were diligent about adding accurate tags every time you saved a note, this is a breeze. Simply tap Tags in the top menu bar of your iPad app, and Evernote sorts all your notes by tag, as shown in Figure 6-14. Tap the stack with the tag you want and then browse the notes.

✔ **Use the Search box.** Type a search term in the Search field, and Evernote searches through the text of all your notes and presents a list of results. It even searches for text in any images you've saved in notes. Suppose that you liked a particular jam and snapped a photo of it as a reminder to buy it later. Search for the name of the jam, and Evernote finds it in the photo, as shown in Figure 6-15. Impressed? The jam was pretty good, too.

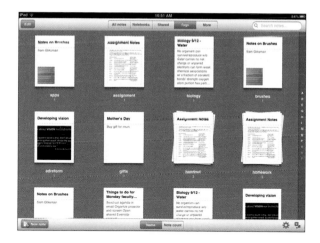

Figure 6-14: Evernote groups notes in stacks according to their tags.

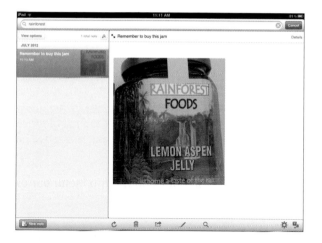

Figure 6-15: Evernote will find text within images in your notes.

Assuming that you have an Internet connection, if you saved a note using an iPad, iPhone, or any other device with GPS services enabled, Evernote knows where you were when you created the note. Open a note in the viewer, and tap Details in the top-right corner. You'll see a map at the bottom of the Details menu, which you can tap to zero in on the exact location associated with the note.

Using Evernote in your classroom

Evernote is the Swiss army knife of tools for your iPad classroom. There are a wide variety of ways to use Evernote. Once you start using it, I can guarantee you'll think of many more. Here are just a few ideas to get you going:

- **Taking class notes:** Students can take class notes and organize them in notebooks for each subject. Even if they don't take the iPads home, they can access their Evernote account and notes on any computer with an Internet connection.

- **Sharing notebooks for group work:** Notebooks can be shared — a point I look at more closely in Chapter 7. Sharing a notebook is a great way for students to work collaboratively on a group project and share research and information.

- **Distributing content to class:** Teachers can share a notebook with students. That's a very simple way to distribute information to the class. Just create a note in the shared notebook and add the content, and it's available for all students to open and access.

- **Submitting work to the teacher:** Sending content via e-mail to your Evernote e-mail address is a fantastic way to easily create notes on an iPad. It can also be used creatively to create a class dropbox where students can submit work to a teacher. You can have each student add the teacher's Evernote e-mail address to the Contacts on his or her iPad. Students then send their work to the teacher's Evernote e-mail address, and bingo — it's automatically filed as a new note in the teacher's Evernote account. Also, by simply giving the e-mail address to students, you don't give them any access to see or open any notes in the teacher's Evernote account. It won't guarantee that students submit their work on time, but each note will indicate the exact time each student submitted it.

If you're starting to feel a little cocky, why not set up a notebook in the teacher's account for a specific homework assignment or project and have the students e-mail it right into that notebook? Check the earlier section on e-mailing to your Evernote account for instructions on how to do that.

- **Blogging:** Get students to set up a notebook, and keep it as a writing journal or blog. They can share it with you so you can access it and add comments.

- **Practicing a foreign language:** Use the recording feature, shown in the figure, in notes as a tool for students to record themselves practicing their foreign language skills. *Es muy increible, no?* Or something like that . . .

- **Reading and speaking:** Use the recording feature in notes as a method for students to record themselves reading or speaking. Notes are kept as a way of gauging progress through the year.

7

Social Networking and Sharing

The future of learning is evolving from the traditional one-to-one exchange between teacher and student to a dynamic model that thrives on networking, collaboration, and sharing. This chapter focuses on how you can start learning with social networking services. That applies whether you're a teacher recognizing the need to continually be learning, a professional updating his or her expertise with new discoveries and practices, or a student working on a school project. I look at learning with Twitter, collecting and sharing information with social bookmarking services such as Diigo, and sharing videos with Showyou. So go ahead and sit back, relax, and invite the world to your living room. It's okay; you won't have to provide dinner.

Teachers typically have been the curators of information in schools, selecting and presenting information, and specifying articles and books for students to read. Then came the Internet. The fact that you can connect to people and information anywhere has raised the very important issue of how to filter the wheat from the chaff. What sources do you use, who published them, and how do you know the information is reliable and accurate? These questions form the basis of an important new ability that many are calling *information literacy*. Children have a tendency to believe everything they see and read on the Internet. We can't just metaphorically throw them out into the midst of a vast information jungle and expect them to navigate their way to the sources they need. If we want them to Google for information, it's vital that they receive training and guidance on how to filter, verify, and analyze anything they find. Information literacy needs to become a staple in the diet of every child's education.

Learning with Twitter

Everyone knows how Twitter is used. It's where you tell everyone about the lousy movie you saw last night and what you ate for breakfast, right? We've all heard the stories about celebrities with millions of followers making the most outrageous comments and politicians who have been caught publishing things they later regretted — no details required. What you haven't heard enough about is that there are millions of users sharing news, opinions, and important information in every field of knowledge, especially education.

I'm an avid Twitter user, and I could easily devote several chapters to using Twitter for learning and professional development. The concept is pretty straightforward. *Tweets,* as they are called, are messages of up to 140 characters that Twitter subscribers post on their accounts, as shown in Figure 7-1. When you have an account, you *follow* people who talk about topics you find interesting. The latest messages from those users show up on your home page for you to read. Don't underestimate your opinion. People will follow you and want to hear what you have to say as well!

Tweets

Hashtags

Figure 7-1: Your Twitter page includes the latest tweets from people you follow.

Twitter users include a hashtag symbol (#) before a relevant keyword (refer to Figure 7-1) or phrase in their tweets to categorize them and make them easy to find in a search. For example, users will include the hashtag #edtech to indicate that a tweet is about educational technology. If you click or tap the hashtagged keyword, you'll get the latest list of tweets from all users who have used that keyword. It's a great way to find relevant information and additional people to follow.

You can set your Twitter account to be private or public. Your Settings page has an option to protect your tweets. If you select that option, other users will need to request your permission to view your tweets. There are good arguments for and against making your tweets public, and you should select this option if you decide to keep your account private. You'll need to use a standard desktop browser to access your Twitter Settings page.

The following steps get you started with an account and using it to find and learn from other users:

1. **Open any web browser, and go to** www.twitter.com.

2. **Tap or click the link to sign up for an account.**

3. **Look for people you know, news sources you read, and so on, so that you can follow them.**

   You'll get information from Twitter users whom you follow. You follow them by finding their accounts and tapping or clicking a Follow button on their pages.

   You don't need to find too many to start; the situation tends to snowball. You can see the people they follow and get information from people whose tweets they *retweet* — repost information that someone else posted in a Twitter account.

Finding people to follow on Twitter

There's no question that celebrities tend to be the one group of Twitter users with the largest followings. That's unfortunate, considering the wealth of important people and information you can access through Twitter. *Time* magazine listed 140 people you should consider following on Twitter. The list includes scientists, historians, political analysts, and yes, even some comedians and entertainers. If you'd like to see the list, search for *Time Magazine 140 best Twitter feeds,* and you'll get the link to the article and list.

4. Follow hashtags for topics that interest you.

As you begin to use Twitter, you'll run into common hashtags that represent your areas of interest. For example, #iPadEd is often used for messages about using iPads in education (as shown in Figure 7-2), #mlearning for mobile learning, and so on.

Figure 7-2: Hashtags with keywords identify and categorize message by topic.

5. Post a message with a link to an interesting article or your opinion about an important topic, and add a relevant hashtag, if you know it.

Get involved. Remember that sharing works best when it flows in both directions.

6. Go to the App Store, and download a Twitter app for your iPad.

You can also add your Twitter account information in the Settings app in iOS 6 (scan the left column for the Twitter menu item), and the Twitter app is automatically installed with your account.

There are Twitter apps for your iPhone, iPad (see Figure 7-3), and most other mobile devices, so you can connect and access your Twitter account and feeds whenever needed.

Once you start using Twitter, you'll be amazed how much important information starts literally landing in your lap every time you access your Twitter page. Opinions, links to articles, debates, latest news . . . it's all there. The more you start using Twitter, the more you'll develop additional connections and get even more information and knowledge. You'll also be making important contact and friendships within a community that you follow.

And of course I'd love to hear from you as well. Sign up for your account, and you'll find me on Twitter as @samgliksman. See you there!

Connecting through Twitter

You wouldn't believe how easy it can sometimes be to connect with someone through Twitter. Here's one example: I was working with an English teacher whose class was reading a book by a contemporary British novelist. We decided to try to locate the author. Sure enough, a quick search on Twitter revealed that he had an account, so we sent a message inviting him to videoconference with the class and discuss the book with the students. Within the next couple of weeks, the author spoke to the students via Skype. They experienced and related to that novel from a completely new perspective — all through the magic of social networking and Twitter. And the author never once told us what he ate for breakfast.

Figure 7-3: The Twitter app for the iPad displays your Twitter account feeds.

Twitter, a great tool for personal and professional development, can be used effectively in a classroom setting. Here are a few ideas to get you thinking, including some hashtags you might use. (I'm appending a unique identifier such as ms6 to the hashtags as an example for a fictitious sixth-grade class in Venice Middle School.) By the way, always check that any hashtag you want to use isn't already being used for some other purpose. You can use Twitter's search function to check whether any existing tweets already reference the hashtag you'd like to use.

- Create a special hashtag phrase for your class, and use Twitter as a classroom discussion forum for communication after school hours (#discuss-vms6). You can review the hashtag discussions the following morning or at any other time.

- Use Twitter as an easy way for students to post questions and comments during lectures and field trips (#comments-vms6).

- Have students adopt the character in a historical event or book, and get them to tweet as that character with other students/characters. Don't forget to use a hashtag to group the tweets into an easy-to-follow discussion (#civilwar-vms6).

- Post a question of the day that requires your students to practice their information literacy skills and search for the answer online (infolit-vms6).

- Ask children to read something and summarize it in a string of 140-character Twitter posts. The skill of condensing issues to their essential core is important to all forms of communication (#novel-vms6).

- Teach vocabulary by having students submit a sentence a day (#vocab-vms6).

Twitter is such a popular service that it has spawned an entire industry of Twitter add-on services. One such app that can be great for educational *or* recreational use (hey, all work and no play . . .) is Twitterfall. Use a standard desktop browser to access `http://twitterfall.com/`, and get a current stream of all tweets on anything you search. For example, say that you're debating the politics and issues regarding gun control. You can type phrases such as **gun control** and **nra** in as searches, and Twitterfall will give you a stream of tweets as they are being published on the web. It's amazing to see the stream flowing down on your screen. You can even look at the difference in opinions within different geographic areas by using the geolocation option and only displaying tweets within a specific geographic area.

A word of warning about using Twitterfall, and for that matter, any public Twitter search: The tweets coming to you through these tools are not filtered. That said, you may run across all forms of profanity and objectionable opinions. Exercise some reasonable amount of caution when using these tools, especially when you are using them with your students.

Group Sharing with Diigo

Diigo is a wonderful tool for organizing and archiving web content. Diigo is often referred to as a social bookmarking tool. Chapter 6 focuses on its bookmarking prowess, but it's that social component that I explore further in this chapter.

If you think that something you find on the web is worth archiving, there's a good chance that your friends and colleagues will consider it helpful as well — and vice versa. Diigo enables the sharing of content in a number of ways:

✔ **Public and private bookmarks:** You can set any Diigo bookmark listing to be private or public. Private bookmarks are still very helpful for archiving and referencing content, but only public bookmarks can be shared and viewed by others.

✔ **My Network:** You can certainly learn from what other people are reading and bookmarking — especially people you know and respect. Diigo has a My Network feature that enables you to add friends and colleagues and see what they are bookmarking. Access your account on any web browser, and tap or click the My Network item on the top menus. Look for the link to Browse and Edit your friends and then add more. Once you have added some people to your network, you'll see everything they have publicly bookmarked in your My Network section.

✔ **My Groups:** Start or join a Diigo group. Groups are formed around a common theme, and members can share their findings with each other. Tap or click the My Groups menu item on the top of the web browser page, and browse for groups with which you share a common interest. Groups exist for everything from teaching mathematics to scuba diving. You can also type a term in the search box, and Diigo drops down a menu of options, one of which is to find groups that are interested in your search term. Tap or click any group in the search results, and you're taken to the group page. You'll see a large button that you tap or click to apply for membership in the group.

As Groucho Marx famously said, "I don't want to belong to any club that would have me as a member." If you feel so inclined, go ahead and start your own group! Just tap or click the Create a Group button on the My Groups page, define your group's topic of interest, and start inviting members. (Just don't grow one of those Groucho moustaches!) After you have a group set up, start sharing:

- **Sharing with a group:** Whenever you save a bookmarked page, Diigo offers you the option to share it with a group. Select any one of your groups, as shown in Figure 7-4, and your finding will be listed and shared on the group's page.

- **Sharing in class groups:** If you upgraded to an Educator account (described in the last chapter), you can set up a private group that includes your students. That's a great way to create and organize class research and to build a knowledge base for your course. You can also create subgroups that can share findings when working on collaborative projects.

The Diigo app on the iPad is an excellent tool for reviewing all the content you've archived along with annotations and highlights. It doesn't, however, currently give you access to the content of any Diigo Groups that you have joined or members you're following. To access that content, use your web browser, and sign in at www.diigo.com. The My Network and My Groups menu item at the top of the page will list that content.

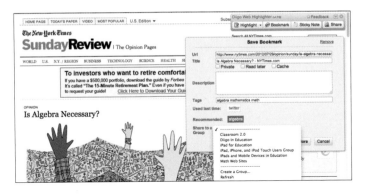

Figure 7-4: Use Diigo to bookmark a page so you can share it with any of your groups.

Sharing Videos with Showyou

So much of our modern communication is gravitating toward multimedia that it helps to have a simple, dedicated method for sharing and accessing video with your friends. That's the singular objective of Showyou, shown in Figure 7-5. Unlike other social sharing services that accommodate a variety of media, the Showyou app does one thing only — and it does it with style. Showyou is a "social video" app that allows you to browse through all the different videos your friends have shared on social networks such as Facebook, Twitter, YouTube, Tumblr, and more.

As shown in the figure, Showyou presents a grid of some of the most popular videos referenced by Showyou members on their social networking sites. If you slide the grid to the right with your finger, you'll see that the content is categorized by subject matter. Tap any topic in the left menus, and Showyou presents the videos in that category. Tap any video in the grid, and it opens and plays. Nice, but Showyou can do so much more.

After you download Showyou from the App Store, you can create a profile that enables you to make connections, find friends, and search for shared videos. Just follow these steps:

1. **Tap the Showyou icon on your iPad home screen to start the app.**

2. **Tap the smiley-face icon on the bottom-right (refer to Figure 7-5) to create a profile directly with Showyou.**

    You can also sign in with your Twitter or Facebook account.

    Once you have signed in, you can start connecting with your friends and colleagues.

3. **Edit your profile by tapping the Edit button at the top-left of the display under your user name.**

You'll land on the Settings page, as shown in Figure 7-6.

Currently popular videos

Video categories

Figure 7-5: Showyou enables you to browse videos friends share on social networks.

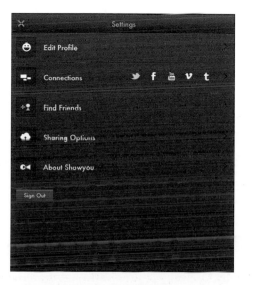

Figure 7-6: Connect to social networking services and add friends to see videos they share.

4. **If you already have accounts with social networking sites such as Twitter, Facebook, YouTube, Tumblr, or Vimeo, tap the Connections option, and turn on the connection to those services.**

   As you turn on any of the options, Showyou will ask you to sign in to that service and verify that you're allowing it to connect.

   Now that you have given Showyou access to your accounts, it can look at your connections and suggest some of your friends who are using Showyou.

5. **Tap the Find Friends menu option in Settings, and you'll get a list of friends whom you can follow.**

6. **Tap the Follow button next to any name, and the videos they share through Showyou will show up on your video grid.**

   It's as though you are creating your own social networking video channel.

7. **Search for videos shared on Showyou by entering a term in the Search field.**

   One powerful way to search is to search by theme. For example, earlier in this chapter, I discuss using hashtags to group Twitter posts by theme. Try using a hashtag in your Showyou search. So, for example, if you search for #ipaded, as shown in Figure 7-7, the results show all the videos on Showyou that were referenced in Twitter using that hashtag. It's a very powerful way to get a video-based overview of any topic that has been discussed on Twitter. It really blew me away the first time I tried it!

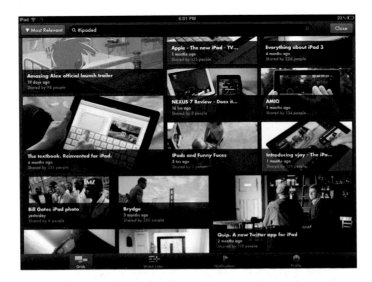

Figure 7-7: Use a Twitter hashtag in a Showyou search to see videos related to that theme.

Part IV
Exploring Applications for Digital Reading and Writing

The 5th Wave   By Rich Tennant

"Has the old media been delivered yet?"

In this part . . .

This Part takes a peek at how the e-book revolution is changing the way people read. It shows you how to find and order whatever you like reading and have it in your hands within seconds. I also explain how to create, edit, and annotate your own documents. You can even record classes and coordinate the sound to play back in sync with your notes. For the more enterprising among you, I take you on a stroll through some options for creating your own digital e-book.

I take a look at how iPads can be used as a tool for inquiry, data collection, and analysis in math and science, and review some model lessons from teachers.

Lastly, I cover how to use assistive technologies to help students with physical challenges such as vision and hearing impairments.

8

Reading on the iPad

*1*f you're old enough to be parenting or educating, you probably love the smell of printed paper just as much as I do. Printed books won't be disappearing quite yet, but there's no question that the whole publishing industry is in a period of transition. Many large retailers have closed, and the number of digital reading devices and e-books sold continues to rise dramatically. The popularity of e-books is partly due to their convenience factor. Browse books online; read samples; and, with the tap of a button, order a book that arrives on your device within a minute or so. However, convenience alone wouldn't explain the degree of change currently taking place in the book publishing industry. We've had books in digital text format for a few years, and their adoption has been relatively slow. Two major factors are now contributing to the growth of e-books:

✏ **E-reading devices are becoming more sophisticated.** Their displays are crystal sharp, books are easier to browse and deliver, and devices are decreasing in price. All that allows users to carry around libraries of e-books in devices that weigh less than a single paperback.

✏ **The nature of what we call a book is evolving.** E-books are increasingly including elements of multimedia and interactivity. Also, e-books are being read on devices that integrate the experience of reading with search tools, dictionaries, highlighting and annotation features, and even elements of social networking.

I still love that smell of walking down the aisle in a bookstore and browsing the titles on the shelves . . . but that experience is becoming rarer, whereas digital reading continues to grow in popularity.

In this chapter, I take a look at different approaches to using your iPad for reading — from book subscriptions to the purchase of individual books, book apps, and even ways to access free e-books. I present different ways to access books for young readers and adults. Finally, I take a peek down the road at the fast-approaching market for e-textbooks that is finally beginning to materialize. Read on!

Digital Reading for Younger Students

It's one of the most commonly asked questions you hear about children using iPads: Should we encourage them to read e-books or paper books? The answer is fairly simple. As long as they are enjoying reading, does it really matter? I vote for an extra hour a day reading either an e-book or a paper book instead of more time wasted with a mindless video game.

Some children love the extra perks that come with reading e-books. Some of the common features include

- **Interactivity:** Touch objects, and they react. Turn your iPad, and things move.
- **Dictionary:** Touch words, and their definitions pop up.
- **Audio and soundtracks:** Characters talk. Background music plays. Sound effects play as events occur in the book.
- **Read aloud feature:** Younger children can have the book read to them, as can those who have visual problems.
- **Language options:** Select the language for text and/or audio.
- **Recording:** Record yourself reading the text and play it back as the audio narration later.
- **Games and activities:** Coloring pages, puzzles, and more are often included in the books.

It's difficult to keep up with the rush of new *digital books* (or electronic books, known as *e-books*) being released for younger readers. The range of options is expanding rapidly as new e-books are being released. The most common terms associated with digital books are e-books and e-pubs, e-book apps, and book subscriptions.

E-books

E-books and e-pubs are essentially the same, and it's more a question of which *e-reader* (electronic device for reading e-books and other digital documents) you use with them. E-books are available from the iBookstore, which delivers them directly to the iBooks app on your iPad. There are also a variety of other e-readers and e-reading apps for the iPad such as Kindle, Nook, Kobo, and more that can be used for reading e-books from other sources.

iBookstore has a Children and Teens section, as shown in Figure 8-1. You can also access the list of best-selling books by tapping the Top Charts icon in the bottom toolbar of the iBookstore and selecting the Children and Teens category. Any book that you purchase is automatically added to your e-books library and available on other iOS devices you may own.

Figure 8-1: The iBookstore has a Children and Teens category.

If you tap the Top Charts icon in the bottom toolbar of the iBookstore and select the Children and Teens category, you'll see the top sellers divided into Top Paid Books and Top Free Books, as shown in Figure 8-2. It's an excellent way to find a wealth of good, free e-books for your child to read.

Figure 8-2: Top-selling books are divided into Top Paid Books and Top Free Books.

Book apps

Many book publishers prefer the flexibility of creating their own book apps. *Book apps* function in much the same way as the books you read in iBooks; however, in creating their own apps, publishers are free to use additional functionality outside the framework of the regular e-book or e-pub formats. Book apps aren't read within an e-reader such as iBooks. Instead, they function as apps and are purchased through the App Store. For example, you'll find the book, *Al Gore - Our Choice: A Plan to Solve the Climate Crisis,* by Push pop Press, in the App Store and not the iBookstore. It opens as its own app — not within an e-reader. Pick objects up and move them around, pinch to open and zoom around images, and interact with objects such as windmills that simulate the generation of power when you blow into the iPad microphone!

The quality of many of these book apps is outstanding. You'll find them listed in the Books section of the App Store. They feature beautiful musical soundtracks, top-quality narration, and amazing illustrations and effects. You'll find reviews of these books all over the web, and even institutions such as *The New York Times* now occasionally feature reviews of e-books and book apps.

The list of quality books is too long to mention, but if you want a sampling of what's out there, consider the following book apps:

✔ ***The Three Little Pigs,* by Nosy Crow:** Featuring excellent graphics and sounds, this book is an excellent choice for younger readers. It tells the traditional tale of the Three Little Pigs . . . with a few twists. It offers lots of interactive surprises on every page and sophisticated animations, and you can listen to the story narrated by children or read it yourself. One of the highlights of the book is that you can help the wolf blow down the houses by blowing into the iPad's microphone!

✏ ***The Fantastic Flying Books of Mr. Morris Lessmore,* by Moonbot Studios:** This beautifully designed book app (see Figure 8-3) is based on a story by William Joyce that was also an award-winning animated short film. The animation sequences in the book are stunning, and the interactive elements will keep the reader entertained and engaged. The story revolves around a man infatuated with books. One day, he's blown away in a storm and finds himself in a remote country house filled with books. It's a poignant story about the power of books and the people who love to read them. The book is also filled with games that children will love, such as spelling in a bowl of alphabet cereal and playing "Pop Goes the Weasel" on a piano.

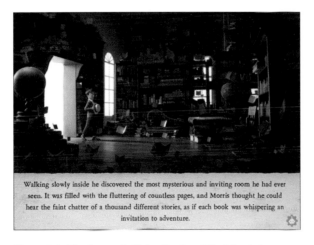

Walking slowly inside he discovered the most mysterious and inviting room he had ever seen. It was filled with the fluttering of countless pages, and Morris thought he could hear the faint chatter of a thousand different stories, as if each book was whispering an invitation to adventure.

Figure 8-3: *The Fantastic Flying Books of Mr. Morris Lessmore* illustrates the potential of e-books.

✏ ***Unwanted Guest,* by Moving Tales:** This stunning book is adapted from a traditional Jewish folk tale. It tells the story of a poor old man living in an old, dilapidated house. He's visited by an unwelcome houseguest, and the story details his attempts to rid himself of his surprising visitor.

This book is beautifully produced. The illustrations are gorgeous (see Figure 8-4), and it also includes sophisticated 3-D animations, original music, professional narration, and sound effects. It's a book that children and adults alike will enjoy.

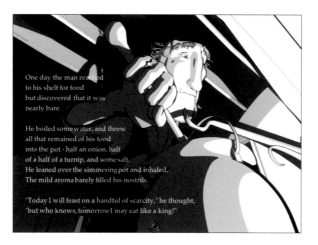

One day the man reached
to his shelf for food
but discovered that it was
nearly bare.

He boiled some water, and threw
all that remained of his food
into the pot - half an onion, half
of a half of a turnip, and some salt.
He leaned over the simmering pot and inhaled.
The mild aroma barely filled his nostrils.

"Today I will feast on a handful of scarcity," he thought,
"but who knows, tomorrow I may eat like a king!"

Figure 8-4: *Unwanted Guest* is an iPad book app that's beautifully produced.

E-book subscriptions

Given the ease with which e-books can be delivered to any computer or mobile device, it makes sense that some companies would start offering subscription services that have you sign up and get e-books delivered directly to your device as needed. At the risk of repeating myself, this sector is evolving, and new options are springing up all the time. In this section, I highlight two existing services.

Storia

Scholastic is a leading publisher of children's books in the United States and is now producing e-books as well. Storia, shown in Figure 8-5, is Scholastic's e-book management app, designed to download, store, manage, and read e-books. Storia comes with five free e-books.

Sign up for a Storia account online, and you'll gain access to a growing catalog of e-books that includes picture, chapter, and interactive books (for purchase and download), all targeted to children from the ages of 3 to 14. Scholastic offers popular and reasonably priced books ranging from the Harry Potter series to *Clifford, the Big Red Dog* and *The Hunger Games Trilogy*. Set up a separate virtual bookshelf for every child. As you purchase e-books, you can assign them to the bookshelf of any child.

Figure 8-5: Storia is an e-reading app with links to Scholastic's library of children's books.

To purchase and add books to your Storia library:

1. **Go to** www.scholastic.com/Storia.

2. **Choose the Shop for e-Books option, and select books.**

   Books can be selected by age, grade, reading level, price, and character or series.

3. **Follow the prompts to purchase your book.**

   You'll need to sign into your Storia account to complete the purchase.

4. **After completing the purchase, open the Storia app on your iPad, and tap the Parent Tools icon in the upper-right corner of the home screen.**

5. **Tap Manage e-Books, download the e-book, and assign it to the appropriate bookshelf.**

You can track an individual child's progress through each e-book, see what new words he learned and how many pages he read, and how long he spends reading each day. Select titles, called enriched e-books, also include word games, story interactions, and animations.

Reading Rainbow

You probably remember *Reading Rainbow*, the TV series hosted by LeVar Burton that ran on PBS for more than two decades. Reading Rainbow is now an app that offers subscription-based downloads of books for children ages 3 to 9.

Children tap a themed island (see Figure 8-6), such as Animal Kingdom, My Friends, My Family, or Genius Academy, which takes them to a selection of books they can browse. Each island also has a selection of "field trip" videos, some of which come from the original series. As was the case with the TV show, many of the stories are read by celebrity actors, and you can elect to turn the narration on or off. Books feature light animations and activities to enhance the story. *Reading Rainbow* currently contains a library of 150 interactive e-books; monthly subscriptions range from $5 to $10, depending on the term of the subscription.

Figure 8-6: The *Reading Rainbow* app is based on the PBS series hosted by LeVar Burton.

Reading Documents with GoodReader

You aren't limited to reading e-books on the iPad. You often need access to all sorts of documents when you're on the move. Fortunately, the iPad makes it easy to download and read them.

I discuss how to get content onto your iPad in Chapters 3 and 6. Options include using a cloud storage service such as Dropbox or Google Docs/Drive and, of course, moving content directly onto your iPad by syncing it through iTunes. One of the issues you'll encounter, however, is that documents come in all formats, sizes, and types. The spreadsheet that looked just great in Microsoft Excel on your Windows desktop computer all of a sudden either doesn't open or looks like a jumbled mess on your iPad. One of the best apps for handling content from a variety of sources is GoodReader.

GoodReader is an iPad app that enables you to download, read, manage, organize, access, and annotate just about any file you have stored — locally or on the web. Many have described it as the all-purpose Swiss army knife of document readers.

GoodReader can download and synchronize content from a wide variety of sources. It will read and display most common file types and is equally comfortable with your 100-page manual as with a 1-page letter or a 30-slide Microsoft PowerPoint presentation.

GoodReader is extremely versatile in the ways it enables you to connect to the different locations where documents might be stored, as I describe in the following list:

- **Open In:** When you tap and hold a document in most iPad apps, such as Mail, the Open In function menu pops up. GoodReader usually appears as an option to open most types of documents.

- **Connect to cloud services:** Tap the Connect to Servers pane, and you can add your account to any of a long list of storage and file synchronization services, such as Dropbox, Google Apps, Box, SugarSync, and more. Tap any option and type your account name and password, and a connection will be established. Now you can view and download any files you have in that account.

- **Connect to a computer:** Tap the wireless icon on the bottom toolbar and follow the instructions to connect GoodReader to your desktop or laptop.

- **Connect to the web:** Tap the Browse the Web pane, and use GoodReader's internal browser to locate any page or document on the web and download it to your iPad for reading. Tap the Sync button on the Web Downloads pane, and your downloaded document will be updated with any changes that may have occurred since you downloaded it.

Remember that GoodReader does more than just download a document to your iPad. Tap the Sync arrow, and GoodReader *synchronizes* a file or folder that updates and incorporates any changes that have been made since the last time you downloaded it.

The Manage Files pane, shown on the left in Figure 8-7, allows you to move and delete files, create folders, e-mail files, and more. Tap the Preview pane, and you can preview any file you have downloaded before opening it. GoodReader built its reputation as being the file reader you want on your iPad. Simply tap any document in the list of downloaded files on the left pane, and GoodReader opens it for reading, as shown on right in Figure 8-7.

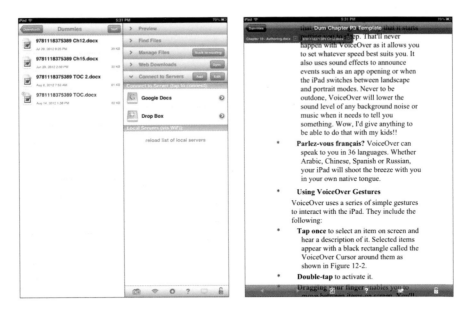

Figure 8-7: Tap a document in GoodReader's downloaded list to open and read it.

Reading Books Electronically: E-Reader Devices and Apps

You can read electronic books two ways: on a portable electronic device known as a dedicated e-reader (such as the Amazon Kindle or Barnes & Noble Nook) that can store and display e-books; or on a device like the iPad, which serves many functions, including acting as an e-reader via an e-reading app. Using the iPad as an e-reader is a great thing, especially with the high-resolution display of the third-generation iPad (if you're lucky enough to have one).

You can read e-books using your choice of a variety of e-reading apps on the iPad. Each app has a unique set of features and often its own store for buying the books. In this section, I compare a few. You can decide which ones to use and when.

iBooks

iBooks is the native e-reading app for the iPad and the most popular book-reading app for users of any Apple iOS device. It's designed specifically for iOS use and cannot be used on other platforms. I discuss the functionality and interface of iBooks in Chapter 4. One of the app's strengths is that it's the only one on the iPad that has a built-in bookstore for browsing and in-app ordering of books. In most cases, you can download samples to read before buying the book. To be fair, some of the other major e-reading apps had in-app purchasing in earlier versions; they were required to remove it from their iPad versions.

iBooks has improved steadily with new releases and is a solid choice for reading on the iPad. The capabilities to change color schemes, increase and decrease font sizes, keep notes, annotate text, and more have made iBooks the standard e-reading app on the iPad.

Kindle

Amazon (www.amazon.com) offers e-reading devices — its Kindle models — and an e-reading app — the Kindle app — that can be used on other devices. Amazon has the advantage of offering the largest selection of paid e-books available, with more than a million titles in its inventory. Download the free Kindle app to your iPad, and when you purchase an e-book on Amazon.com, you have the option of downloading it to the Kindle app on your iPad. You can also purchase hundreds of newspapers and magazines and download them to your Kindle device.

The Kindle app, shown in Figure 8-8, is available on a wide variety of devices, including Android devices, Windows Phones, iPhones, Windows PCs, and Mac PCs. In addition, the Kindle's WhisperSync feature saves your last page read, bookmarks, and notes so that you can pick up any other device and synchronize with where you left off on another device. Amazon also offers free samples for download so you can review books before buying them.

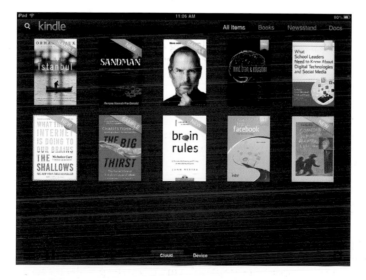

Figure 8-8: Amazon's Kindle offers the widest selection of e-books for purchase.

Nook

Barnes & Noble (www.bn.com) offers an e-reading device — the Nook — as well as an e-reading app that can be used on iOS and Android devices. Barnes & Noble created the Nook app to promote and bolster its sales of e-books.

Barnes & Noble offers a large selection of paid and free e-books, as well as magazines and newspapers. The free Nook app is also available for your Mac, PC, and smartphones, and it syncs your reading status between devices. Unfortunately, B&N hasn't yet found a way to deliver a hot cup of coffee and pastry with the book.

Kobo

Kobo (www.kobo.com/ereaders) has various models of e-readers, and its e-reading app shares many features with other e-reading apps. You can purchase books from Kobo's online store; it has apps for several devices (including the iPad and iPhone); the app synchronizes your account between your devices. You also can change text size, add notes, annotate text, and more.

What really distinguishes Kobo from other e-reading apps, though, is its Reading Life feature. Reading Life is an example of a new trend called *social reading*. You're probably familiar with social networking — possibly the most powerful phenomenon sweeping the Internet — and it has reached the world of reading. You may think of reading as a rather solitary activity, but book clubs have been around for a long time. Book club members meet in someone's living room and, over a drink and some snacks, discuss a book everyone has read. The advent of social reading is born out of book clubs . . . except in a social reading club, you can meet any time of day you want, at any place you happen to be, and discuss books with countless readers from all across the planet. You just have to bring your own tea and snacks.

Kobo is one of a new generation of e-reading apps that is moving the social networking experience into the realm of book reading. Tap the cover of any book in your library and let your friends on Facebook and Twitter know what you're reading. Select any text in the book and then post and share it — along with your comments — on your social networking sites.

The Kobo Pulse is a spherical icon at the bottom of each page in the book, as shown in Figure 8-9. It grows and gets darker on pages that have a lot of activity. Tap the Kobo Pulse to get the following information:

- *Who is currently reading the book.*
- *Any comments that have been left.*
- *How many people have liked the book.*

In addition, you can add comments of your own or reply to other comments.

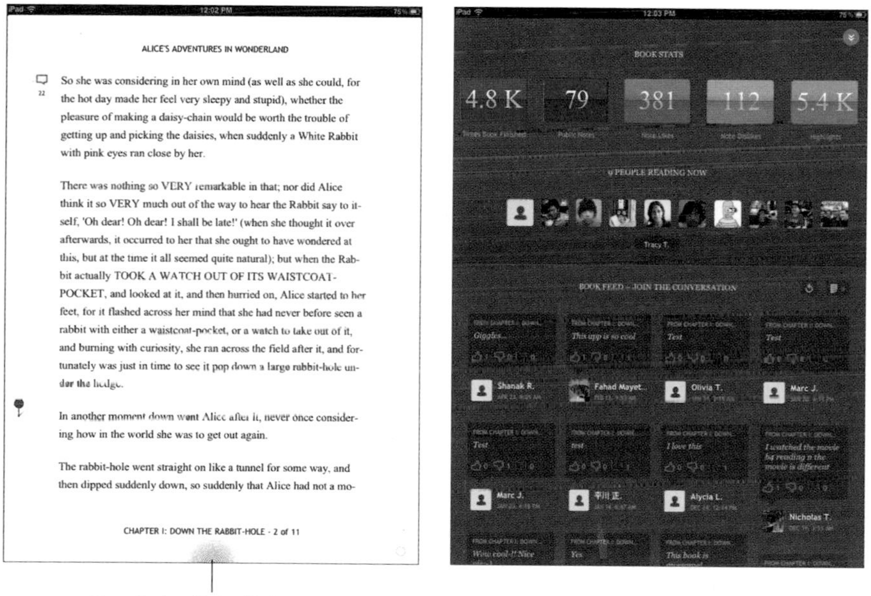

Touch the Kobo Pulse . . .   . . . to interact with other readers.

Figure 8-9: Tap the Kobo Pulse icon on any page to interact with readers and share comments.

Tap the top menu bar on your Kobo home screen or bookshelf to reveal the Reading Life icon. Tap it to explore statistics about your reading. Find out how long you have been reading, the average pages per hour, time you take to read a book, and more. Sign up with your Facebook account and see what your Facebook friends have been reading and recommending.

Getting Free E-Books

There's no such thing as a free lunch, right? That may be true with regard to eating, but when it comes to reading, there actually are a few ways to get your hands on lots of free e-books. One of the best ways to access thousands of free e-books is through the Project Gutenberg website (www.gutenberg. org). Just download, read, and enjoy.

Project Gutenberg is a volunteer effort to digitize, archive, and distribute public-domain books. The project was founded in 1971 and offers more than 40,000 free e-books that can be downloaded or read online. The books are primarily older books, the copyrights of which have expired, and include many of the classics you grew up reading. Downloading them to your iPad is simple: Go to www.gutenberg.org, and browse the books in the archives or type your search term in the Search field at the top of the page. You can search for a complete title, any part of a title, or an author. (For example, a search for *Oscar Wilde* lists all the books he wrote.) You have various formats to choose among for the download, but select ePub to view items in iBooks (see Figure 8-10).

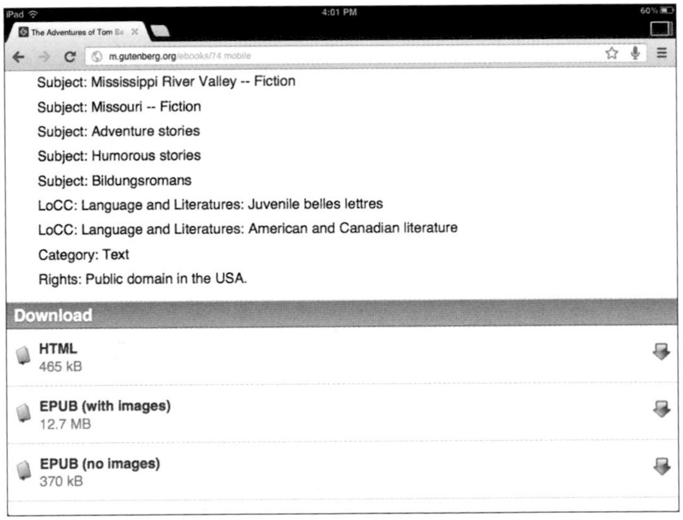

![Screenshot of Project Gutenberg download page showing book subject details and download format options]

Subject: Mississippi River Valley -- Fiction
Subject: Missouri -- Fiction
Subject: Adventure stories
Subject: Humorous stories
Subject: Bildungsromans
LoCC: Language and Literatures: Juvenile belles lettres
LoCC: Language and Literatures: American and Canadian literature
Category: Text
Rights: Public domain in the USA.

Download

HTML
465 kB

EPUB (with images)
12.7 MB

EPUB (no images)
370 kB

Figure 8-10: Download free books from Project Gutenberg and open them in iBooks.

Another website I recommend checking is www.baen.com/library. It also has a nice election of free e-books that you can download and read on your iPad. Remember to select the ePub format.

Goodreads (www.goodreads.com), which has an iPad app, is a great way to keep track of your reading lists and preferences and then share them with friends. Keep track of what you have read and want to read by adding books to your shelves. Check what your friends are reading, and read their book reviews. It's a great way to discover new books to read. As a bonus, Goodreads has a library of more than 2,000 free public-domain books you can download.

Entering the E-Textbook Era

How many of us see our children leave for school in the mornings carrying backpacks filled with heavy textbooks that could break a lumberjack's back? We've finally reached a period of transition where many traditional publishers are recognizing the need to publish and promote e-textbooks. In addition, smaller publishers and even individuals now have the technology to create and distribute their own textbooks — something that wasn't possible when textbooks had to be mass-produced and sold through traditional sales channels.

The dust is still settling, and a variety of e-textbook formats are on the market. In the case of the iPad, Apple has released a free software program for the Mac (requires 10.7.2 or higher), called iBooks Author, which I discuss briefly in Chapter 10. iBooks Author was released with the specific intent of allowing authors to create e-textbooks for the iPad and distribute them through the iBookstore. The iBookstore now has an iBooks Textbooks category (see Figure 8-11), and the content in it has started growing rapidly.

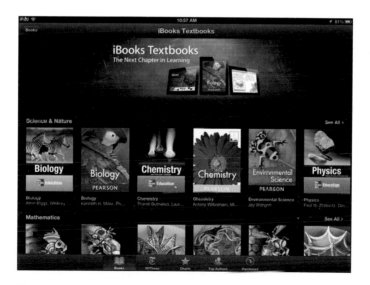

Figure 8-11: The Apple iBookstore now includes an iBooks Textbooks category.

Other publishers are releasing interactive textbooks as apps. That gives them more capability to add features such as monitoring and reporting on student progress. Sites such as Inkling (www.inkling.com) focus solely on interactive textbooks and have apps for a variety of platforms, including iPads.

9

Creating, Editing, and Annotating Documents

*Y*ou may tire of hearing me talk about the fact that modern communications have progressed from being primarily text-based to an evolving mixture of multiple digital media formats. If we want school to remain relevant, students need ample opportunities to express themselves in all forms of media. Pushing education into the 21st century doesn't mean leaving all 20th-century skills behind entirely, however. Theoretically, you could sit through a long business meeting sketching everyone around the table and recording audio of all the conversations, but it would probably be a lot simpler to jot down the important points and create a quick list of tasks to complete. Even longer reports may include references to the web, images and links to video, but they often still require a substantial amount of writing. So let's not throw out the baby with the bathwater: Taking notes, creating documents, and editing or annotating text all remain vitally important. They also are what this chapter focuses on.

If you're an adult who just started using an iPad, I won't need ESP to mind-read your first complaint: "I can't type on this thing!" You might use slightly more colorful language, but you get the point. I agree. Whether you use the onscreen virtual keyboard or go out and purchase a physical keyboard that works with the iPad, it does take time to get accustomed to creating text on your device. I mean, did you pick up a pencil when you were a kid and immediately start writing a 50-page thesis? New skills take time and practice.

You need to determine how and where you want to use your iPad and then decide how best to use the appropriate apps and skills. As you'll see, you have many options that range from simple note-taking apps to full-featured word processing and handwriting apps. There are hundreds of excellent apps for creating and editing text on the iPad — yes, even for those of you who still insist you did write a 50-page thesis when you first picked up that pencil as a kid.

Determining Your Objectives

I'll be honest. If you look in the satchel that I take to work most days, you'll find both an iPad and a MacBook Air. They are neatly slotted in the section next to the cheese sandwich I forgot about last week. I take both because there are days I need to attend meetings and take brief summary notes; the iPad is ideal for this task. Other times, I have time to sit somewhere quiet and really write. At those times, I prefer having the full-size keyboard and larger screen that the MacBook Air provides.

Some days, I have to jot notes in my lap because I'm taking a long plane ride and the big guy with the stained blue checked shirt next to me in seat 26B insists on spreading out and monopolizing the armrests while slurping that soft drink. (You know who you are . . .) Other times, I have access to a desk and lots of space to stretch out. There are times I can complete all my notes in a quick session and times I'll need to finish writing later at home. You get the point. As they say in Australia, "different horses for different courses," meaning that what's suitable for one purpose may not be for another. So ask yourself a few pertinent questions:

- **Are you usually taking short notes for a class or meeting?** If so, look for a simple note-taking app without a lot of frills.

- **Do you need to share notes with others or file them somewhere that will give you access on all devices?** That will require that your app connect to a *cloud storage* service such as Dropbox (www.dropbox.com) that stores your files on the Internet and enables sharing of folders and files with other users.

- **Are you more comfortable typing (see Figure 9-1), or do you prefer handwriting?** If handwriting is your preference, consider using an app that supports note-taking by handwriting with a stylus.

- **Are you writing something that's longer and may be continued later?** You'll require a more robust word processing application, and cloud storage is important.

- **Will you continue the file on a device other than your iPad?** If that's the case, you need to make sure that you use an app that has the capability to save or export the file in a format you can use in other software applications (Microsoft Word document, Pages file, and so on).

✔ **Do you often need to access files for review and editing?** You'll need cloud storage and annotation features.

I review solutions for all those situations later in the chapter. Determine your priorities, and you can mix and match the various options as needed.

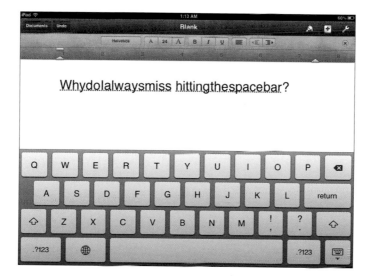

Figure 9-1: Are you more comfortable typing on the virtual keyboard or handwriting?

Taking Notes

Whether you're sitting in class, meeting with clients, or attending a board meeting, there are times you want to create short notes as a synopsis of the event for later referral or study. You could create documents and store them somewhere for later retrieval, but a good note-keeping app would satisfy the following requirements:

✔ **Simple and quick:** It needs to be quick to open and get to the point at which you can start taking notes. You don't want to always be leaning over, asking the person next to you to repeat what was just said. Typing should be simple, without the need to work out complex margin settings, hanging paragraphs, line spacing, and more. You need to get that text down quickly and easily.

✔ **Organized:** You're usually taking notes as part of some ongoing process. Ideally, the system or app you use has a built-in format and flow for organizing your notes. Set up one folder for Biology and another for English. Set up a folder for one client and subfolders for individual projects. Notes should easily fit in the right category and have a simple flow so that everything you need is there in sequential order.

- **Always available:** Apps that have an accompanying website service and interface are always my preference. I like to know my notes are available in a common location that every device supports. These days, every computer and device has a web browser, so I need an app that provides secure web access.

- **Cloud storage and backup:** Back in the day, if you lost your folder with months of notes, you'd more than likely start hyperventilating. Digital storage is simple these days. Don't use an app that uses the iPad as its primary storage location and relies on you to synchronize your files in order to create a backup. Select a solution that allows simple and automatic cloud storage.

- **Search:** A bonus is the capability to tag your notes with keywords and an effective search function to find whatever you need easily.

- **Images, sketches, sharing and more:** You're using an iPad! Your note-taking app should take advantage of the capabilities it provides. It's helpful to use that camera to add a quick picture of a document or a whiteboard to your notes. Sketch something in your note with your finger or stylus. Record a snippet of important audio. E-mail your note to someone else who needs it, or even better, share it so that groups of people can have access.

Following are two of the best apps for note taking:

- **Evernote:** I discuss Evernote in significant detail in Chapter 6. For my money, Evernote has all the features you want from a note-taking app. It excels in organization, storing notes in notebooks that you can create and share, while allowing you to add all types of digital content within your notes, including audio, images, and even websites. Your account is also available from any device and through the Evernote website itself.

- **iA Writer (see Figure 9-2):** iA Writer is a fantastic app for simple text editing — but it's text and only text. One huge feature is a much-needed extended keyboard (hello, Apple?) that adds keys for those simple functions such as moving through text letter by letter or skipping through it word by word. Dropbox and iCloud integration is provided as well, but organization of notes is not very intuitive.

If you prefer creating handwritten notes, don't panic. I discuss some great apps for that later in the chapter.

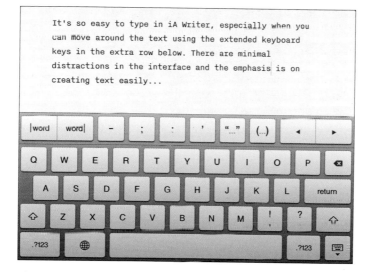

Figure 9-2: iA Writer's focus is simple text with an extended keyboard to simplify editing.

Word Processing with Pages

There are many full-featured word processing apps for the iPad, but if I have to choose only one, it would have to be Pages (shown in Figure 9-3).

Return to Documents page   Undo   Format Insert

Tools

Figure 9-3: Pages has full support for text styles, charts, images, and more.

Pages is packed full of functions you expect from a word processor, adapted for use with the touch interface of the iPad:

- Templates with preselected formatting of colors, backgrounds, and fonts to get you going.

- Full page and paragraph formatting options, such as margins, line spacing, columns, bulleted and numbered lists, and more.

- Support for text and paragraph styles.

- Easy addition and formatting of images. Options for editing photos are simple to use, and you can add 3D charts and tables as well. Set text to wrap around your image automatically.

- Full support for multitouch gestures such as pinch to zoom in and out, touch to select, and swivel to rotate images and more.

- The ability to step back through changes with Undo even after you next open the document.

- A Page Navigator that allows you to browse and change pages by tapping on thumbnail previews.

- Automatic document saving.

- Tight integration with iCloud. Options can be set to synchronize documents across devices, even to the point that you can continue from the point at which you left off on another device.

- Microsoft Word- and PDF-friendliness. Open Word and PDF files and edit them in Pages. You can also export your document as a Word doc or PDF.

If you've used a word processor before, using Pages will come pretty easily. Tap the Pages icon to start the app and then stick with me through the following bullets as I hit the highlights of using Pages:

- **Using Pages with iCloud:** The first time you open Pages, it will ask you whether you want to use it with an Apple iCloud account. I strongly recommend opening an iCloud account, if you haven't already, because it will allow Pages to sync your documents and data among all your devices and computers. I am keeping one ace up my sleeve, though. Check out the "iCloud versus ALL cloud" sidebar for a great tip about syncing Pages with other cloud services for a fabulous alternative. I believe that's called a "teaser" in the book business.

- **Starting or opening a document:** You start on your main documents page, which contains any files and folders you have created. If you have any documents on your iPad that you'd like to open and edit, you can simply tap them.

To create a new document, tap the + sign in the top-left corner and select Create Document. Select one of 15 preformatted templates, or tap the blank template option to start from an empty page.

✔ **Editing documents:** Tap anywhere in the document to enter editing mode. The keyboard will slide up, along with the ruler and formatting bars across the top of your display. I strongly suggest turning your iPad to landscape orientation because it makes the keyboard larger and easier to use. You could also consider using it in portrait mode if you were using an external keyboard. Some of the main editing features include the following:

- *Font sizing:* Adjust the appearance of your document using the Font button located on the left side of the top toolbar. Pages allows you to adjust font style, size, and color. Select any text by tapping and holding it, and then choosing Select. You can expand your selection by tapping and dragging the handles of the selection box. Tap the Font button on the top toolbar and scroll through the font styles to find the one you want. Font families have little arrows next to them. Tap the arrow to reveal and select one of the styles.

- *Text selection:* Double-tap to select a word. Triple-tap to select a whole paragraph. Tap and drag the selection handles to select a block of text.

- *Replacements and definitions:* Double-tap a word for the options Cut, Copy, Paste, Replace, Define, and Style. (You'll see them by tapping the More button in older versions.) Replace gives you the option to replace your misspelled word with a similar word. Definition brings up the dictionary definition, and Style gives you the option to copy the style.

- *Text styles:* Triple-tap to select any block of text, tap the Format button, and then choose format options from the menu that appears (see Figure 9-4).

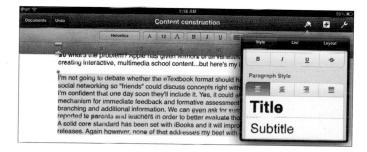

Figure 9-4: Use the Format tool to change styles.

The menu has three tabs:

Tap the Styles tab for preset styles that you can use to ensure that titles, headings, body, and captions match throughout your document. You can also change text alignment and font selections and style.

Tap the List tab for bulleted- or numbered-list options.

Tap the Layout tab to create columns or tweak line spacing.

- *Ruler:* Tapping and dragging the arrows pointing up adjusts your margins, and the flat button adjusts the paragraph indentation on the first line. Tap and drag a right-facing arrow to adjust column width.

- *Document Setup:* Tap the Tools icon (the wrench) and select Document Setup (see Figure 9-5) to make changes that apply to every page in the document:

Figure 9-5: Document Setup allows you to change headers, footers, margins, and more.

Tap to add or edit headers, footers, and page numbering.

Tap and drag the page edges to adjust page margins.

Tap the Insert icon to add logos and images.

Tap the Format icon to set document styles.

- *Page Navigator:* To find and jump to any page, tap and hold your finger anywhere against the right edge of the screen until the navigator appears, displaying a thumbnail image of a document page, as shown in Figure 9-6. Drag up or down to view the thumbnail images of any page in the document. When you get to the page you want, lift your finger straight up from the screen to jump to that page. To release the navigator without leaving the current page, swipe to the right.

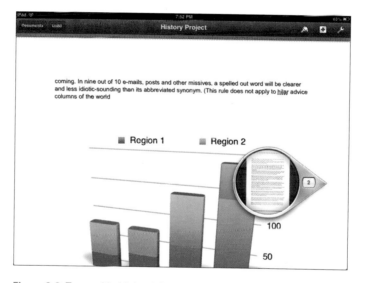

Figure 9-6: Tap and hold the right edge of the screen until the Page Navigator appears.

- *Image insertion:* Tap the Insert icon to select and insert photos from your iPad.

To resize a photo, tap drag the selection handles in the corners.

To move, tap the image and drag it to any location.

To rotate, tap and select the image; then rotate it with two fingers.

Tap and select the image; then tap the Format icon for Style options such as borders and effects. You can also tap the Arrange tab to move the photo in front or behind other objects and set the way text wraps around it.

Double-tap to mask the image and determine which portion of it appears. Slide the image within the masked area and tap outside the picture to save your new cropping.

- *Tables, charts, and shapes:* Tap the Insert icon to select and insert tables, charts that map data visually, and different shapes.

✔ **Managing your documents:** Your Documents screen displays thumbnails of all the documents on your iPad. From there, you can do the following:

- *Rename a document* by tapping and holding the document name and then typing the new name in the text field that pops up.

- *Group documents* into folders by tapping the Edit button in the top corner. Tap and hold a thumbnail image until the documents start to jiggle, and then drag one document onto another. That automatically creates a folder and prompts you for a folder name. Tap outside the folder area to close it.

- *Remove a document* from a folder by tapping the folder to open it. Touch and hold until it jiggles; then tap, drag, and drop the document outside the folder.

- *Delete a document* by tapping Edit, tapping to select the document(s), and then tapping the Trash icon in the top toolbar.

✔ **Sharing documents:** When you're ready to present your work to the world, tap the Tools icon, and tap the Share and Print option from the menu, and you can e-mail or print your document, or send it to your iTunes account or to a WebDAV server. Don't forget that Pages gives you the option of sending the document as a Pages, Word, or PDF document. Of course, if you have an iCloud account and set it to synchronize documents, your document will automatically find its way floating up to the cloud and over to all your other devices without your having to do anything.

As of the latest release, Pages still offers sharing via iWork and iDisk, which have both been discontinued in favor of the newer iCloud service (www. icloud.com).

iCloud versus ALL cloud

iCloud is a wonderful service, but many other options are out there when it comes to cloud storage services. I love my Dropbox account, and I also use Google Drive extensively. I could sync my Pages documents with iCloud and create another, third storage location, but I'm a "keep it simple" sort of guy: The idea of having to organize all these different storage accounts just makes me nervous. Of course, you know I wouldn't bring it up unless I had a great solution, right?

Otixo gives you access to all your cloud accounts from a single location. So I recommend that you rush to the Otixo.com website (www.otixo.com) and open an account. Whether you use any combination of Dropbox, Google, Box, CX, or something else, just add them all to your Otixo account and let it be the single access point for all the files in those accounts. Here's the great part . . . it's accessible right from within Pages.

To save your Pages document, follow these steps:

1. **Tap and hold to select the document in the Documents view, and then tap the Share arrow in the upper-right corner.**

2. **Select WebDAV.**

Otixo uses a WebDAV server, which talks directly to all of Apple's iWork products, which include Numbers and Keynote.

3. **Sign in by entering your Otixo server address as** https://dav.otixo.com, **and add your username and password.**

   You need to sign into your Otixo account only once.

4. **Tap to select a file format.**

   Your choices are to save the document as a Pages, Word, or PDF document.

5. **Select a cloud account.**

   If you have already added all your different accounts at Otixo.com, they are all now available to you. In my case, I get my Dropbox, Google Docs, and CS storage accounts as options for saving the copy of my Pages document.

The same applies if you want to open a document from a cloud account. Use the WebDAV option, and use your Otixo account to open it from anywhere. Just remember that you are copying the document. If you change it elsewhere, it doesn't synchronize with the copy on your iPad.

Many of us have been using Microsoft Office for several years, and the switch to using an iPad feels less than harmonic. There's help to bring harmony, though: Consider an app called CloudOn (see Figure 9-7). It links it to your Box, Dropbox, and Google Drive accounts, enabling you to open any document you have stored in those accounts. Once you open your Office documents, you'll be presented with an interface that feels very much like home.

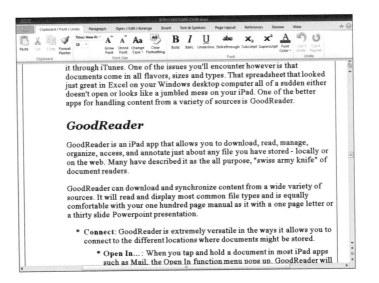

Figure 9-7: CloudOn provides a Microsoft-like interface for creating/editing Office documents.

Annotating PDF Documents

Here I am, supposed to be providing you all the answers, yet I spend so much time asking you questions. If you want to look into marking up and annotating PDF documents, I have to ask you, "What's your objective?" Depending on your answer to that question, I do have apps to suggest:

✔ **Filling out forms? Consult the PDF Expert (**http://readdle.com/products/pdfexpert_ipad/**):** If your primary need is to fill out forms and sign them, I recommend looking at an app called PDF Expert. Like most PDF annotation apps, it links to your cloud accounts so that you can download documents easily.

PDF Expert reads most document types and provides standard highlight and annotating functions. Use the keyboard or write on the form with your finger or a stylus. Annotations are saved within the document in PDF format.

The app excels in its support of PDF form fields and functionality created in Adobe Acrobat. Special fields such as text fields, check boxes, radio buttons, and other form elements all function as needed, and all information you enter is saved inside the form — including, of course, any signatures.

✔ **Writing serious, heavy-duty annotations? Try iAnnotate (**www.branch
fire.com/iannotate**):** If you're looking for a robust annotation app
that can be used for everything from grading papers to marking up
important business documents, take a look at iAnnotate (shown in
Figure 9-8).

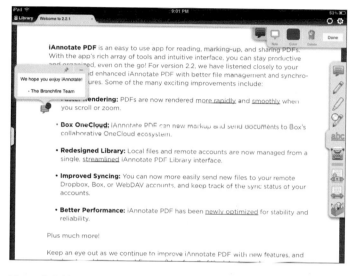

Figure 9-8: iAnnotate provides a robust set of features for heavier
annotation needs.

iAnnotate provides a wide range of annotation features, including
annotation tools such as a pen, highlighter, typewriter, stamps, notes,
underline, strikethrough, photo, date stamp, and even voice recording.

- *Create your own custom stamps, including even your signature.*

- *Organize, insert, and delete pages.*

- *Organize files with the graphical file manager.*

- *Use the navigation and search tools to find any text you need
anywhere in your library.*

✔ **Going the simple yet effective route? PDFpen is what you need**
(http://smilesoftware.com/PDFpen/index.html)**:** PDFpen
(shown in Figure 9-9) lacks the organization and management features
of apps like iAnnotate, but it provides all the features you'd need for
annotation within a simple and effective interface. You can add text
boxes, notes, comments, highlights, and strikethrough, for instance,
and many other features make it simple to mark up any document you
retrieve from the cloud.

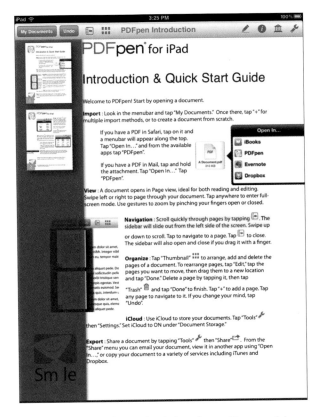

Figure 9-9: PDFpen has a simple interface with powerful tools for marking up documents.

Handwriting and Sketching

That virtual keyboard may not be a good fit for you. Maybe you tried using a Bluetooth keyboard. Some people, however, still feel more comfortable handwriting, and when you start to look at the features included with the leading handwriting apps, you'll realize that they offer so much more than just doodling a few squiggles on a page.

Touring Notability

When comparing the features of multipurpose handwriting apps, it's difficult to look past Notability (www.gingerlabs.com/cont/notability.php). Notability is a note-taking app for the iPad that gives you the power to integrate handwriting, typing, drawings, audio, pictures, and PDF annotation all into one document. It's easy to go from typing to sketching and then adding media to your page.

But the killer feature of Notability is the capability to add audio recordings that automatically link to your notes. Tap Record to keep an audio track as you take notes. When you read your pages back, just tap a word to hear what was said at that very moment you were writing that note. How many times have you looked at your hastily scribbled pages, trying to decipher what you'd written? Was it *exogenous zones* or *erogenous zones?* Tap to listen to the audio, and it's easy to find out. You can also use the recording feature to add your own voice to notes and memos.

It's a wonderful tool for students in middle school through college and into the workplace. Whether you want to take notes, keep memos, or capture your own ideas, Notability has a rich set of features (see Figure 9-10) for any note-taking objective. And Notability can be an especially effective tool for people who have difficulties taking notes.

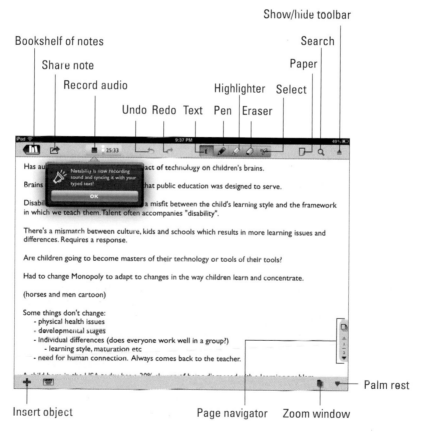

Figure 9-10: Use Notability to take handwritten or typed notes with synchronized audio.

Notability offers the following:

- **Full-featured handwriting:** Select different paper and pen styles. Use the palm rest to make handwriting easier and prevent unwanted marks and smudges. You can even set handwriting to left-handed mode.

- **Zoom capability for more detail:** The zoom window helps you clearly draw every detail or take detailed notes. Change pen colors and widths easily.

- **Document markup:** The same tools that help you take beautiful notes in Notability equip you to annotate PDFs. You can import pictures or PDF files; then you can highlight or take notes directly over them.

- **Word processing:** Notability isn't just for handwriting. Use your keyboard for typed text as well. It has many word-processing features, like styling, outlining, text boxes, spell check, bullets, bold, italic, underline, and more.

- **Flexibility:** Create notes that are as vivid, visual, and informative as required by the occasion.

    - *Move and even restyle objects with a scissors tool.*

    - *Enhance your notes by adding pictures from your photo library or iPad camera.*

    - *Insert web clips, figures, or drawings to complement your notes.* Don't worry; your text will automatically flow around the images.

    - *Crop, resize, and draw on your images to make them more detailed.*

- **Organization:** Organize your notes into subject folders. Within any note, tap the page navigator icon to scroll through your pages in a pop-up sidebar, rearrange them, or add and delete pages as needed.

Using Notability

I'm just as eager as you are to start using the app. The following sections break down using Notability into a four-step process.

Getting started

To create a new note, tap the Compose icon in the Library. Tapping the Bookshelf icon at any time returns you to the Library, and your note will automatically be saved.

Choose a paper background by tapping the Page icon on the top toolbar. Examples include graph paper, lined paper, canvas, colored paper, and so on.

Writing, typing, sketching, and recording

Notability has a powerful set of tools that can accommodate all your note-taking needs and preferences. In the following list, I review some of your options:

✔ **Text:** You can type text notes using the following techniques:

- *Tap the Text icon in the top toolbar; then tap in the document wherever you want to type; the keyboard slides up.*

- *Tap Outline (the icon to the left of the Font icon in the keyboard toolbar) to select your outline style: bullets, numbers, or plain text.*

- *Tap the Font icon (Tt) to select your font, color, size, and style.*

- *Create a text style by setting the font size, style, and color, and then tapping and holding a font preset button (Aa, Bb, Cd, or Dd).* Tap the Keyboard icon to lock it. (Note that the keyboard needs to be closed for the button to appear.)

✔ **Keyboard toolbar customization:** You can customize your keyboard toolbar (see Figure 9-11) by tapping and holding the toolbar above the keyboard to open the tool window. Simply drag the tools onto the keyboard toolbar to create your ideal tool set, including font presets, bold, italic, underline, cursor controls, and bullet or numbered outline styles. Tap Done when you're finished.

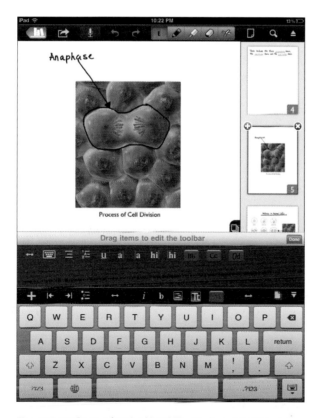

Figure 9-11: Customize the Notability keyboard toolbar with your favorite functions.

✔ **Finger or stylus writing:** Double-tap the Pencil icon to select color and line width; then proceed to write with your finger or stylus.

Notability improves the look of your handwriting, giving you smooth and organic-looking strokes, as shown in Figure 9-12. It mimics the way a marker writes by creating lines with varying thickness that give you the tapered look of a natural marker stroke.

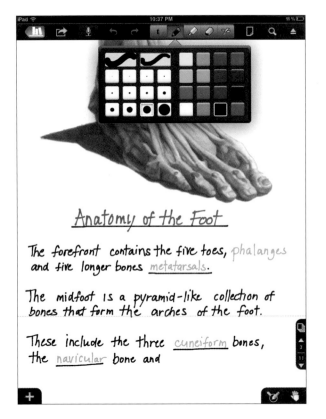

Figure 9-12: Double-tap the Pencil icon to select the color and line width.

✔ **Highlight:** Tap the Highlighter icon to draw attention to information in your note. As with the pencil, tapping it a second time will display options for color and width.

✔ **Eraser:** Tap this icon to erase handwriting or drawings. It removes whole strokes as a single object, which makes it quick to erase but doesn't allow fine control.

✔ **Scrolling:** Use two fingers to scroll through a note.

✔ **Palm rest:** Tap the Palm Rest icon to lay the heel of your hand on the iPad without making marks on the page (see Figure 9-13). One superb addition to this tool lets you adjust the palm rest to a height that suits you by tapping and dragging the icon with three horizontal bars on the top right of the palm rest.

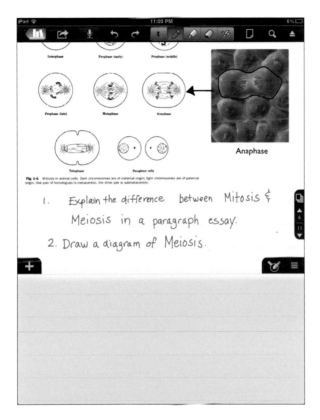

Figure 9-13: Adjust the palm rest height by tapping and dragging the horizontal bars icon.

✔ **Zoom:** Tap the Zoom icon to open the Zoom window and a zoom *target box* (see Figure 9-14) that you can move around the page to magnify any area. Write or sketch in the magnified zoom window to gain finer control over handwriting, sketching, filling out forms, adding notes or details on a drawing, or writing small captions. Resize the zoom target box by dragging the lower-right handle.

Figure 9-14: The Zoom box magnifies areas of your note that require finer details.

✔ **Cut/copy/paste:** Tap the scissors icon and circle an area with your finger or stylus to cut, copy, paste, and restyle content you have handwritten or sketched. Move the selected object anywhere on the page, or tap it to display menus with options to cut, copy, or change styles such as color and line width.

✔ **Left-hand capability:** Don't fret if you're a lefty; you haven't been forgotten. Tap the Library icon and then tap the Settings icon on the bottom toolbar. Scroll down to the Other Settings section (using two fingers, of course) — and smile as you turn on Left Handed mode.

✔ **Synchronized audio recording:** The audio recording feature really makes Notability stand out from many other handwriting apps. It's a simple way to listen to important audio that's synchronized with the notes you were taking at the very same time! To use this feature, follow these steps:

1. *Tap the microphone icon to start recording at any time.*

2. *Tap the Stop button when you're ready to stop the recording.*

   Any notes taken during a recording are synchronized to the audio taking place at the same time.

3. *Tap the Playback button to listen to the recording.*

4. *Tap any text or media object to hear what was said at that point in the recording.*

   Playback options include volume control, fast forward, rewind, and deletion of recordings.

I know I'm repeating myself, but I'm awed by the possibilities this feature presents. Whether you have attention deficit problems, difficulty hearing or processing audio, or just plain don't understand anything being said during an important class, you'll absolutely love the recording option.

✔ **Page navigation:** Tap or drag the pages icon on the right of the screen to open the Page Navigation tool, as shown in Figure 9-15. A window slides open along the right of your screen, with thumbnails of all the pages in your document. Add, delete, or reorder pages, or simply tap to go to a specific page.

✔ **Media insertion:** Tap the Insert Media + icon on the bottom left to insert web clips, photos, figures, text, and writing boxes into your note:

- *You can write or draw over the top of any media.* It's a great way to add notes and little captions for additional detail on images. Text will automatically wrap around images.

- *Tap with two fingers on any media object to select it and display the menus.* Tap edit to enter the figure editor, where you can crop, use prebuilt shapes, or use a pen to edit your media.

- *Tap the caption field at the bottom of any image to insert your caption text.*

- *Tap the Web Clip icon to open a browser and select a page to insert into your notes.* Once you've inserted it, you can add notes and highlights.

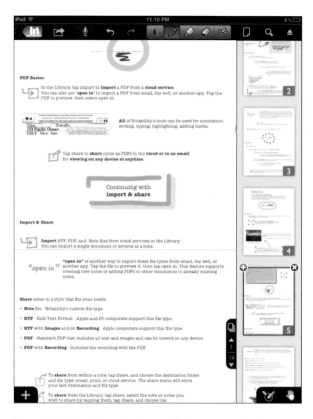

Figure 9-15: The Page Navigator slides open to display thumbnails of all your pages.

TIP

Use the Text media object as a great way to fill out forms, annotate PDFs, or move text anywhere on the page. Tap the Insert Media + icon; then tap to select Text. You can tap anywhere on the page to insert your text box and then start typing in it.

Importing, annotating, and sharing notes

From the Library, tap the curved arrow Import icon on the right of the top toolbar to bring in a PDF from a cloud service. You can also import RTFs and .Note (Notability) files.

Use Notability's tools for annotating your document, including writing, typing, highlighting, and adding media.

To share from within a note, tap the curved arrow Share icon, and choose whether to e-mail, print, or upload to a cloud service, where you can select the specific folder and file type. To share from the Library, select the notes to share by tapping them and follow the same process.

Organizing your notes library

I could go into mind-numbing detail on this topic, but you probably need a break and a cup of tea as much as I do. Tap and hold, drag, and look for the Edit button in the top-left corner of the Library. Here's a short breakdown that you can read while your tea water is boiling:

- ✔ All the organization takes place in the Library, as shown in Figure 9-16.

- ✔ Set up Categories that contain Subject folders. Your notes are stored in the Subject folders. Add and delete as needed. Your subject folders are listed and color coded in the left column.

- ✔ Notes are filed in folders and listed on the right side with thumbnails.

- ✔ Add, delete, file, sort, rename, search, move . . . it's all there and pretty intuitive to use.

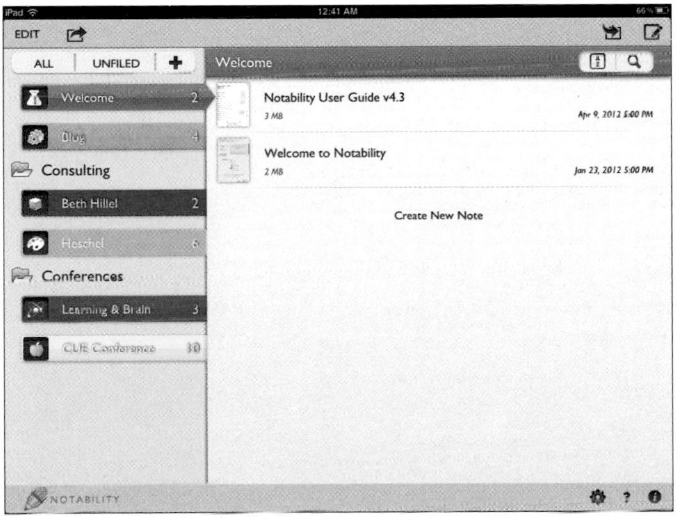

Figure 9-16: Notes are organized in the Library by category and subject.

On that note (pun intended), it sounds like the water is boiling. Enjoy!

10

Becoming a Digital Author

Remember those days you'd come to school with your assignment on a large sheet of cardboard, little pictures stuck randomly around it and punctuated with large headings you wrote with bold markers? If you think I am going to dissuade you from encouraging your students to create those types of projects, you are wrong. There's always a place for such hands-on work, and you should continue to encourage it wherever appropriate. As parents and educators, however, it's also important for us to recognize that the landscape is changing at a rapid rate and that there are some compelling, digital alternatives that need to be incorporated into education.

The whole notion of writing is changing. Being an author used to mean having an agreement with a book publisher to distribute and sell your book. Don't get me wrong: It's still a good idea for those of us in that situation! The publishing market, however, is in a period of transition: We're seeing a range of tools that make it simple to create and publish your own digital content. Those tools range from simple blog formats where you can post opinions and articles to full-blown book authoring tools that enable any prospective author to create a book and use online publishing channels to sell and distribute it.

Anyone, of any age, can now create and distribute books — textbooks, story-books, personal accounts, class assignments, and more. The whole notion of publishing is changing with the amazing growth of the Internet and technologies such as social networking These days, anyone — even the students in your class — can express herself to a worldwide audience. Tools exist to make the process simple and to incorporate digital publishing into any grade level and academic discipline.

This chapter focuses on the different ways you can use these book authoring tools — from the simpler apps that empower young children to create and distribute their work to the more robust tools that can create full-blown interactive and multimedia experiences.

With a little enthusiasm, creativity, and resolve, today may be the day you start helping your students develop their voices as expressive writers. In the immortal words of Mark Twain, "Apparently there is nothing that cannot happen today." (Well, he also said, "Cauliflower is nothing but cabbage with a college education," but I couldn't find a way to work that quote into the paragraph.)

Choosing an E-book Format

I admit. It's confusing. You have Pages documents that won't open in Microsoft Word. Then there are Microsoft Word documents that don't open in older versions of Word itself. You have HTML files that look all messed up wherever you open them. And, of course, PDF files . . . well, nobody wants you messing with their formats.

You're already having a hard enough time handling the different programs and files you have on your computer, and now I start tossing in new terms such as *e-books* and *iBooks*. Well, don't throw this p-book (yes, that stands for *paper book)* at me quite yet. Give me a moment to take a stab at explaining the various terms to you.

It's important to understand the difference because it helps determine your options in creating e-books — and other digital files — and the apps you'll use when reading them. I'll take a stab at clarifying some of the common terms:

- **Documents:** Unless they are very basic text files, most documents are associated with editing software. The most common formats include Word documents and, to a lesser degree, Pages documents. They are primarily designed to be opened and edited within the software that created them — a fact we all encounter when we get that all-important e-mail attachment we can't open.

- **PDF files:** Also known as Acrobat files, they share a common formatting standard used by the Adobe Acrobat software. Generally, anything that can be printed can be turned into an Acrobat document. PDF files are easily distributed and read by anyone who has the free Acrobat reader on her computer.

  Both word processing documents and PDF files are essentially designed to be printed on paper. Of course, they can be read onscreen, but the paper size and formatting options are directed at printed output. Then along came e-books.

✔ **E-books:** An e-book can be a digital version of a printed book but doesn't have to be. The distinguishing feature of an e-book is that it's designed to be read on a computer or portable e-book reading device. E-books can normally be purchased and/or distributed online.

Many e-books are PDF files or in the ePub format, which is an open standard designed to work across a wide variety of reading devices. Traditionally, e-books were just text and images; they now incorporate more multimedia and interactive elements. They provide a pleasant screen reading environment, with tools for changing colors, text size, searching, bookmarking, and more.

✔ **iBooks:** Apple's e-book reading app, iBooks opens books made with iBooks Author, ePub books, or PDF documents. Of course, it also links to the iBookstore, where you can purchase and download e-books.

So if you want to create e-books, you have a variety of options. You can turn an existing document into an e-book, or you can use a variety of apps to create e-books — from the very simplest levels you might use in lower grades all the way up to sophisticated multimedia and interactive books that older students or teachers might consider. Options abound.

Distributing Documents for e-Readers

One simple way to distribute content is to create any document and convert it to a PDF file. Distribute it via e-mail or the Internet; just about any e-reader will open it.

Add your PDF documents (and ePub) books on to your iPad in the following ways:

✔ Drag and drop them into the Books Library in iTunes on your computer. Select your device in the sidebar and then click the Books tab. You'll see your content listed there. Check the books you want to sync and click Sync to move them onto your iPad.

✔ Use the Open In function on your iPad to open the document in iBooks from any e-mail or app. Tap and hold the attachment for a few seconds and then choose Open in iBooks (see Figure 10-1) from the pop-up menu that appears.

Creating a standard text document and turning it into an e-book is quick, simple . . . and sooo 20th-century. Take a little stroll on the wild side and try some more adventurous alternatives. A growing number of apps are designed specifically to create e-books that integrate interactivity and multimedia. I review a couple of the most popular ones in the following sections.

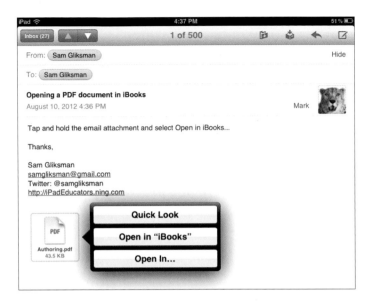

Figure 10-1: PDF files can be opened and added to your iBooks library.

Using Book Creator for Simple Projects

Book Creator is one of the simplest iPad apps for creating your own e-books. It's a great solution for a range of projects from children's picture books to cookbooks, storybooks, and more. Your completed book can be read in iBooks and sent to family and friends, or you can even submit it to be published in the iBookstore. Maybe the next J.K. Rowling is sitting at the back of that second-grade class you're teaching!

Book Creator, shown in Figure 10-2, is a simple app to use, and it's a great tool for school projects. It uses a fixed layout format for its e-books. In practice, that means that the author controls the exact design and position of every element on the page. You create each page with elements that have a fixed position and size that cannot be changed. The reader can usually zoom in and out but can't change settings such as the text size and have elements reformat and flow onto other pages. It's well suited to shorter books with a lot of images.

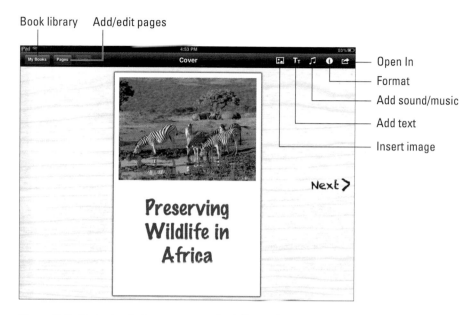

Book library   Add/edit pages

Open In

Format

Add sound/music

Add text

Insert image

Figure 10-2: Students of all ages can use Book Creator's tools.

The basic steps involved in creating a book are simple; just follow these steps:

1. **Tap the + sign on the opening screen.**

2. **When prompted, choose a portrait, landscape, or square size for your new book.**

3. **Tap the Insert Image icon (refer to Figure 10-2) to insert an image, and tap the Add Text icon to insert your title text.**

4. **(Optional) Insert a soundtrack or record an introduction by tapping Add Sound, tapping the red Start Recording button (shown in Figure 10-3), and then speaking narration.**

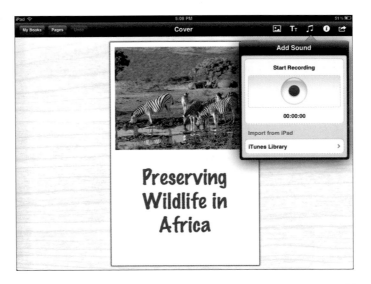

Figure 10-3: Record a narrative for your book or add music from your iTunes library.

5. **Tap the Next button on the right side of the screen to start editing your pages.**

   The Pages button on the top left of your display enables you to add, edit, and organize your pages as needed:

   - *Pages can contain text, images, or embedded sound.* Insert them anywhere on the pages by tapping the icons on the top toolbar.

   - *Format text and choose among more than 50 fonts.*

   - *Add pictures or video from your Photo library.* Move, resize, and rotate them on the page.

   - *Record any sound or narration directly, using the app's built-in audio recorder.* It drops a little speaker icon on the page, which plays when tapped. You can also import audio from your iTunes library.

   - *Guidelines and snap positioning help you lay out and align objects on the page.*

   - *Reorder pages.* Tap the Pages button and tap Edit; then drag pages by their lined icons in the right column.

   Your book is automatically saved on your iPad.

6. **Tap the My Books button in the top left.**

   You'll see it listed in your book catalog. The book is formatted as an ePub file by default and can be read by the many readers that support the ePub format.

7. **Tap the My Books button (in the top-left corner of the Book Creator interface).**

   You're returned to the My Books page (your Book Creator library). As you scroll through your books, notice the row of icons under each one.

8. **Tap the cloud icon to see the Export options (shown in Figure 10-4):**

   - E-mail your books.

   - Print using AirPrint or a printer app.

   - Send it to iTunes on your computer as an e-book or PDF.

   - Open it in any of a slew of other apps as an e-book or PDF document.

Figure 10-4: Export options for Book Creator books.

Book Creator uses a fixed layout format. That means that the books you create don't give readers the flexibility to change colors and fonts. It's targeted primarily at the creation of shorter books with images and brief text rather than longer, text-based books.

ScribblePress for Beginning Authors

ScribblePress is an app that gives kids the tools to author, illustrate, share, and publish an e-book. When you open the app, note that it is divided into three sections: My Books, My Drawings, and Gallery, as shown in Figure 10-5.

My Books and My Drawings include your unique creations, whereas Gallery is stocked full of books created and shared by others that you can download and read. Who knows — maybe you'll decide to share some of your own.

Figure 10-5: ScribblePress is divided into sections for My Books, My Drawings, and Gallery.

It's similar to Book Creator in the sense that it uses fixed layout pages that include text and image elements, and you can add and edit pages as needed. It doesn't have the audio capabilities included in Book Creator, but it does offer the following features:

✔ **Story templates:** When you start a new book, you can create your own story from a blank book or select among 50 story templates — as shown on the left in Figure 10-6 — to get you started.

✔ **Drawing tools:** You can create and save your own drawings in the My Drawings sections or draw within the pages of your book as you create it. The app contains a cool set of drawing tools, including markers of various colors and types, as shown on the right in Figure 10-6.

✔ **Stickers, stamps, and photos:** Select and add images from a collection of stickers and stamps. Take photos or choose one from one of your existing photo albums.

✔ **The capability to add a book summary and short author bio:** Write a short synopsis of the book to let potential readers know what to expect, and include a short biography of yourself as well.

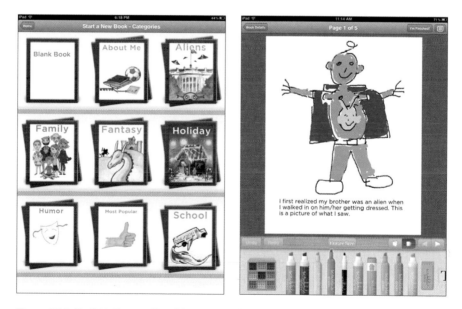

Figure 10-6: ScribblePress offers 50 story templates and several drawing tools.

When your e-book is finished, you can

- ✔ **Download it from the Gallery:** Download and read books that others have shared in the Gallery.

- ✔ **Send it to iBooks:** When you tap the icon to Send to iBooks, the app converts your book to an ePub file. You then can open it in iBooks or any other e-reader app that supports ePub.

- ✔ **Share it or print it:** You can upload your book to the Gallery for others to read or order printed copies from ScribblePress for a fee.

When sharing a book, you're presented with a Sharing Policy form onscreen. You're required to select one box to verify that you're either over 13 years old or the parent/guardian of the author. A second check box asks you to agree that you have verified that there's no personal information or photos included in the book. It's obviously important to take precautions whenever sharing anything in a public forum, but it's also simple for anyone to select the boxes and upload the book. I recommend using it as an opportunity to discuss important issues of privacy and public sharing of information on the Internet.

Publishing with iBooks Author

Now it's time to bring out the heavyweights. Apple released its iBooks Author software in January 2012 as a means for creating and publishing a new generation of e-books that integrate different media, interactive elements, 3D objects, and more. It's designed to differentiate e-books by including compelling, interactive content that was never possible on the printed page. It's no coincidence that Apple announced the release of iBooks Author at the same event that introduced the new iBookstore category for e-textbooks. One of the more popular applications of iBooks Author is intended to be the creation and self-publishing of textbooks for the education market. The software works on Mac computers running the Mac OS X operating system (10.7.2 or higher) and is available for free download in the Mac App Store.

Creating interactive multimedia e-books could certainly be the subject of a book all its own — an e-book of course. I only scratch the surface of it in this section. The interface will be somewhat familiar to anyone who has used word processing or presentation software, and it's particularly close in nature to Apple's Keynote presentation software, as you can see in Figure 10-7.

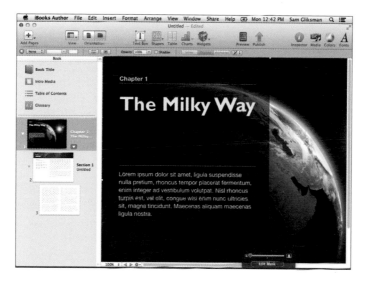

Figure 10-7: The iBooks Author interface is similar to the Keynote interface.

The highlights of iBooks Author includes the following:

✓ **Templates:** Start by selecting a template (see Figure 10-8) that has pre-designed layouts you can select and adapt.

✓ **Text import feature:** You can import text from any Word or Pages documents directly into the Book Navigator.

✓ **Image implementation:** Drag and drop any images on to the page and your text will automatically flow around the object.

✓ **Widget power:** Including widgets for interactive photo galleries, movies, keynote presentations, animations, interactive images, and 3D objects (see Figure 10-9), this feature gives users the capability to create truly customizable objects in books. If you know some coding, you can even get your hands dirty creating HTML widgets that display custom content.

✓ **Chapter reviews:** Add chapter reviews for readers to measure their understanding. Question types include multiple choice, choose the correct image, label the image, or a mix of all three. What's more, authors can include up to six alternative answers to each question.

✔ **Publishing:** Preview your e-book on your iPad. When you're ready to publish, you can submit it to the iBookstore for purchase or free download. You can also export and share your e-book on iTunes U or give it to anyone with an iPad. You can review the conditions and common distribution questions on the Apple support website at `http://support.apple.com/kb/HT5071`.

Figure 10-8: Start authoring your e-book by selecting a style in the Template Chooser.

Figure 10-9: The power of iBooks Author comes from the use of its interactive widgets.

11

The Mathematical and Scientific iPad

We tend to split science and humanities as though they were separate branches of life. But no matter what profession we choose — artist, plumber, historian, or salesman — we all use some form of scientific inquiry in our daily lives. We learn about the world around us through the same vehicles of experimentation, trial, error, and experience. We use scientific inquiry to learn about the world around us.

Today's interconnected world demands that the doctor, engineer, pharmacist, and scientist increasingly master skills that used to be classified within the domain of the arts. Skills such as communication, presentation, effective writing, among others, are now vital to all walks of life. In addition, scientific inquiry, critical thinking, exploration, and experimentation have never been more important skills than they are today. If we expect to produce independent learners who can thrive in a society that's constantly changing, it's vital that we educators search for opportunities to hone those skills in our students at every turn.

More than any other academic disciplines, science and math draw their meaning by relating to life in the "real" world outside the classroom. They seek to understand the world by inquiry and investigation. Giving children ample opportunities to develop sound investigative skills at an early age is essential to nurturing their ability to think critically and scientifically as they get older. Reading and learning about plants in a book is a far less meaningful experience than planting seeds and watching them grow. If you discuss the various needs of plants and then hypothesize and experiment with differing amounts of sunlight and water, you have a scientific experience that imbues children with a more intimate and fundamental understanding of what it takes for any living organism to grow.

Granting students the freedom to inquire and explore makes them the investigators of life's mysteries. In the process, they are sharpening their all-important critical and creative thinking skills. Technology offers fantastic opportunities for the application of critical thinking skills toward an understanding of real-world questions and answers. It can be used to gather information about the world around us so that we can investigate real-world questions and test their answers. That's the focus of this chapter. You find numerous apps that deliver content about botany or algebra, but I want to focus on how you can use technology to have students experience that knowledge from the inside out.

This chapter looks at tools that can be used with the iPad to help you investigate phenomena and collect data. After you collect that data, you look at tools that help analyze the information and present conclusions. You focus less on apps and instead discuss the "application" of mobile technology within a more inquiry-based approach to science and math education. It should be fun!

Whether it's geometry, physics, or chemistry, scientific method starts with research, discussion, and the development of a hypothesis about the phenomenon being examined. A substantial amount of space in this book is devoted to research, communication, organization, and sharing of information — all important elements in the research and development stage. You start by jumping to the next step: using the iPad for investigating and gathering data for analysis.

Exploring Tools for Scientific Inquiry

The iPad is an ideal tool for investigation. The capability to be mobile and communicate over a Wi-Fi or Bluetooth connection makes it possible to gather data with external sensors that send data to an app on the iPad. Here's a small sampling of some of the possibilities.

SPARKvue HD and PASCO Probes

Integrate sensor-based data collection into the learning experience with the SPARKvue HD app for the iPad, which communicates with any of the 70 sensors from PASCO (www.pasco.com). The connection between the sensor and iPad is facilitated by PASCO's AirLink 2 Bluetooth interface, which enables you to connect a sensor; then it wirelessly sends data to the SPARKvue HD app on your iPad. See Figure 11-1.

Measure a wide range of phenomena, including pH, temperature, force, carbon-dioxide level, and much more. Use sensors in experiments — anything from weather to cellular respiration, from sound levels in an elementary school classroom to advanced optics in physics. In addition, you can capture images with the iPad cameras and use SPARKvue HD's image analysis capabilities. Or collect and display live acceleration data with the iPad internal accelerometer.

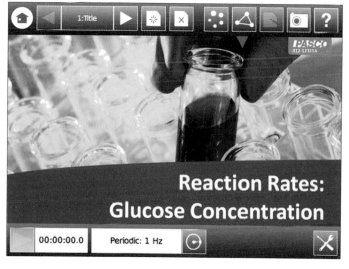

Image courtesy of PASCO Scientific.

Figure 11-1: PASCO probes collect and transmit external data to the SPARKvue HD app.

ProScope Mobile

ProScope Mobile is a wireless hand-held digital microscope for iOS devices. ProScope sends live video and captured stills to multiple iOS devices simultaneously via Wi-Fi. Use ProScope in the field, classroom, or lab to zoom in on any object of interest and project it to a host of devices. ProScope lenses vary from 0–10X to 400X.

ProScope Mobile creates its own Wi-Fi network and can be used simultaneously with up to 253 iOS devices. ProScope Mobile works with the AirMicroPad app on the iPad.

Users can view live images, freeze them, and capture them. Imagine a classroom filled with iPads. Each student would simultaneously see what the teacher is showing with the ProScope Mobile. When the teacher taps the Capture button on the ProScope Mobile, that image is captured in the photo album of each student's iPad at the same time. Students can then study and mark up that image.

Cameras, apps, and more

Your iPad comes equipped with perfect tools for investigating and recording phenomena:

- Use the camera to snap events and video processes.
- Record notes in any of the many note-taking apps.
- If you're using any of the sensors or hardware listed earlier, they generally come with their own iPad apps to record, analyze, and present data in multiple representations.
- If you're using the old tried-and-true methods of observation and documentation of data, you'll want a way to record and analyze the data you collect. Use a spreadsheet such as Numbers to record and statistically analyze the data. Use the charts feature to present your data visually.
- Presentation apps such as Keynote, Explain Everything, and iMovie are ideal for presenting a dynamic and media-based summary of your findings.

The Investigative iPad Classroom

This section includes a few short samples of how iPads were used in science and math classrooms to research and construct knowledge. They are cited less as specific lesson plans to follow and more as examples of how the iPad can be integrated as a tool into processes of research and scientific method. I'm sure one or two may inspire you to come up with your own ideas.

I'm extremely grateful to the wonderful and talented educators who contributed to this list of sample lessons, including Dr. Randy Yerrick, professor of science education at State University of New York at Buffalo; Julie Hersch of Temple Israel of Hollywood Day School; and Sivan Lipman of New Community Jewish High School.

Finding the effect of watering solutions on germinating beans

Submitted by	Sam Gliksman
Grade level	4th- to 6th-grade science
Objectives	Students learn to measure and collect data about botany and plant growth, and learn simple techniques for statistical mapping and mathematical analysis.
Apps/tools	iPad 2 (or higher), time-lapse photography app such as TimeLapse Pro or StopMotion Recorder, photography stand for iPad, Numbers app
Materials needed	Packet of mung beans, 4 glass jars or beakers filled 75% high with sterilized potting soil, tap water, salt, dish detergent, coffee powder, 4 100ml beakers, 1 measuring cylinder, 1 digital weighing scale, black marker and/or labels

This experiment uses TimeLapse Pro (see Figure 11-2) to test how different solutions used to water plants affect growth. The results will be measured and recorded by students while also being captured on time-lapse video.

The following points outline the process:

- The independent variable is the solution used to water the plants — plain water, coffee-and-water mixture, salt water, and water-and-detergent solution.

- The dependent variable is the growth of the mung-bean plants. This is determined by measuring the height of the plants every day.

- The constants (control variables) are the size of the container, the amount and concentration of the various solutions added daily, the amount of sunlight, and the temperature of the environment (room temperature).

- Fill the four glass jars or beakers three fourths full with the sterilized soil. Plant 12 mung beans in each pot, and allow them to germinate for 5 days, using the same amount of water on each plant. (You need ten seeds to germinate; add two extra just in case some don't germinate. When you are ready to record your data, make sure you have only ten germinated beans.)

- Plug in the iPad, mount it on a stand, and set up your Time Lapse app. Set the time lapse to take one picture every five minutes. For the first five days, you may choose to do a close-up of just one of the plants to capture the mung-bean germination in full close-up. The resultant time-lapse movie is truly magical.

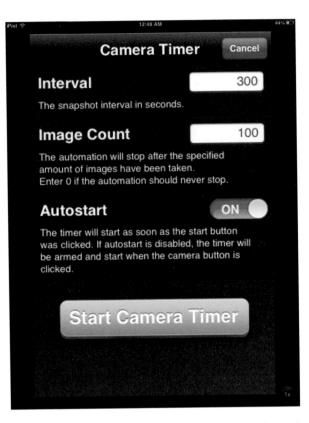

Figure 11-2: TimeLapse Pro records your experiment by setting the number of images and intervals.

- After the first five days of germination, you need to have a clear view of all four plants so that you can compare the growth of the plants and the effect of the different solutions. Make sure that you are looking at them from the same angle so that perspective will not be a factor.

- Water the four plants with tap water only for the first five days, allowing the seeds to germinate. After five days, record the average heights in a spreadsheet in the Numbers app. Discuss the meaning of "average" growth and how it can be calculated in the spreadsheet. Obtain the average height by measuring the height of the ten plants in each pot, adding them up, and dividing by 10.

- Prepare your four solutions in the 100ml beakers. For the coffee mixture, add 10g of coffee to 100ml of water, and label it Coffee. For the detergent mixture, mix 10ml of detergent to 100ml of water, and for the saline solution. add 1 g of salt to 100ml of water. Label each beaker accordingly. (You could also prepare enough solution in advance for all ten days by preparing a liter of each of the mixtures.)

↙ Label the four plants Water, Coffee, Detergent, and Saline. Over the next ten days, water the pots once a day with 100ml of each solution, according to the labels on the pots. Make sure you turn the plants halfway through the experiment period to ensure that each side of the plant is getting adequate sunshine. Check to make sure that the soil is not too soggy and there is no water pooling at the bottom of the container. Adjust the quantity of liquid if need be, but be sure to give each plant the same amount of liquid as the others.

↙ Measure and calculate the average height of the mung-bean plants every day for the next ten days. Record all calculations in a Numbers spreadsheet.

↙ Discuss linear graphs and their meaning; then have the students use the different growth rates to create a linear graph.

Demonstrating mathematical proofs

Submitted by	Dr. Randy Yerrick, professor of science education, State University of New York at Buffalo
Grade level	8th- to 12th-grade math
Objectives	Have students demonstrate knowledge of mathematical proofs.
Apps/tools	Keynote, Explain Everything app
Materials needed	n/a

Following the lesson where math teachers demonstrate the construction of an algebraic or geometric proof, students are given the opportunity to create their own. Using media-based presentations and audio recordings of their own voices, students create and share a narrated slide-show presentation.

Keynote is Apple's presentation app that enables students to build a slide-based presentation with text and media, which they then present live in front of an audience.

The Explain Everything app (detailed in Chapter 17) enables students to build and record a series of narrated slides with picture, text, and media content that explains and demonstrates a concept to an audience. Essentially, once students put the slides in the order they choose, they tap Record and step through their slides, explaining, highlighting with color, and accentuating with the laser pointer feature. The Record function also enables students to pause or to rerecord their presentation so that they can practice before presenting it to the class. Explain Everything also includes members' libraries and upload links to such social media sharing sites as Dropbox and Facebook, making student sharing of work easy and manageable.

Students were given the option of using the preceding apps to explain some of the data that can be retrieved from scientific agencies such as the U.S. Geological Survey (USGS), National Aeronautics and Space Administration (NASA), and the National Oceanic and Atmospheric Administration (NOAA). Students used the latitude and longitude of approaching hurricanes to learn Cartesian coordinates and plot them. For example, one student provided an explanation of the calculated arrival time of a tsunami across the Pacific Ocean from an image acquired from the USGS.

This is also a scenario in which students can use apps such as GarageBand or iMovie to collate specific photos they gather into a podcast or movie and explain what they know or how they apply the concepts to examples in the real world.

Exploring properties of humanmade materials

Submitted by	Dr. Randy Yerrick, professor of science education, State University of New York at Buffalo
Grade level	2nd- to 7th-grade science
Objectives	Students learn to collect microscopic data with tools, recognize patterns in manmade materials, develop hypotheses regarding why things are soft, and compare predictions of softness and observed patterns to offer explanations for why some objects are soft and others are not.
Apps/tools	ProScope Mobile for the iPad, AirMicroPad app from Bodelin
Materials needed	Tissues

Children are rarely asked to explore their own ideas in science. In this activity, students can explore their own personal theories and offer supporting evidence through the digital microscope.

This activity begins with a discussion surrounding the question "What makes things soft?" Students openly discuss their ideas and compare drawings and explanations. Then students are asked to predict what a softer tissue (Kleenex or Puffs) will look like compared to others. Students are sent out around the school to collect samples and images of tissues from teachers' purses (with said teachers' permission, of course!), restrooms, and elsewhere.

To gather data, students need to turn on the ProScope Mobile and enter the IP information into the AirMicroPad as they select the new network. After launching the app, ProScope Mobile will broadcast live images, as shown in Figure 11-3, to any iPad within range of its network. To save time and necessary equipment, tissues can be gathered in advance, and students can log into the ProScope Mobile network through the AirMicroPad so that all the children can take their own photos broadcasted live from ProScope.

Once the photos have been collected, a blind softness test is conducted by students to rank the tissues for softness. Students should see features such as consistency of fibers, size of fibers, and distance between fibers. They should see evidence that some of the common predictions have no basis. For example, students regularly predict cottony and poofy tufts for soft tissues, for which there is rarely evidence. Students also predict finding oils or lotions they have heard from advertisements, but there is rarely evidence of this either.

Students should see that highly uniform, regular, and small threads make for soft tissues. This is analogous to thread count for sheets.

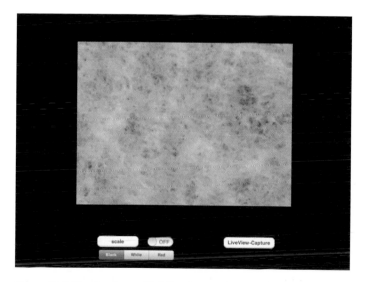

Figure 11-3: The ProScope Mobile microscope broadcasts live images to any iPad within range.

Observing animal behavior

Submitted by	Sivan Lipman, New Community Jewish High School
Grade level	9th- to 12th-grade science
Objectives	Learn the practice and process of studying animal behavior; learn research procedures, including the collection and analysis of data; and recognize different patterns of animal behavior, such as territorial behavior, aggression, courtship rituals, communicative behavior, and so on.
Apps/tools	iPad 2 (or higher), note-taking app, Reflection app with Mac laptop or desktop, photography stand(s) for iPads, Numbers app
Materials needed	n/a

Students observe gibbons at a reserve near Los Angeles. They start by silently observing the animals, trying to identify at least six common behavior patterns, taking notes and photos to document their observations. As a group, students then discuss and analyze notes, images, and video and agree upon six common behavior patterns.

Students then return to observe and record the six common behavior patterns. One of the challenges is that the gibbons are in an environment that isn't their natural habitat, and the presence of observers tends to inhibit their natural behavior. One possible solution is to use a series of iPads on stands pointed toward the enclosure. With the cameras turned on, students can watch the recordings nearby.

Using the Reflection app on a central MacBook, you can mirror the image of multiple iPads simultaneously on the MacBook screen, enabling students to watch the iPads from a central location. Double-tap the Home button on each iPad, and swipe to the right in the lower multitasking tray to display the quick access controls. Tap the AirPlay button and select your computer to mirror the iPad on your Mac.

You might even consider using QuickTime on the MacBook to record events. Note that the iPads and MacBook would need to be on the same Wi-Fi network. (Consider creating your own wireless hotspot, if necessary.)

A fantastic optional extra is to broadcast the iPads live on the Internet and invite anyone to watch. Once you have them mirrored on your MacBook, open a Google hangout and display your screen. Anyone you invite to the Google Hangout can observe the gibbons. It would also be possible to use QuickTime recording on your MacBook screen for an extended period of time, enabling students to return and view activity that occurred in their absence.

Some students will be tasked with recording the data as it occurs, while others control any video recording of the gibbons. The results can later be collated and analyzed.

Hunting for geometric treasure

Submitted by	Julie Hersch, Temple Israel of Hollywood Day School
Grade level	3rd- to 4th-grade math
Objectives	Students learn about the properties of concentric circles by relating them to objects in the real world.
Apps/tools	iPad 2 (or higher); iOS 5.1 (or higher); presentation app such as Keynote, iMovie, ShowMe, Explain Everything
Materials needed	Anything in the immediate environment

Using visual prompts, students break into groups and discuss the properties that distinguish and define concentric circles. Once they arrive at a consensus, students are sent on a scavenger hunt in pairs to find examples of concentric circles around campus and take photos of them. They come back with examples that include sink drains, door knobs, cart wheels, clocks, and more. Each group prepares a narrated presentation of the images that they found. One interesting departure was that some students wanted to create a quiz with their images, some of which looked like concentric circles but weren't. As one example, there was a series of hula hoops hung up on a wall that looked like concentric circles but didn't actually have the same central point. It's interesting how students were able to deepen their knowledge of a concept by presenting patterns that actually didn't match the required definition.

Calibrating spring length with physics and math

Submitted by	Dr. Randy Yerrick, professor of science education, State University of New York at Buffalo
Grade level	9th- to 12th-grade math or physics
Objectives	Students create a mathematical model for physical phenomenon and apply their conceptual understanding of trigonometric functions and physics to explain how a spring loses energy over time.
Apps/tools	iPad 2 (or higher), iOS 5.1 (or higher), Video Physics app by Vernier, Data Analysis app or Numbers app
Materials needed	A weight attached to a large spring

Here is one of the ways to combine physics and math to help students think beyond algorithms:

Hang a weight from a large spring from the ceiling or ring stand. Be sure there is a meter-stick near the spring to calibrate the spring length. To do the extension activity simultaneously, hang the PASCO Airlink and Accelerometer from the end of the spring.

Ask the students to use their iPad to predict the shape of the graph of a y distance per time for the oscillating spring. Once the students' ideas have been made public and debated, pull down the spring, release, and begin the experiment. The spring should have just enough tension to give a large amplitude but not enough to cause jumping or erratic motion outside the up and down y-axis.

Students collect the video through the camera app. This can also be done with the Video Physics app (see Figure 11-4) using the New Video Capture function. The video will be analyzed for its motion over time.

Once the video collection is stopped, open the video in the Video Physics app; set the scale for the meter-stick length' and tap the position of the Airlink, marking the position with a dot every tenth of a second automatically. Each tap will create a y versus t graph and also automatically advance the frame.

Swipe to the next screen after data collection is finished. Examine the previous predicted models, and compare them with the actual data.

Export data to the Data Analysis or Numbers app, and find a best fit for the collected data.

Exploring celestial mysteries

Submitted by	Dr. Randy Yerrick, professor of science education, State University of New York at Buffalo
Grade level	4th- to 12th-grade astronomy
Objectives	Navigate the sky for recognizable celestial objects; identify and name constellations, stars, galaxies, and planets.
Apps/tools	iPad 2 (or higher), iOS 5.1 (or higher), Star Walk app
Materials needed	n/a

Figure 11-4: Measure and analyze motion with Video Physics.

Some of the best science apps created for the iPad are those geared toward the teaching of astronomy. An example is the Star Walk app, shown in Figure 11-5. One benefit of these apps is the integration with the built-in accelerometer and GPS information systems that enables users to simply point to the sky to obtain vast updated information about where they are looking. Celestial navigation is made simple through the interactive interfaces that allow the user to turn on and off the available layers of information when pointing at the night sky.

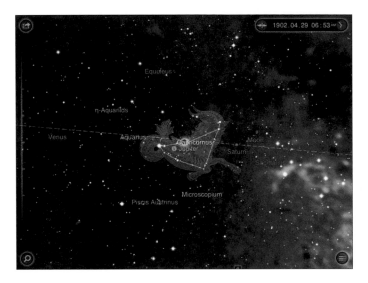

Figure 11-5: Explore the night sky with Star Walk, an interactive astronomy app.

Teaching with the Star Walk app can be as easy as taking an independent evening stroll with the self-lit app in hand and noting the relative positions of the objects in the sky. At the same time, this app adds a robust environment to explore important questions such as

- Does the sun really rise in the east? Does that change?
- Where do all the planets appear in the sky? How can you tell a planet from a star or galaxy?
- Can people in the Southern Hemisphere see the same stars as people in the Northern, Eastern, or Western hemispheres?
- Where do stars go during the day?

The power of this app can be seen in a very simple activity for children up through adulthood. Ask students, "How many planets are there? More important, how do you know?" Have students point out any objects in the sky that they think are planets, and before they use Sky Walk, ask them to point to any they can see. Ask them to draw where those objects would appear at night, and explain what they would look like.

Additional Apps for Math and Science

The primary focus of this chapter is on processes that stress investigation, experimentation, and real-world application of scientific and mathematical principles. That isn't to say that there aren't many excellent apps that also provide important instruction, simulated experiences, opportunities for differentiated learning, and excellent game-based approaches to the learning of important principles.

The list of apps changes rapidly; you can refer to the updated recommended apps on `http://list.ly/people/SamGliksman` or at `http://iPad Educators.ning.com`. Here are a few to start with.

Frog Dissection

The ethics of animal dissection have been debated for quite some time. Calling itself the "greener alternative for teaching dissection in the classroom," the Frog Dissection app (see Figure 11-6) is geared toward middle-school students who are learning about organs and organ systems as part of their life-science curriculum.

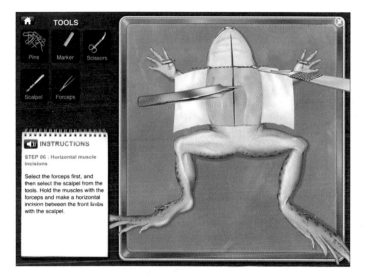

Figure 11-6: The Frog Dissection app enables students to dissect a virtual specimen.

Rather than dissect an actual animal, students dissect a virtual specimen with all the trappings that come with the real procedure. The app comes with all the dissection tools and detailed instructions to complete the procedure. Once dissection is complete, the frog's organs are exposed for further study. With the aid of vivid 3D imagery, students are able to visualize the internal organs very effectively.

The Frog Dissection app is an excellent example of the educational promise offered by a rising tide of vivid, realistic simulations offering students experiences that may otherwise be unattainable.

DragonBox

With all due respect to the many excellent algebra teachers out there, many of us have had that teacher who droned on with endless explanations of formulas and solutions. DragonBox uses a game-based approach that has students solve puzzles by moving cards around onscreen. The principles required to solve the puzzles are based on . . . (keep this to yourself) fundamental algebraic concepts! Yes, you learn the principles of algebra by playing a fun game. That does seem to break all the rules, now, doesn't it?

Khan Academy

If you've been on a remote safari in the Panamanian jungle for the last few years and haven't heard of Khan Academy (see Figure 11-7), it contains more than 3,000 tutorial videos on a wide variety of topics in math and science. Granted, it isn't always Oscar-winning material, but when it's late at night and you really need help understanding Negative Exponent Intuition (seriously? I have no clue whatsoever . . .), you can just open the Khan Academy app and watch the video.

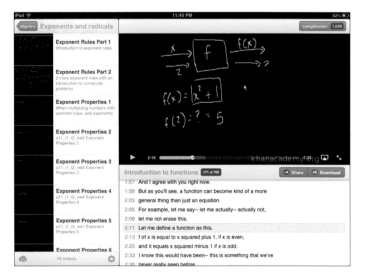

Figure 11-7: The Khan Academy app contains 3,000-plus tutorial videos in math and science.

The nifty subtitles feature enables you to tap any line of dialogue listed and jump right to that point in the video. It isn't quite as effective without the interactive exercises that are available after each video on the Khan Academy website, but apparently, they should also be available in the iPad app soon.

Monster Physics

With Monster Physics (see Figure 11-8), you can build your own virtual machines, from cars to rocket ships, using parts including wheels, wings, propellers, magnets, rockets, and claws. Kids learn physics by building and refining their inventions and completing missions.

Build virtual machines by combining different wheels, rockets, propellers, cannons, magnets, claws, wings, and more. Monster Physics renders your creation, and then you can actually operate it in real time. Drive your car, pilot your rocket into space, or try flying that thingamajig you built that doesn't look like it'll ever get off the ground! Learn physics by solving missions and building and refining your inventions. Monster Physics challenges you with 50 missions to solve, from simple to mind-bending. Many missions can be solved with a wide variety of solutions, enabling you to test all sorts of creative approaches.

If you believe, as I do, that having fun is a key element to learning, try building a contraption that solves some missions. You may learn a few key physics concepts along the way!

Figure 11-8: Learn physics by building inventions and solving missions in Monster Physics.

12

Utilizing Assistive Technologies

Schools have traditionally adopted a "one size fits all" philosophy when it comes to mainstream education. Students are grouped by age and academic discipline and are then expected to use the same textbooks, sit in the same lectures, do the same homework, and submit the same (typically written) assignments. It's the easiest way to deal with large numbers of students, but it doesn't accommodate the sometimes vast differences in learning styles, preferences, and individual challenges faced by so many students in our schools. The past decade has seen a positive movement toward more differentiated learning, and many students now receive assistance and accommodations that enable them to learn more effectively and remain within standard school environments.

Apple has typically built features into its hardware to assist anyone who has difficulties with vision, hearing, communication, motor skills, and more. iPads are no exception, and the educational sector that has benefited most from iPad use is probably special education. Built-in features for screen reading, support for playback of closed-captioned content, and other universal access features make it a natural for students with special needs. They simplify use for students with vision impairment or difficulty hearing, or those who have a physical disability. Further, as you discover throughout this book, there's a thriving market for every need, and there are certainly some standout apps that assist students with special learning needs.

In this chapter, I take a look at the assistive technology features built into the iPad. The three main categories of features are vision, hearing, and physical and motor skills. I also take a quick survey of some of the leading apps that are being used successfully by students with special education needs. One of the most satisfying benefits of these innovative new technologies is that you can leave that "one size fits all" model in your rear-view mirror and instead offer genuine assistance to students with learning challenges.

Accessibility Features on the iPad

The following steps show you how to find the iPad's accessibility features:

1. **Tap the Settings icon on your iPad home screen.**

2. **Tap General in the menu on the left of the Settings screen.**

3. **Scroll down and tap Accessibility to access all the accessibility features.**

   They are organized into Vision, Hearing, Learning, and Physical & Motor categories, as shown in Figure 12-1.

You can also activate VoiceOver using iTunes on your computer. Select your iPad in the Devices category in the left panel and then click Configure Universal Access at the bottom of the Sync Options page.

Figure 12-1: The iPad's accessibility features are listed in the Settings page.

Vision

Featuring the VoiceOver screen narrator, the iPad comes with many accessibility features that simplify the user interface for anyone with impaired vision.

VoiceOver

VoiceOver is a gesture-based screen reader that enables you to interact with the iPad even if you can't see the screen. You discover and interact with screen elements by touching the screen and having them spoken to you. For example:

- **Touch anything onscreen to hear a description of it.** Touch apps on the home page or elements in a web page or an app, and their text or functional description will be announced.

- **Double-tap to select.** A single tap announces the description, and a double tap selects any item or icon.

- **Scroll with three fingers.** Scroll up@nddown or left@ndright by swiping with three fingers.

- **Drag your finger to hear about elements on any screen.** Drag your finger around the iPad home screen, and as it passes over an app icon, VoiceOver will announce the name of the app and remind you to double-tap the icon to open it. The same applies to any web page or screen within an app. Place your finger in the top corner, and drag it slowly around the page. VoiceOver helps you discover and understand the location and context of items on the screen.

- **Have notification alerts read aloud:** As you receive notifications onscreen, VoiceOver detects and announces them to you.

- **Receive system information:** VoiceOver also gives you information about your device. Tap the icon for battery level, network signal level, or time of day, and VoiceOver announces the data to you.

- **Adjust the speaking speed:** Have you ever had that friend who talks so quickly, you never understand a word that's being said? Even worse might be the person who drones along so slowly that it starts putting you to sleep. That'll never happen with VoiceOver: It allows you to set whatever speed best suits you. It also uses sound effects to announce events such as an app opening or when the iPad switches between landscape and portrait modes. Never to be outdone, VoiceOver lowers the sound level of any background noise or music when it needs to tell you something. Wow! I'd give anything to be able to do that with my kids!

- ***Parlez-vous français?*** VoiceOver can speak to you in 36 languages. Whether you choose Arabic, Chinese, Spanish, or Russian, your iPad will shoot the breeze with you in your preferred language.

Using VoiceOver gestures

VoiceOver uses a series of simple gestures to interact with the iPad. They include the following:

- **Tap once** to select an item onscreen and hear a description of it. Selected items appear with a black rectangle around them, called the VoiceOver cursor, as shown in Figure 12-2.

- **Double-tap** to activate it.

- **Drag your finger** to move between items onscreen. You'll hear a click as you move off one item and onto another, and VoiceOver will begin reading the next item.

- **Flick left or right with one finger** to move between items. Can't find an app or a menu choice? You could search for it by dragging your finger around the screen, but you can also simply flick left and right to move the VoiceOver cursor to the next or previous available item. By flicking, you can make precise choices without having to physically find an object onscreen. For example, imagine you're trying to find a specific e-mail in your e-mail app. Keep flicking, and VoiceOver will read each e-mail down the list until you find the one you want. Double-tap anywhere on the screen to open the e-mail.

This item is selected.

Figure 12-2: The VoiceOver cursor is a black rectangle around the currently selected item.

✔ **Use a two-finger double tap** to play or pause (music, video, speaking).

✔ **Use a three-finger tap** on the home screen tells you how many pages of apps there are and which page you're currently on.

✔ **Flick three fingers left or right** to move between your different home screens.

✔ **Flick three fingers up or down** to scroll one page at a time.

✔ **Flick two fingers up** to read everything on the current screen, including menus and buttons.

✔ **Flick two fingers down** to read everything from the current position forward.

✔ **Use a three-finger double-tap** toggles between VoiceOver speech off and speech on.

Triple-clicking the Home button

Triple-tapping the Home button can be set as a quick and easy way to toggle VoiceOver on and off. Tap Settings, General, and Accessibility, and you find the option to turn on Triple-tap Home at the bottom of the Accessibility page, as shown in Figure 12-3. (Note that the option if actually named *Triple-click Home*, but rest assured that it's for triple-tapping.)

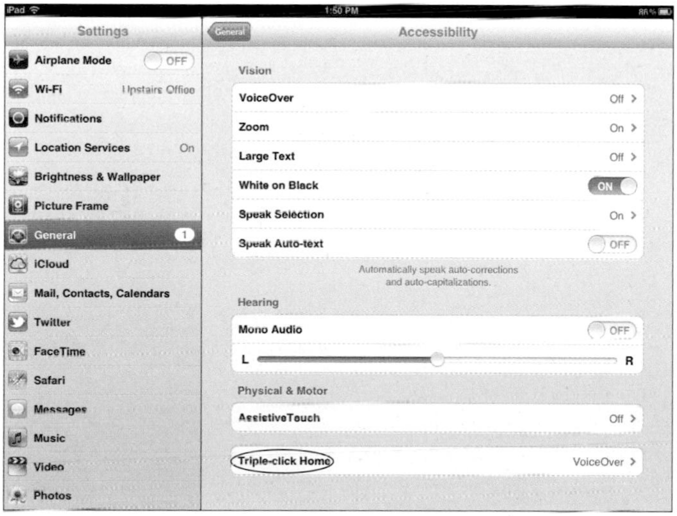

Figure 12-3: Triple-clicking Home can be set to quickly toggle core assistive features.

This can be an extremely helpful feature if your iPad is shared between users who need a quick method for turning VoiceOver features on and off. It's particularly helpful when VoiceOver is turned on and you have to work with it while trying to get to the Accessibility menu and turn it off.

You can set the Triple-click Home button option to toggle other features, such as Zoom and Invert Colors.

You might think of VoiceOver as a function strictly for people with visual impairment. Everyone has way too much to do these days; there's never enough time to sit and read quietly. Many of us spend large chunks of our day on the move, going from place to place. Setting VoiceOver to be activated with a triple tap of the Home button enables you to easily call on a digital reading companion whenever you can't read yourself. Whether you're using your treadmill or sitting in traffic, opening an e-book or pulling up an article from the web, triple-tap the Home button to activate VoiceOver, and let it read the content to you. When you're done, a simple triple tap turns VoiceOver off again.

Typing with VoiceOver

Tap Settings, General, Accessibility, and VoiceOver, and one of the options you see in the menu is Typing Feedback. Use that option to set the way VoiceOver responds when you type. VoiceOver can speak each character, word, both, or nothing, as shown in Figure 12-4. The default setting is set to have VoiceOver speak each character as you type and then the whole word when you finish it by entering a space or punctuation.

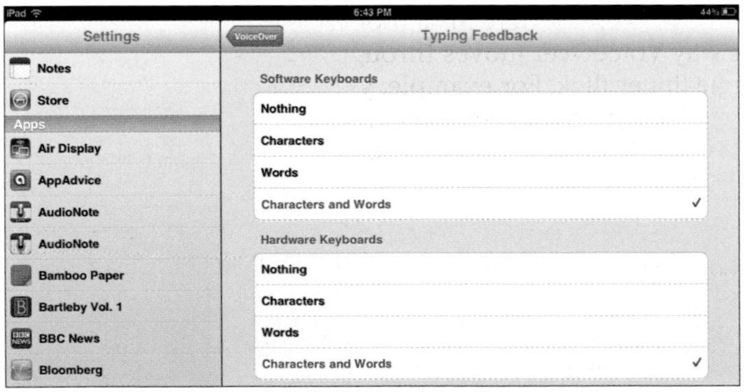

Figure 12-4: When you type, VoiceOver can speak each character, word, both, or nothing.

Accessibility features in iBooks

iBooks has several features built in that customize the reading experience for all users, including those with vision impairment. You can switch between reading in portrait or landscape orientation, depending on your taste. Text fonts can be changed, and the font size can be set larger or smaller. The page background color can be altered, and iBooks also works with the Invert Colors text setting.

When you're using the keyboard, VoiceOver speaks each character you touch and repeats it again in a different voice to confirm that you just typed it. Use one hand to select the keys, sliding your finger on the screen to the key you want, and then tap the screen with any finger on your other hand to insert the character in the text.

It takes a little practice, but once you get the hang of the slide–tap combination, it gets a lot easier. You can also move your cursor left or right in the text by flicking up or down.

Other VoiceOver features

VoiceOver offers quite a few options to keep it as customized as possible. Some of the options include the following:

- **The rotor:** The rotor is a virtual controller that you activate by rotating two fingers on the screen as though you were turning a dial. It changes the way VoiceOver moves through a document with an up or down single-finger flick. For example, you might be reading an e-mail, and a single flick reads the e-mail character by character. That makes it difficult to get through the text. Use the rotor and change the flick to read the e-mail text word by word.

- **Spoken hints:** VoiceOver continually gives you spoken hints. That setting is on by default and can be useful when you're first learning how to use it.

  After a while, you'll probably be comfortable enough to turn these hints off. Tap Settings, General, Accessibility, and VoiceOver. The first item on that menu is SpeakHints, and you can tap to turn it off.

- **VoiceOver in iBooks:** VoiceOver works effectively within iBooks. With a single flick in any e-book, you can have your books read aloud. When you want to browse for new books, VoiceOver will help you access and look through selections in the online bookstore.

✔ **Audible Alerts:** Activate audio alerts for events such as incoming and outgoing mail and calendar appointments.

✔ **Braille support:** The iPad supports and connects to Bluetooth Braille displays. They can be used to read VoiceOver output, and input keys and other controls can be used to control the iPad when you have VoiceOver turned on.

Zoom

Several apps on the iPad have a built-in zoom function, and it's as simple as a single pinch onscreen. The zoom function in Accessibility, however, lets you magnify the entire screen and helps you get a closer look at your iPad display at any time, whatever you happen to be doing. Zoom works on your home screen, the Spotlight search screens, and in any app.

Using Zoom is simple:

1. **Tap the Setting icon.**

2. **Tap General in the left menu.**

3. **Select Accessibility.**

4. **Tap Zoom, and toggle the switch to On.**

    Double-tap with three fingers to instantly zoom in 200 percent. Double-tap with three fingers again, and the iPad returns to the normal 100 percent display. If you want more control, double-tap and drag three fingers.

    As you drag your fingers upward, the display increases the zoom up to 500 percent; drag them down to reduce the zoom level. Once you set the level of magnification, you can move around the zoomed-in screen by dragging with three fingers in any direction. All your familiar iPad functions and gestures continue to work as normal.

Large Text

Use this feature to enlarge the font size on text. You can go up all the way to 56-point text.

Invert Colors

Some people prefer their display in higher contrast. If you are one of those people, you may consider using the Invert Colors option (see Figure 12-5), which changes your iPad display to white on black. Like Zoom, this works across all apps, and it can also be used with Zoom and VoiceOver. Turn it on in your same Accessibility menu in Settings.

Vision		
VoiceOver	Off >	
Zoom	Off >	
Large Text	Off >	
Invert Colors	ON	
Speak Selection	Off >	
Speak Auto-text	OFF	

Figure 12-5: The Invert Colors option applies a reverse video effect to your iPad display.

Speak Selection

You may not require VoiceOver to be active when you use the iPad, but there may be times you'd like the iPad to read a certain few words to you. The Speak Selection option in Accessibility does just that when turned on. Select any text in a website, e-mail, or anywhere else, and Speak Selection reads the highlighted text aloud. It also gives you formatting options, such as cut, copy, and paste.

Speak Auto-Text

If you have the Speak Auto-Text feature turned on, the iPad plays a sound effect and the suggested word is spoken automatically as you type. To accept the suggestion, tap the spacebar. To ignore it, keep typing.

Hearing

Education with iPads uses a variety of media and audio and is certainly an increasingly important method for communicating and expressing knowledge. The iPad offers features to help those with hearing difficulties:

✓ **Mono audio and channel balance:** This option combines the left and right stereo channels into a single mono audio signal output. Mono Audio enables users with hearing loss in one ear to hear both channels in the other ear. Tap Settings, General, and Accessibility; Mono Audio is the Hearing category toward the bottom of the screen. Tap to turn it off.

You can also adjust the balance of the output between the left and right channels by using the slider directly under the Mono Audio option in the Hearing section, as shown in Figure 12-6.

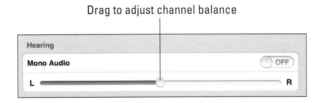

Figure 12-6: Set Mono Audio or adjust channel balance for those with hearing impairments.

- **Headsets:** In addition to the standard speakers, the iPad comes with an audio jack you can use to plug in earphones, earbuds, noise-canceling headphones, and amplified speaker systems. It also works with Bluetooth wireless headsets.

- **FaceTime:** FaceTime is a great tool for people who want to communicate using sign language or by lip reading. Video chat allows users to see hand and finger gestures, as well as facial expressions.

Learning

Guided Access is a new feature introduced in iOS 6 that helps students with disabilities such as autism remain on task. When Guided Access is enabled, a parent or teacher can limit use of the iPad to one app by disabling the Home button. It also allows you to restrict touch input on certain areas of the screen.

To start Guided Access, first turn it on in the Accessibility options of the Settings app and then triple-tap the Home button in the app you want to use.

Physical & Motor Skills

The iPad has a wonderfully designed interface with lots of intuitive multi-touch gestures that enable users to interact with it in simple yet powerful ways. Some users, however, such as the elderly and those with a physical disability, have difficulties with fine motor skills and multitouch gestures. Swiping, pinching, and other gestures can be challenging. Apple released an AssistiveTouch feature in iOS 5 specifically designed with those users in mind. The AssistiveTouch feature allows you to mimic most of the multi-touch gestures and button clicks with a single tap onscreen.

Turn AssistiveTouch on in the Accessibility settings. Remember that you get there by tapping Settings, General, and then Accessibility at the bottom of the display. The Accessibility page has a category toward the bottom for Physical & Motor features, and that's where the AssistiveTouch feature is listed. Tap once to enter the AssistiveTouch page, and tap again on the button to turn it on.

The first thing you'll notice is that a large round dot appears in one of the corners of the display. Whenever you press the dot, it displays a menu, shown in Figure 12-7, of single-tap AssistiveTouch options for Gestures, Device functions, Home, and any Favorites you may have defined. Everything can be maneuvered with a single tap of the options onscreen.

Figure 12-7: The AssistiveTouch menu allows users to control the iPad with single taps.

Assessing Accessibility Apps

Much of the power of the iPad lies in the fact that developers have created very innovative and helpful apps for specific purposes. That is certainly the case with accessibility apps, and the following sections describe just a few of the most popular options.

Proloquo2Go

It's estimated that around 2.5 million Americans are speech-disabled to the extent that they experience significant difficulty being understood by other people. This can be due to a variety of reasons but is often caused by amyotropic lateral sclerosis or, as it's more commonly known, Lou Gehrig's disease. Many people who suffer from this combination of vocal and motor skills weakness often purchase and use an Augmentative and Alternative Communication (AAC) device. These devices allow users to select combinations of symbols, words, and sounds, and convert them to synthesized speech. A typical AAC device can cost several thousand dollars.

Proloquo2Go is an AAC app that works on an iPad and provides similar functionality to these expensive AAC devices for a small fraction of the cost. That's because it uses the existing hardware features of the iPad. Proloquo2Go includes a library of more than 14,000 symbols, automatic conjugations, word prediction, multiuser support, and the capability to fully customize vocabularies for users along a broad continuum of abilities, from beginning symbolic communication to full literacy. Proloquo2Go provides a range of natural sounding text-to-speech voices, both male and female, adult and child, and with American or British accents.

You build phrases by tapping symbols (see Figure 12-8) with words and phrases under them. For example, the home screen offers categories such as "I want," "I need help," "food," "drinks," and so on. Tapping one gives you underlying words and phrases. As you tap a symbol, the phrase is added to the top and spoken. The built-in logic takes you to connected phrases automatically to help complete the sentence. In addition, the interface is extremely flexible and customizable; you can add words and phrases to the app's vocabulary. It's a terrific communication aid for users with this type of disability.

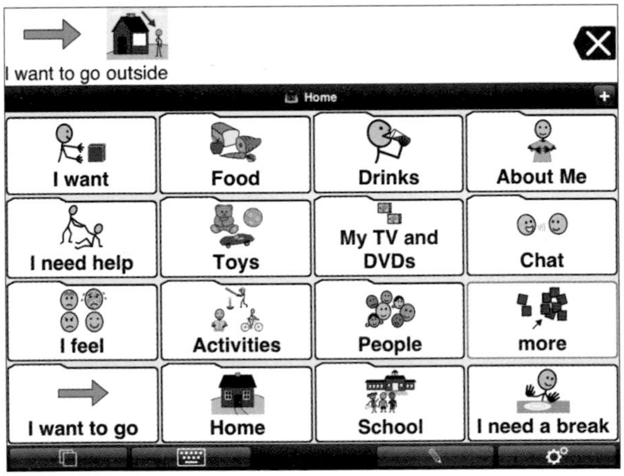

Figure 12-8: Proloquo2Go enables users to communicate by tapping on symbols.

Digit-Eyes

Digit-Eyes (see Figure 12-9) is a wonderfully creative iPhone app for those with serious visual impairment. Digit-Eyes enables people without vision to create and read bar-code labels. Simply use your iPad or iPhone to scan product packaging for UPC/EAN codes, and Digit-Eyes automatically identifies the code and tells you the name of the product. Turn on your device's VoiceOver function — as described earlier in this chapter — and it will read aloud for you. With the aid of Digit-Eyes, you can scan and hear the names of more than 7.5 million products, often including the full description, usage instructions, and ingredients — and in ten languages.

Figure 12-9: Digit-Eyes helps the visually impaired by identifying and reading bar codes.

If that were all Digit-Eyes did, it would be a great product. It also, however, enables you to print your own bar codes directly from the Digit-Eyes website (www.digit-eyes.com) on ordinary labels. You can then attach those labels to anything that you want to scan and identify.

Now I'll take that concept one step further. The Digit-Eyes bar codes you print may contain text that VoiceOver reads or can be used to record audio on your iPad that's played when the label is scanned. Why would you do that? Suppose that you bought a packet of fresh salmon from the supermarket. When the bar code is read, Digit-Eyes correctly tells you that the package contains salmon. Now assume that you get more salmon. Which is the older package? Print any standard label and use Digit-Eyes to record yourself saying "Salmon bought on Tuesday, March 17." Your problem is magically solved . . . well, unless your guests hate fish.

Here's a clever thought: Print and record audio for bar codes that you put on containers. You can rerecord the audio labels for those bar codes as often as you need. Every time you put something new in the container, use Digit-Eyes to record a new audio label, and you'll know what's in it. If you use plastic containers for perishable food items, simply bar-code the container and record the date of anything you put in it! Great idea, huh? I think I'll record some applause for the bar code I just printed.

Eye Glasses

Sometimes, really smart ideas are very simple. The Eye Glasses iPhone app is one example. Open Eye Glasses, and it uses your device's camera, adding the capability to use 2X, 4X, 6X, or 8X magnification levels for anything the camera is displaying (see Figure 12-10). It's an extremely simple tool that offers powerful results for the visually impaired. Think of it as a digital magnifier that uses your device's camera as its eyes. Just point the camera and hold it about five inches from anything you want to magnify, whether it's text, an image, or even that curious and potentially dangerous bug that just landed on your hand. It's a clever little solution for anyone who has trouble reading fine print or needs to see an object in greater detail.

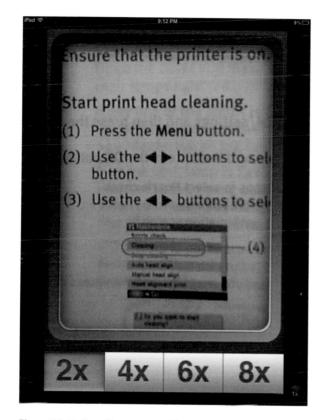

Figure 12-10: Eye Glasses magnifies anything you see through your device's camera.

SpokenLayer

The developers of SpokenLayer proudly announce that their iPhone app lets you "read the web with your ears." While I wouldn't go quite that far, SpokenLayer is a simple app that collects the latest articles from a catalog of sources such as the Associated Press, TechCrunch, *The Atlantic,* Engadget, and more. Simply tap to select a source and article, and SpokenLayer will read it for you — wherever and whenever you want. It's a great solution for the visually impaired, but also handy if you want to listen to articles while driving or working out. It's a simple idea that's nicely implemented. Just remember to bring along some earphones any time you might want to use SpokenLayer.

SoundAMP

Shown in Figure 12-11, SoundAMP does for hearing what Eye Glasses does for sight. SoundAMP amplifies the sounds of the world around you. It uses either the device's built-in microphone or a headset with mic to amplify any nearby sound.

Use SoundAMP when you are talking to a friend nearby, watching TV, listening to a lecture or concert, or are at a party or anywhere else where it's difficult to hear. You can adjust volume, tone, and background sound levels and even create recordings that you can listen to later.

Figure 12-11: SoundAMP uses the iPad mic to pick up and amplify the sounds around you.

Part V
Expressing Yourself with Media

In this part . . .

Part V is all about harnessing your creativity for digital storytelling. From creating story boards to producing iMovies, puppet shows, and animations — you can do it all. I also show you how to produce podcasts and screencasts and release your inner artist (bonus: no brushes to clean afterwards!) with some terrific tools for all ages.

13

Digital Storytelling in Education

*W*e tell stories. We've always told stories throughout human history. They can be fictional or nonfictional. Stories can be the creation of imaginative fables, the recording of personal or historical experience, or an expression of knowledge. They always reflect the perspective of the storyteller and are subjective and personal by nature. Storytelling is an integral part of education that spans all ages and academic disciplines.

Storytelling is how we make sense of the world around us. It's how we pass knowledge, cultural traditions, narratives, and more from one generation to the next. It's what connects us to the generations that came before us and what binds us to the generations that will come after our time.

Digital storytelling is simply the ancient art of telling stories enriched through the use of multimedia technologies. The skills and literacies developed through digital storytelling are increasingly important as more of our communications rely on multimedia. As I discuss in this chapter, communications have become very rich and diverse. With its built-in microphone and cameras (iPad 2 and higher), the iPad offers a wide range of alternatives for students to express themselves with media. I cover some of the most popular options in the chapters that follow.

Understanding the Role of Technology in Digital Storytelling

The digital aspect of storytelling raises the art to a new level of experience. The emergence of technology and digital media has resulted in some significant departures from the traditional role of storytelling in education:

Stories have become media-rich experiences. Billions of mobile devices are in the hands of people worldwide, and an ever-increasing percentage of those devices contain video cameras, still cameras, and microphones. Whenever anything of personal significance happens, it can be captured and chronicled in digital media (as shown in Figure 13-1) that we edit, process, and publish. Within minutes, that moment is available to friends and family around the world. Media has become the language of today.

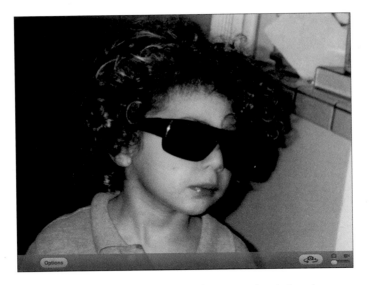

Figure 13-1: Any moment or event can be captured and shared instantly using digital media.

Don't get me wrong. Reading and writing remain crucial educational components. However, if you want to prepare students for life in 21st-century society, it's essential to help them develop and use a broad range of communication skills. Schools have begun to recognize the importance of multimedia use in education. Fortunately, with its built-in microphone, camera, and a host of multimedia apps, the iPad is an extraordinary tool for creating and integrating multimedia into education.

When you think of storytelling from a traditional perspective, you might conjure up any of these images:

- Danny Kaye telling a story to a group of children seated on the ground. (If you don't know who Danny Kaye is, look up the movie *Hans Christian Andersen.*)
- A kindergarten teacher reading a book to a group of young students.
- A parent reading a bedtime story to a child.

The common thread is the clarity of role definition: The adult tells the story, and the child listens; the teacher imparts knowledge, and the students listen and learn. (That's the theory, anyway.) All those images show a clear relationship between adult and child, expert and learner, craftsman and apprentice.

Then we reached the information age. Technology is expanding knowledge at accelerating rates. Passively absorbing information that is then regurgitated can't pass for learning any longer in the information age. Students must develop the skills necessary to constantly learn by searching for, interpreting, and analyzing information, and then applying what they've learned to real-world problems throughout life. Students are becoming producers of knowledge: digital storytellers who use technology to express themselves. And it's a role that's become an integral part of their lives outside school. Facebook, YouTube, Twitter, and more. . . technology has turned everyone into a story producer in one form or another.

Students traditionally produced a product for an audience of one: their teacher. Thanks to the Internet and the power of social networking, those digital stories can now be shared worldwide in an instant. Producers of a digital story today can communicate with people and communities anywhere around the globe through the power of a device — such as an iPad — that they hold in their hands.

Engaging Learners through Digital Storytelling

If you own an iPad (and I presume you do, since you are reading this book!), you have access to a host of apps and tools for creating digital stories. Use them for creative expression, communicating information, entertaining, expressing comprehension, tutoring purposes, and much more. Here are just a few ideas:

- Create a narrated slide-show story to demonstrate the understanding of new vocabulary.

✔ Use a video or *screencast* (a recording of interactions on a computer or iPad display) to explain a complex scientific concept.

✔ Create an audio or video interview of your grandparents for a family history project.

✔ Create a historical narrative of a pivotal event using images and audio.

✔ Create a first-person audio journal of a person who lived during a significant event in history.

✔ Explain a mathematical concept by creating a screencast tutorial.

✔ Use audio podcasting to practice reading and speaking in a foreign language.

✔ Demonstrate a portfolio of work with personal narrative describing each piece, its objectives, and development.

✔ Narrate a character story or a personal journal with a musical soundtrack.

Digital storytelling makes for engaging lessons that allow students to create and publish content rather than just passively consuming it. It empowers every student with the opportunity to develop his voice and personalize it through the use of media.

Throw away that lesson plan that calls for students to "read Chapter 5 and answer questions." You have a wide variety of options for applying digital storytelling to your curriculum. I discuss a few of them in the next few chapters.

14

Lights, Camera, Learning

In This Chapter

▶ Examining the different steps in a multimedia project

▶ Creating a movie storyboard with Popplet

▶ Producing short narrated movies with StoryRobe

▶ Trimming video directly in your iPad's Camera Roll

▶ Creating multimedia productions with iMovie

▶ Exploring other creative options for video editing

*O*pen your browser to a popular news page such as Yahoo!, and the lead story is often some scandal about an actor or actress. Movies have become mainstays of our culture, and there's no denying their popularity. We love watching and creating movies, and they definitely have their place in education. And although creating and editing video used to require special cameras and expensive desktop software, we're now able to discuss how to produce movies easily and inexpensively with a simple mobile device.

Creating a short movie can be a great way to narrate a story with new vocabulary words, practice a foreign language, "interview" a famous figure, create a school news broadcast, and so much more. Students love creating videos. Their enthusiasm for learning activities tends to skyrocket when they can express themselves with video. Frankly, between the two of us, I've conducted many teacher workshops with video activities, and I can tell you that adults aren't really any different.

Just as reading and writing occupied a special place in our learning, video has become an important component in the education of our children and students. It doesn't replace the role of reading and writing — in many respects they work together. Students will read and research background information for a movie project and write a script before performing in front of a camera. The use of media has a place in education, from the first-grade vocabulary project to the more complex productions of high-school students.

In this chapter, I demonstrate how you can integrate video into a variety of educational settings. I show you how to create and edit short narrated slide-show videos as well as more intricate video productions. This chapter also guides you toward many of the creative educational applications that these multimedia projects offer across grade levels and throughout the curriculum.

Planning Your Production

I've heard many people express the thought that multimedia projects aren't "serious" schoolwork. They're right from the perspective that a digital storytelling project shouldn't be the school equivalent of that 30-second pet cat video on YouTube. Student work often reflects the standards and expectations that the teacher has expressed.

Any educational project or activity benefits from careful forethought and planning; that's most certainly the case with a multimedia production. The objective isn't to stand in front of a camera spontaneously and start recording. It also doesn't mean dispensing with more traditional forms of story crafting, such as researching facts, interviewing people, writing the story, or scripting the dialogue.

Many important phases should precede the production of any significant multimedia project:

- **Collaborate:** Multimedia assignments make great team projects. They include multiple phases with opportunities for each student to gravitate toward his or her particular strengths, whether those are research and reading, organization, writing, visual design and editing, performing, or something else.

- **Research:** Any project worth its weight requires students to do some digging and massaging of information. Don't forget that effective research is more than grabbing some facts from the first link in a Google search. For example, suppose they had to prepare a narrated slide show on the life of a U.S. president. That's an opportune time to discuss the elements of effective research with students. You can pose questions to your students such as these: How do you decide where and what to search? What factors about the president are important to your project? You'll more than likely come up with boatloads of information. How are you filtering the search results? Is the information accurate, and how can it be verified?

- **Select and create supporting materials:** Collect and/or create materials such as images, music, and more. Discuss the impact of visuals. What images match the sentiment students are trying to express? How does music set the scene for a story? One teacher I know demonstrates this very effectively by showing short political election advertisements. It's very revealing to note the way images and music are selected to positively or negatively reflect upon candidates' positions.

✔ **Discuss copyright issues:** Consider discussing issues such as copyright, ownership, and usage rights.

✔ **Create a storyboard:** Plan and organize. One way to do this effectively is to create a storyboard that maps out the project visually step by step.

✔ **Write a script:** Just because we're advocating the use of multimedia doesn't mean that we abandon important traditional skills such as writing. Writing an accompanying script can be a vital part of the multimedia project, and you certainly should consider asking students to submit their script along with their final digital media.

Assessments should reflect the elements of a project you consider educationally important. That can extend beyond the final media piece to include elements such as the storyboard, the script, and even the research or collection of resources used in the project. Create and clarify your assessment rubric. It will communicate the project elements that you consider important and result in a more thorough final product.

One effective method for planning any form of media project is to create a storyboard that clearly lays out all the steps or scenes. A storyboard is a form of flow chart that visually maps out how to progress from one step to the next in a project. Each step can also include the relevant details, images, links, and text.

One popular iPad app that lets you map your ideas visually is Popplet Lite, which also comes in a paid version called Popplet. It has a simple interface (see Figure 14-1) that enables you to create and place notes called Popples on a board. Add content to your notes and move them around so they connect to other Popples and form relationships. It's simple and cool, and can serve a wide variety of functions. This list gives you the basics of getting started with Popplet:

✔ **Meet the Pinboard.** When you first open Popplet, it presents a blank area called the Pinboard. You create your visual map by placing Popples on the Pinboard.

✔ **Place some Popples.** Double-tap anywhere on the Pinboard to place a Popple, which is a digital note. Grab the corner to resize it, and tap the Popple itself to move it around on the Pinboard. Add content such as images, text, or a freehand drawing to it by tapping any of the icons on the bottom. You can even take a live photo with your camera!

✔ **Connect the dots!** Did you notice that each Popple had a little circle on each side of it? Go ahead: Tap it and drag the little circle to a new location. A new Popple is automatically created with a line connecting the two of them. Pretty easy, wasn't it? You can also double-tap the Pinboard to create a new Popple and then pull out a line between it and another Popple to make a connection.

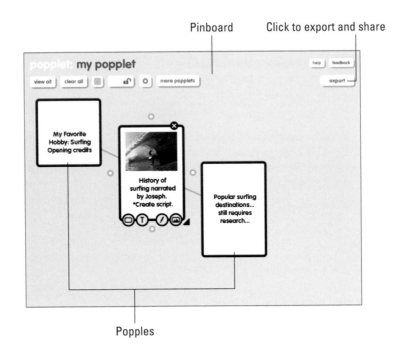

Figure 14-1: Popplet Lite enables students to map out storyboards of steps in their projects.

✔ **Keep going as far as you want.** If you're putting a lot of information into your Popples, you'll run out of room on your iPad screen pretty quickly. Just place your finger anywhere on the Pinboard and slide it out toward the edge to get additional space. The existing Popples slide out the side of the screen as you get more space for new ones. If you start to feel insecure and need to see all your Popples at once, tap the View All button on the top of the Pinboard. Have faith: They're all still there!

✔ **Share from Popplet Lite.** Tap the Export button in the top-right corner when you're done. If you're using the Lite version, you can e-mail your work as a PDF document or a JPG image. If you purchased the full version, you have additional options to collaborate with other users, share Popplets online, and more.

We live in a visual world. Many things that can be written can also be mapped visually. Popplet is a great tool for creating storyboards (see Figure 14-2). It's also actually a great tool for a variety of other purposes, such as planning a section in a book's chapter. You can also use it to map out a period of history, graph a family tree, demonstrate the relationships between factors that contribute to a scientific outcome, list resources for a course, map themes in a novel, show steps in a cooking recipe, and more. The more options we can give learners for connecting with information, the more we can accommodate and differentiate between alternative learning preferences.

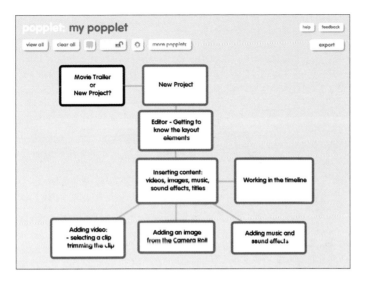

Figure 14-2: Using Popplet to plan the writing of a section on iMovie.

Designing Short, Simple Movies with StoryRobe

An increasing number of us walk around with constant access to a smartphone with a built in camera. Combine that with mobile Internet access, and you can take and distribute images and video anywhere on the planet instantly. And that's increasingly what our students are doing outside of school. Our families may have searched old shoeboxes for snapshots when we were kids, but today's students create complete digital libraries that they share on websites such as Facebook. They're very comfortable communicating with images and video.

In this section, I show you methods that can be used to create short movies. These methods can certainly be used with any age level, but they're so simple that they are especially suited for use with younger children.

All you have to do is select some images and start narrating as you flip through them. The end product is a video of up to three minutes in length. Using the StoryRobe app is really that simple. StoryRobe is actually an iPhone app, but as you may know, iPhone apps also work on the iPad — just at a lower screen resolution. (If you didn't already know this, flip back to Chapter 2 and read about it.) The video quality from StoryRobe may not win you that Oscar you've always coveted, but it will be sufficient for your educational needs.

I don't recommend spontaneously recording yourself without any preparation. Take some time to prepare your movie before you begin to create it. Think about the story you want to tell, and write the narration that will accompany the slides. Create your video story using the following steps:

1. **Start a new StoryRobe movie by tapping Create Story on the opening screen.**

   You're presented with the Choose Photo screen shown in Figure 14-3; it contains a menu of options to select your images (from your iPad's Camera Roll or image libraries). You can even select a short video clip.

Figure 14-3: Create a StoryRobe video by first selecting images.

2. **Select an image or video from your photo library or Camera Roll by tapping it.**

   For the brave-hearted, you can also take a live photo on the spot by tapping the Take Picture option, which activates the iPad camera. Feel free to experiment. Once you snap your photo, you're presented with buttons to Retake or Use your image. Tap the Use button when you're satisfied, and your image is brought back into StoryRobe.

StoryRobe will prompt you after you add an image and ask if you want to add another.

3. **Continue selecting images until you're done; then tap View Photo on the menus at the bottom of the display.**

    The next screen is the View Photo screen, where you can delete or rearrange images. All your images are presented as thumbnails onscreen, each with its own Edit button in the right column (see Figure 14-4).

4. **(Optional) Tap the Edit button, and you can tap and drag the lined icon to the right of any image to a different spot in the order.**

Figure 14-4: Tap an image's Edit button to change its position in your StoryRobe movie.

5. **(Optional) Tap the red Delete button on the left of a thumbnail to remove an image from your list.**

   Don't worry, it isn't being deleted from your iPad. It's just being removed from the list.

6. **Tap the Record Story icon.**

   The Record Story icon is on the bottom right of the screen (refer to Figure 14-4). After you tap it, you're taken to the Record Story screen shown in Figure 14-5. The middle image of the slide show appears along with thumbnails of other images in the slide show and three buttons: Next Image, Record/Pause, and Stop.

Figure 14-5: Narrate your StoryRobe video over the images.

7. **Tap Record, and, speaking clearly, narrate the script for this image.**

   You can tap the Pause button at any time to stop and collect your thoughts and then tap it again to resume.

8. **When you're ready to move to the next image in the slide show, tap Next Image, and continue recording.**

9. **Tap Stop when you're done.**

   StoryRobe presents you with a screen to name your video.

10. **Tap in the Video Name box, type the name of your new creation, and tap the Create Video button.**

    StoryRobe creates and saves the video. It actually creates two files: a StoryRobe file that you can open and edit in StoryRobe later, and a standard video file in your Photo app. You'll find yourself on the Open Story screen with a list of all your StoryRobe files.

11. **Break out some popcorn, sit back, and tap the View Story icon to view your video masterpiece.**

12. **Tap the Close icon on the top left of the Open Story screen to close the movie.**

From the opening menu screen, you can share your creation:

1. **Tap the Share button.**

   The Share Story screen displays a list of your StoryRobe projects.

2. **Tap any project to select it.**

3. **Tap either the Upload to YouTube or Email Story icon.**

   Note that you'll need a YouTube account to upload it and an e-mail account set up on your iPad to send it via e-mail.

StoryRobe is one of the simplest ways to create a digital movie on your iPad. I love the look on children's faces when they create their first video in StoryRobe. It's such a simple process, and the results can be quite magical. Try it out for yourself and see.

Allocate adequate time for students to work on their narration and slides before recording, and make this a clear and essential priority. If they have to rush into the creation of the videos without adequate preparation time to research, plan, and script, you won't exploit the full educational potential of multimedia projects.

Creating and Editing Video

The fantastic capabilities of the many apps that use the iPad's camera tap into the creative potential that exists inside all of us. And if you're lucky enough to have a third-generation iPad, you also benefit from features such as 1080p HD quality video and image stabilization. Chapter 2 delves into how to shoot video with your iPad. Now go ahead and put that video to good use.

Here are some tips for taking effective video on the iPad:

- ✔ The first and most obvious thing to keep in mind is to keep your educational objectives front and center. It's unlikely that you'll be applying for any Academy Awards. Students certainly can produce amazing results with video, but if you're after dramatic cinematic effects, you'll probably want to use a more robust video editor on the Mac.

- ✔ The best way to use and put together video on iPads is to keep your clips fairly short and entertaining. Long video clips often make it difficult to hold the viewer's attention.

- ✔ Make sure you have abundant light available and preferably not shining directly into the camera. Also, don't move from one lighting situation to another while shooting video. If you have to shoot under different lighting conditions, turn off the camera and start a new clip at the second location after giving the camera a few seconds to adjust to the new lighting conditions.

- ✔ Don't combine clips taken in portrait mode with landscape photos.

- ✔ Video gets a little scary and blurred if you get too close to your subject. Stay a minimum of an arm's length away when shooting.

- ✔ Whether you have an iPad 2 or higher (which have an image stabilization feature), keep as still as possible when taking your video. Motion blur is disturbing; too much of it will make your viewers seasick.

- ✔ Everyone knows where the lens is on a regular camera . . . but that isn't always true on an iPad. Know where the camera is located physically on your iPad and then do yourself a favor by keeping your fingers clear of it — something I didn't do while snapping Figure 14-6. The greatest video on Earth will be ruined by the sudden appearance of a giant forefinger in the frame!

- ✔ Resist the urge to show off, waltzing around taking video while holding the iPad in one hand. Hold it with steady in both hands with your elbows tucked in to your sides.

- ✔ Experiment and have fun with the video. Trim your clips creatively and put them together with interesting transitions. Try adding an interesting soundtrack. Pan and zoom where appropriate.

Figure 14-6: Know where the iPad camera is located, and keep your fingers clear!

Trimming video in the Camera Roll

To be perfectly honest, despite all my protests to the contrary, my family insists I'm no Steven Spielberg when it comes to shooting movies on my iPad. I guess there's no accounting for taste. Don't worry, we can all keep our moviemaking reputations intact and trim video right there in the Camera Roll before anyone else gets a look at it. It'll be our little secret. Here's how:

1. **Select a video by tapping in the Camera Roll.**

   It is displayed onscreen.

2. **With the video displayed, tap the screen to reveal the trim controls.**

3. **Drag the slide control to the start or end of the frame viewer at the top of the screen (see Figure 14-7).**

4. **Tap the Play button to preview the trimmed version; then tap Trim when you're satisfied.**

5. **Save the new version over the old copy or save it as a new video.**

Video files, especially high-definition video files or large and long movies, will eat up your iPad's space faster than anything else. Review your Camera Roll frequently and trim or delete your videos. Don't forget that you can remove them by synchronizing them with your computer and moving them elsewhere. Refer to Chapter 3 for details on synchronizing your iPad's content.

Figure 14-7: Drag the slide control over the frame viewer to trim your video.

Using iMovie

You'll usually want to do more than just trim your movie clip. In those cases, it's well worth considering an app such as Apple's iMovie. iMovie has been around on the Mac for a few years and is part of the Mac's iLife suite of software products. Apple released a version of iMovie for the iPad. It has fewer features than the full Mac version because the iPad version is designed for quick, on-the-go movies. Although it isn't intended for heavy movie editing, it does offer enough options to enable casual filmmakers to shoot video, use some simple editing tools, and turn out a memorable movie in a few short minutes. It's a perfect tool for most video applications in education.

You begin your movie venture with a simple tap of the plus (+) icon on the bottom of iMovie's opening marquee screen (see Figure 14-8). The marquee screen is where you start a new project and access and share existing projects. A pop-up menu prompts you to start a new project from scratch or choose a new trailer from iMovie's movie trailer themes. I take a stroll through both avenues.

Start a new trailer

Movie trailers are theme templates that are already set up for your movie. Themes include elements such as a custom title screen design, transition effects, and theme music. All you need to do is customize the movie by inserting your content into the theme's prearranged slots.

TIP

Shooting video with your iPad versus pro equipment

I've been asked, "When should I use an iPad for creating and editing video and when should I get more professional equipment?" You may have used digital video cameras and editors such as iMovie for the Mac. The iPad video camera is always available, mobile, and simple to access and integrate into any learning process as needed. It's important, however, to

retain a realistic perspective when using iPads for video projects. They're tremendous tools for smaller projects, but you won't be shooting the next *Lord of the Rings* with your iPad. Don't get me wrong. Motivate your student to shoot for the moon: Just make sure to keep your own expectations firmly on the ground.

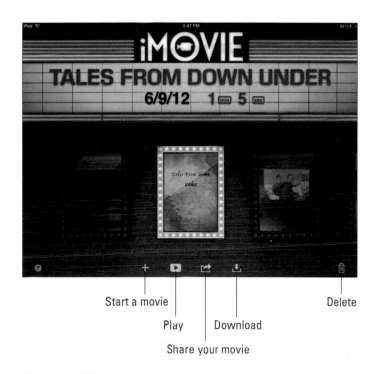

Start a movie

Play

Share your movie

Download

Delete

Figure 14-8: iMovie's screen is where you start new projects and access existing ones.

Themes encompass popular movie categories such as Scary, Romance, Narrative, Retro, and Superhero (see Figure 14-9). For example, if you have footage of the kids at Halloween, you may select the Scary theme. It comes complete with a scary background track, titles, effects, and more. You could select the Expedition trailer for the video you took of last summer's holiday. And of course, the footage of you stumbling into first base in the staff softball game would be a perfect fit for the Swashbuckler theme.

Figure 14-9: Select and customize an iMovie trailer theme for quick and simple movies.

To create a movie using a Trailer theme, follow these steps:

1. **From the iMovie home screen, tap the + sign and select New Trailer from the pop-up menu.**

    Preview the themes by tapping the Play button. When you've decided on one, tap the Create button on the template preview screen to select the highlighted theme. Now you're ready to start customizing it with your content.

2. **Tap the Outline tab (see Figure 14-10), and tap in any text field to edit the Movie Name, Credits, and more.**

3. **Add content to the Storyboard text and Video wells.**

    The Storyboard tab is where you'll edit the various components of your trailer:

    • Edit any title of a slide by tapping in the text field in the Storyboard and changing the text.

- The Storyboard also includes a number of Video wells to which you can add video. The placeholder image suggests what type of video to add (Action, Group, Closeup, and so forth). Tap any Video well to edit it.

- Your available videos will display in the video browser in the lower-right corner of your screen. If the videos aren't displaying, tap the Movie strip icon directly beneath the browser. Tap any video clip to highlight it and then tap the little blue arrow that pops up to add that video to the selected video well.

- You can tap any filled Video well to edit the video in it in the Video browser window. Turn on that video's audio by tapping the volume control at the top right of the clip. You can select which portion of the video plays by tapping and dragging the video through the yellow selection outline in the browser window. Play your selected portion at any time by tapping the Play button.

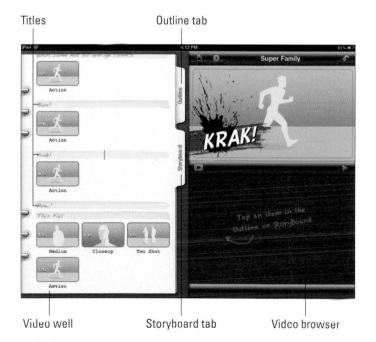

Figure 14-10: Tap an item in the Outline or Storyboard tab to add text and video.

Trailers are an easy way to create quick, simple movies — so easy that it may only take a few minutes to customize the Outline text, add some photos and movie clips into the Storyboard, and go order the popcorn. With butter, please.

Start a new project

You also have the option to start a new project when you tap the + icon on the bottom of iMovie's opening marquee screen. Choose this when you're creating and editing a movie from scratch by yourself. You're taken to the iMovie editing screen, which is divided into three sections (see Figure 14-11):

✔ The top-left section displays the available media on your iPad.

✔ The top-right section is your movie preview window.

✔ The bottom section is the movie timeline.

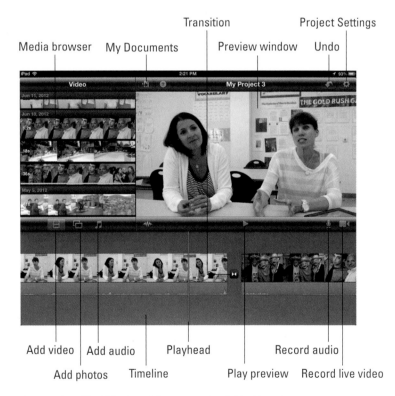

Figure 14-11: The iMovie editing screen is divided into three parts.

To create a movie from scratch, follow these steps:

1. **Tap the + icon on the bottom of iMovie's opening marquee screen.**

   The iMovie editing screen appears (refer to Figure 14-11). iMovie gives you a number of content options, and these steps show you the process of adding content. Note that if you've already added content, it appears in the Timeline at the bottom of the screen. Any additional content will be added to your movie at the current insertion point — the *playhead* (a red vertical line) — in your Timeline.

Make sure to position the playhead at the right point before inserting new content.

2. **Tap the Video button on the toolbar in the middle of the screen.**

   All your available video clips in the Media Browser are displayed. You can

   Preview any clip by dragging your finger along it in the browser.

   Add an entire clip by tapping to select it and then tapping the blue arrow that pops up immediately afterward.

   Trim the clip before adding it (when you tap and select any clip, yellow trim handles appear at either end of it) by dragging its trim handles so that they encompass just the part of the clip you want to use. When you're ready, tap the blue arrow to insert your clip.

Note that it's always good practice to shoot a couple of seconds before your action and a couple of seconds after it ends. Having those extra seconds gives you footage to trim so you can capture exactly what you need.

As you insert videos into your project, iMovie adds an orange outline on the bottom of the clip in the Media browser. Even though you can use videos as many times as you want in a project, that little orange line makes it easy for you to see which clips you've already used and which you haven't. They do think of everything, don't they?

3. **Tap the Photos button on the top of the Timeline to display the images in your Camera Roll and Photo library.**

4. **Tap any image to insert it into your Timeline.**

   If your Playhead is in the middle of a video clip, the photo will be inserted at the start or end of the clip, whichever is closest.

   Photos will display for a few seconds and automatically get a *Ken Burns effect* (a panning and zooming effect named after the famous American documentary filmmaker) applied to them.

   You can easily edit those photo timings and effects. I take a peek at how to do that in the next section.

iMovie enables you to take photos and video on the go as you create and edit your movie. See the little camera icon on the right of the Timeline toolbar (see Figure 14-12)? Tap it to bring up your iPad camera, all ready for you to snap an image or take some video footage. Just say "Cheese" and shoot whatever you like, and the image or video is automatically added to your movie. Easy peasy.

Figure 14-12: Tap the Camera icon in iMovie and start the Camera app to add live footage.

5. **Tap the Music icon on the toolbar to add a soundtrack.**

   You'll see a selection of menu choices:

   > *Theme Music* lists audio tracks that come included with iMovie, and a number of choices such as Playlist and Artists allow you to access and use music in your iTunes library.

   > The *Sound Effects* category even gives you a library of entertaining audio clips to use in your project. (What project would be complete without a rooster crowing?)

6. **Add narration to your movie by positioning the Playhead in your Timeline and tapping the microphone icon on the toolbar.**

7. **Tap Record on the pop-up menu to start recording and tap Stop when you're done.**

8. **Tap the gear icon in the top-right corner to access the Project Setting menu and choose a theme.**

   iMovie comes with a collection of themes. Each theme has specific default style for the title screen, transitions, and theme music. You'll see themes ranging from Modern to CNN iReport, and each one gives your movie its own distinct flavor. You'll also see an option to turn the theme music on or off.

9. **Swipe, split, and edit in the Timeline.**

   Here's just a short selection of some simple but powerful options to edit your movie project:

   - *Zoom in and out.* Unpinch your fingers in the Timeline to zoom in and see a more detailed frame view of your movie. That will be helpful if you need to be more precise when splitting clips, adjusting background music, and more.

- *Split a video clip.* Scroll the Timeline so that the red Playhead is positioned where you want to split the video clip. Select the clip in the Timeline by tapping it. You'll see it highlighted with an outline. Without lifting your finger off the screen, swipe down to split it at the Playhead. Splitting a clip is useful for trimming parts, and adding transitions, titles, and more.

- *Delete a clip or photo.* Double-tap the element in the Timeline; a Settings dialog pops up. Tap the Delete button. You can also tap and drag an element out of the Timeline to delete it.

- *Add titles.* You can add a title to any clip or image in the Timeline. Double-tap any element in the Timeline, and a small Settings dialog pops up. Tap Title Style and select a style option; iMovie adds a text box to that clip or image. Tap the text box in the Preview window and add your own custom title text.

- *Edit transitions.* Every time you add an element in your project Timeline, iMovie adds a default transition into it. The transitions are based upon the project theme that you selected, but you can change them easily.

  To change a transition, double-tap the icon for the transition you'd like to edit. You can select Cross-Dissolve, Theme, or None to remove it altogether. You can also slide the duration of the transition to the desired time in the list of options.

- *Add a fade-in and fade-out to the project.* Tap the Project Settings icon in the top right of the editor screen. Turn the options on for Fade in from Black and Fade out to Black.

- *Change the volume in a clip.* Double-tap the clip in the Timeline and slide the volume control to the desired volume in the Clip Settings dialog. Turn it on or off altogether by tapping the On/Off button.

10. **When you're done editing, tap the My Projects icon (the document with the star) on the top toolbar to return to the home marquee screen.**

11. **Scroll and select a project on the marquee screen by tapping it.**

12. **Tap the large name of the your project on the top of the screen to edit and rename it.**

13. **Tap the Play icon on the bottom of the screen to prepare and play back your movie . . . then enjoy the show.**

14. **Tap the curved-arrow icon on the bottom of the screen to pop up a list of sharing options.**

Options include preparing a final, compressed version of your video that's placed in your Camera Roll and uploading to YouTube, Vimeo, or Facebook. You can also send your iMovie file to your iTunes account, where it can be easily transferred and edited on another device.

Respect copyrights

Although iMovie allows you to access and use any iTunes song as the soundtrack for your video, you still have to respect the content owner's copyright. The doctrine of "fair use" allows limited use of copyrighted material within the context of classroom instruction.

Using a small snippet of a Beatles song may sound great as the backdrop to part of your History project, but don't plan on including the entire White Album and posting the video on a public web forum!

Exploring other video apps

Although iMovie is the most popular option for creating and editing movies on the iPad, there are certainly many other apps that offer additional features . . . and many more are released all the time. Here's a quick rundown of a few of them to consider:

- **Avid Studio:** Avid Studio has a very intuitive user interface and most of the same features for adding and editing content as iMovie. There's a handy selection of additional features for the adventurous among you who want to venture out and explore your creative options. Here are a few:

  - Avid Studio allows you to add and edit up to three additional audio tracks in your movie. Use them to create complex sound effects, audio transitions, and more sophisticated background audio.

    Transition effects between clips are enhanced with a far larger range of options, including high-quality dissolves and fades.

  - Create picture-in-picture effects.

  - Create professional titles with full control over fonts, sizes, colors, rotation, and more.

- **Reel Director:** This is another popular video editing app for the iPad. Reel Director excels with impressive tools for adding titles and subtitles, and includes an impressive range of transition effects.

- **Silent Film Director:** This is actually an iPhone app but takes an extremely unique and creative slant on videos by turning them into old-fashioned silent movies. Add music, titles, and transition cards, and vary the playback speed of the video. If you update with the in-app purchase, you'll get additional functions, including the option to add retro music to your silent movie.

✔ **CollabraCam:** You thought that just taking and editing video on a mobile device was a leap forward? CollabraCam (shown in Figure 14-13) allows you to simultaneously control, shoot, and edit live video from multiple cameras on other iPads, iPhones, or iPod touches. Each device would need to have CollabraCam installed on it and be on the same wireless network. One device acts as the "director," viewing, recording, and editing live video streams from up to four other devices. You can also silently communicate with your camera operators and pass along instructions. The final assembled video is exported to the Camera Roll on the director's device.

Figure 14-13: CollabraCam allows you to control and shoot live video from multiple cameras.

15

Animating Your Lessons

In This Chapter

▶ Staging and recording a sock-puppets show

▶ Designing, writing, and sharing comics

C ommunication is the heart of learning, and we adopt different communicative techniques at the various stages of our lives. When you're a kid, you love to express yourself by using your imagination in all sorts of creative ways: You role-play, dress up, and make up stories with colorful characters. Playing in these ways — animating, if you will, the stories and ideas you imagine — is a vital part of growing and learning about the world around you. It's also an important part of the learning process in school, and many iPad apps seek to tap into the potential of learning by creating colorful stories. I discuss two such apps here: Sock Puppets (which enables you to create animated shows featuring those lovable critters) and Comic Life (which helps you create your own cartoon strip).

Staging a Sock-Puppets Show

We all played with puppets at some point in our childhood. My daughter's first joke was when she pulled a sock over her hand and pretended it could talk. Children will give the puppet a name and character, and use it to make up stories that exercise their imagination and express their feelings.

One digital equivalent is an iPad app called Sock Puppets (shown in Figure 15-1). It's an adorable app that lets you create sophisticated little sock-puppet shows . . . and it's impossible not to have fun using it. There's a free version and a paid version called Sock Puppets Complete that comes with additional content and longer recording time. Both are available in the App Store.

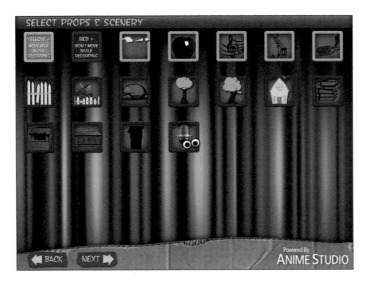

Figure 15-1: Select puppets, props, and backgrounds for your Sock Puppet show.

Create puppet shows by selecting your puppets and positioning them on a stage with backgrounds and props. Tap the Record button and start talking. Tap one of the puppets, and it will lip-sync while also applying a cute little cartoonish effect to the audio of your voice. If you want to tap your inner Spielberg, you can even develop your plot by switching backgrounds and moving your puppet extravaganza to different locations. When you're done, the show is converted to an entertaining little movie that you can watch and force on your friends . . . um, I mean share with your friends.

Always try to structure activities with your educational goals in mind. Integrate use of the Sock Puppets app into your lesson plans. Why settle for the same stale old vocabulary exercises every week when you can occasionally have children work together and use vocabulary lists in puppet shows? Be creative. Ask children to create and retell stories, review books, explain simple math or science concepts, act out appropriate behavior in social situations, and more. As always, remember to stress the importance of preparation before recording. Often, it's the preparation time where most of the learning will take place.

Yes, I know the Sock Puppets app is designed for kids, but let's be honest: We both know that you can't resist trying it out for yourself. So go ahead and put on your director's cap and create your very own puppet movie. Here's how:

1. **Tap the Sock Puppets icon on your iPad home page to start the app and then tap the New option on the opening-screen menu.**

   This starts a new story.

You're presented with a row of puppet characters.

2. **Tap the puppets you'd like to cast in your movie (any amount you'd like), and tap the Next arrow (at the bottom of the screen).**

Note that you can purchase additional puppets, backgrounds, and props from the opening-menu screen.

The next screen offers a selection of backgrounds to use as sets in your show. Remember that you can use more than one and switch between them during the show.

3. **Select and tap the backgrounds of your choice, and then tap the Next arrow.**

Backgrounds sit behind your characters and cannot be moved.

Now you're ready to decorate your puppet sets with props, such as podiums and microphones, and scenery. Props with a red frame will be placed in a fixed position, and those that have a yellow frame can be moved wherever you'd like them.

4. **Tap the props and scenery of your choice, and they will be placed in your show; tap Next when you're done.**

The app sets up your stage, and you're ready to start recording.

5. **Move your puppets and props into their positions.**

If you selected more than one background, you'll see a strip with your background icons along the top-right corner of the screen (shown in Figure 15-2).

6. **Tap any background to select it.**

7. **Tap the round Record button on the top of your screen to start (and it becomes a Stop button).**

Keep the following in mind while you're recording:

- *Talking puppet:* If you've selected more than one puppet, you'll see one of them has a little arrow over its head. That means it's the actively selected puppet, and as you start talking it will lip-sync to the sound of your voice. Tap any other puppet when you want it to become the active puppet.

- *Moving puppets, props, and backgrounds:* You can change the positions of puppets and props during your show by tapping and dragging them. Change the background and move your show to a new location by tapping any of the background icons on the strip at the top-right corner of your screen.

- *Recording time:* When you record, you'll see a timer on the screen. It counts down from 30 seconds, which is the maximum length of the show. You can purchase an option for extended recording time in the App Store.

Record/Stop Play   Save   Share   Options   Home   Backgrounds

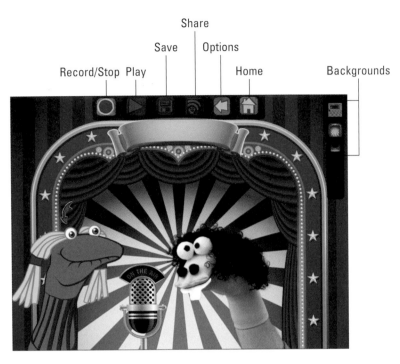

Figure 15-2: Puppets lip-sync to the sound of your voice during the recording.

8. **Tap the Stop button when you're finished.**

9. **Tap the Play button to view your show.**

The first thing you'll notice is that you sound like you've inhaled a mouthful of helium. That's the cute little effect the app has applied to the voices in your movie. You can control the pitch of the effect in the Settings option on the home screen.

The puppet show will play back with all the sound and movement that you recorded.

10. **Save your project by tapping the Disk icon on the top row.**

11. **Share your show on Facebook or YouTube, or save it to your Photo library by tapping the Share icon.**

One issue I have with Sock Puppets is that the current basic version allows sharing puppet shows only on YouTube and Facebook. Although you theoretically could create a private class account, such sites are blocked in many school districts. You'll need to arrange the purchase of an additional in-app option that adds the capability to save video to the iPad Photo library. The developers should have recognized the importance of that option to classroom use and included it in the basic version.

Puppet Pals HD

Another impressive app for creating puppet shows is Puppet Pals HD, which works in much the same way as Sock Puppets: You select and position puppets, backgrounds, and props. A nice additional feature is that Puppet Pals allows you to create your own puppets — *actors,* as they are called in the app — by cropping existing photos or using the iPad camera to take a photo. In that way, students can insert themselves into their puppet shows. You can also create videos that are exported directly to your Camera Roll.

Many apps offer the choice of purchasing additional content and features from within the app itself. In the case of Sock Puppets, you can purchase items such as additional backgrounds and puppets. You can also purchase a feature that extends the recording of the app from 30 seconds to 90 seconds. Apps that offer in-app purchasing usually have a button that allows you to buy the additional options using your iTunes account. One important difference to note for educators is that apps can often be purchased through Apple's Volume Purchasing Program (VPP) at an average 50 percent discount in larger quantities. At the moment, there isn't any method for purchasing in-app options through the VPP at a discount; you pay the full fee per copy.

Living the Comic Life

I absolutely loved reading comics as a kid. Intrigue, superheroes, mysteries, or comedies — it didn't matter. The characters were imaginative, and the colors brought the stories to life so vividly. The minute I finished one story, I'd want to start another.

Now with the assistance of digital tools, you can do more than read comics: You can create them! What's more, you don't have to be a master artist to create your own comics. The Comic Life app is the iPad version of a software program that has been popular for several years. Comic Life makes it easy to select a template; drop in balloons, captions, and images; and create comics that you can read on your iPad, print, or share via e-mail or Facebook. The latest version also has an In Tray option, which enables you to share your comics with other iPads nearby.

If you think of comics as simply another method for creating stories that have a specific visual style, you'll recognize that they can have wide use in education:

- ✏ Research an important historic event such as Columbus's voyage to discover America or the Apollo mission to the moon and create a comic that retells the story in detail.

✔ Imagine reading an act in *Hamlet* and asking students to condense the essence of the plot into a comic rewritten in their own words and using modern-day characters.

✔ Create a comic that uses a story to teach important principles such as first-aid or safety. Show students the start and end scenes, and have them write what happens in between.

✔ Practice the use of foreign-language skills by creating a comic in another language.

✔ Create a comic book detailing the life cycle of an insect or animal.

Making your comic

Creating your own comic is simple and requires just a few steps. You don't even have to run off to a phone booth and change into your Superman costume! Okay, if you're under 30, you probably don't even know what a phone booth is...

To make your own comic, open the Comic Life app by tapping its icon on your iPad's home screen. Then follow these steps:

1. **Tap the + icon on the opening screen, and select Create a New Comic.**

   The screen switches to showing you templates. Swipe through the previews to see all the options; a blank template enables you to create your own style.

2. **Tap the template of your choice.**

   Now you can choose a title for your comic, plus captions, images, word bubbles, and more. (see Figure 15-3).

3. **Customize your comic.**

   Although you have many options, customizing your comic is easy and quick:

   • *Editing placeholder objects:* If you selected a prestyled template, your page will be arranged with customizable placeholders for the title, images, and text captions. Double-tap any object to edit it. In Figure 15-4, I'm ready to add a title. You can also tap and drag any object to move it to a different part of your page. The basic elements of your page include titles, text captions, panels for images, and text bubbles.

   • *Adding panels:* Panels are the primary objects for adding and placing images in your comics. To add a panel, drag the panel icon from the Element Tray at the bottom of the screen to any part of your page. See that little photo button in the center of your empty panel? Tap it to add an image from your photo library or take a picture with the built-in camera.

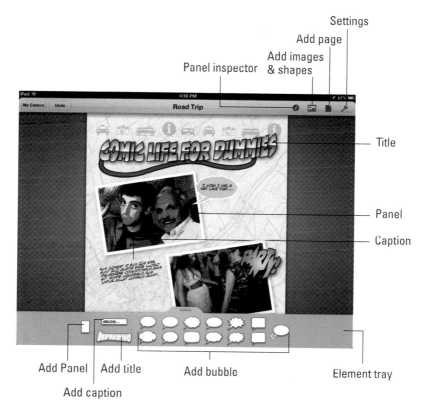

Settings
Add page
Add images & shapes
Panel inspector
My Comics
Undo
Road Trip
COMIC LIFE FOR DUMMIES
Title
I WISH I HAD A HAT LIKE THAT...
Panel
Caption
PARTY!
Add Panel
Add title
Add bubble
Element tray
Add caption

Figure 15-3: Select a Comic Life template, and customize it with captions and images.

My Comics
Undo
Road Trip
Cut
Copy
Paste
YOUR TITLE HERE
return

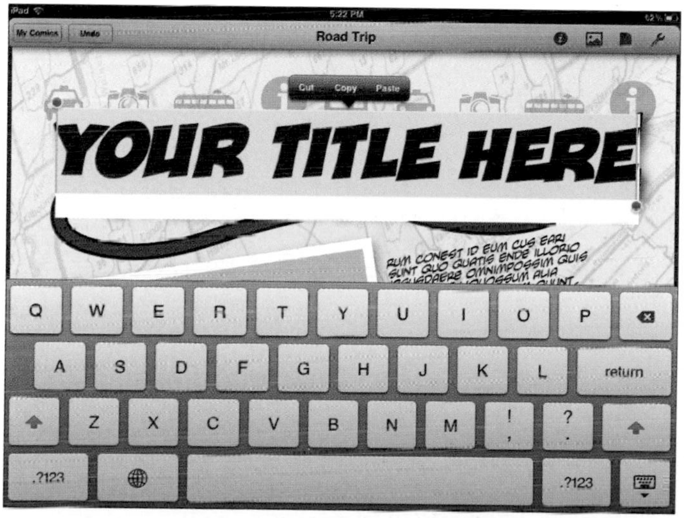

Figure 15-4: Double-tap an object to change its contents.

Add titles, captions, and bubbles: The Element Tray at the bottom of the screen has additional objects that you can add to your page. Tap or drag one onto your page to add; then tap again to edit it.

- *Changing styles with the Panel Inspector:* Experiment and give your comic a personal touch by playing with styles and effects in the Panel Inspector. Tap any object on your page to select it and then tap the Panel Inspector icon on the top toolbar to change the look and feel of it. For example, change the color and shape of your panels, the style of your titles and captions, or select an image and apply an effect to it, as shown in Figure 15-5.

Figure 15-5: Apply effects with the Panel Inspector.

- *Add, reorder, and remove pages:* Tap the Page icon in the top toolbar, and you'll see three tabs:

The Comic tab shows you thumbnails of the different pages in your comic. Tap any page to make it the current editing page, and tap the empty page with the + icon to add a new page. Tap the selected page, and a pop-up menu gives you options to duplicate or delete it. Last, tap and drag any page to change the order of where it appears.

The Template page enables you to browse the predefined pages included in the template you've chosen. Tap any thumbnail to add it to your comic after the current page.

The Layout tab contains predefined pages with different arrangements of panel layouts. Tap one to add it to your comic.

Your comic is automatically saved.

4. **Tap the My Comics button to return to the screen with all your comics.**

Sharing your comic

Your comic deserves an audience.

Who would have saved the world from the Green Goblin if the creator of Spider-Man never shared his comics with the rest of the world? You can also distribute and share your comic — and you have a number of choices. All your comics can be browsed in the My Comics view. If you're editing your comic, just tap the My Comics button on the top left to go to My Comics.

Select any of your comics by tapping it. Tap the curved Export arrow in the row of icons under the preview and take a look at your options (shown in Figure 15-6):

- ✓ **Copy To:** Select this option to see a variety of options to copy your comic off your iPad. Your options include exporting to your iTunes library or to a Dropbox account or WebDAV server if you have either.

- ✓ **Share:** Tap the Share option on the menu, and you'll have options to share your comic on your Facebook or Twitter account (provided that you have either), send it via e-mail, or save it to your Photo Library.

- ✓ **Print:** Tap the Print option on the menu, and select your printer. For more information on setting up a printer, refer to Chapter 22.

Figure 15-6: Print and share your comic in the My Comics view.

You can also send your comics to other iPads using the In Tray feature. This feature is seriously cool. Each version of Comic Life can be set up with an In Tray to receive comics sent by other users. Follow these steps:

1. **Tap the Settings icon (wrench) in the top-right corner of the My Comics view screen, and select Open In Trays from the menu.**

   Any In Trays that are open for receiving comics on nearby iPads will be displayed.

2. **Select a destination In Tray.**

   The In Tray will slide down to the bottom of the screen, enabling you to choose comics from your collections.

3. **Tap and drag any of your comics down to the destination In Tray.**

   A progress meter will appear as the comic is copied.

16

Speaking Your Mind with Podcasts

*A*s the name suggests, the term *podcasting* derives from a mixture of the words *iPod* and *broadcasting*. What generally separates podcasts from live radio broadcasts is that podcasts are usually stored online and can be subscribed to and heard at any time.

Although it's true that the concept of sharing audio broadcasts was popularized with iPods, podcasts can now be created with almost any mobile device or computer and accessed in a variety of ways over the Internet. Also, podcasting is not restricted to audio any longer. Podcasts can include images, videos, and more. Traditionally, podcasts are also posted on a site or a service such as iTunes so that others can subscribe to them and be notified as new podcasts within their subscriptions become available. iTunes remains popular, and now the iTunes U section has been split into a separate app, which includes college and K-12 educational courses with podcasts (see Figure 16-1). However, podcasts can be shared through many different web services and methods.

Figure 16-1: iTunes U has its own app with courses for colleges and K-12.

So when I talk about podcasting, it can mean many things. In this chapter, I focus primarily on audio podcasts. I discuss how to use, enhance, and share them using iPads.

If you want to get the most educational bang for your podcasting buck, podcasting should be integrated into larger lesson plans and objectives, require students to do some planning and possibly research, and may involve some postproduction editing. In fact, you could break down the process of podcasting into several distinct stages:

- ✔ **Preparing:** Including both teacher and student preparation and encompassing technical and educational questions.
- ✔ **Recording:** Looking at the different iPad options for recording your podcasts.
- ✔ **Editing:** Did it come out as intended? Is it too long or too short? Do you want to add soundtracks or images, or edit it in any other way?
- ✔ **Publishing:** Will it be public or private? Where will it be uploaded and available?

I could get all technical about digital formats and discuss sampling rates, bit depths, compression formats, and more, but I'm even boring myself, and you'd be snoozing before you got halfway through the chapter. I keep the technical complexities to a minimum and instead focus my efforts on ways to keep your podcasting simple, fun, and of course educational. Read this chapter, practice a few times, and then you'll be ready to go on air.

Putting an Educational Perspective on Podcasting

You may have noticed an annoying habit I have of always asking "Why?" It's probably a hangover from the days I made my parents crazy asking them the same question. However, it's important to evaluate what you do, especially before plunging into a time-consuming commitment like podcasting. If schools spent more time debating "why" in schools rather than simply following the "what and how" of things that have always been done, we might end up with a system that better serves the needs of our students. So . . . why podcast?

- ✔ **The quick and obvious response is partly that you can.** We've always known the importance of vocal presentation skills, but technology now allows us opportunities to have students easily record, submit, and share podcasts. It's an ideal way for students to develop their abilities to express themselves verbally. In an era where you can chat or video call anyone in the world for a few cents, cultivating verbal presentation skills has become even more important.

- ✔ **Podcasts can be published and shared.** You can opt to share within your local school community or even a worldwide audience. Traditionally, work was given to a single teacher. It's amazing how much it motivates students to know that they are producing work for an audience.

- ✔ **Podcasting is an effective collaborative activity.** Different group members can focus on skills such as research, planning, media, presentation, and more. Podcasting can also be cross-curricular.

- ✔ **Technology offers you the opportunity to shatter that one-size-fits-all model of education.** Some students are better writers, and others are more effective speakers. Give them an opportunity to develop their talents by occasionally allowing them to create podcasts instead of the traditional written assignment. Remember that opportunity can still include a written component such as research and scripts.

- ✔ **You can podcast from anywhere.** The places are almost endless — from a school sporting event, an interview with someone in the community, a school or family trip . . . anywhere you can take your mobile device.

- ✔ **Most conversations in class are dominated by the same handful of students.** Podcasting, which can be kept private and within the class, is a simple way to allow all students to voice opinions and showcase their talents.

- ✔ **Podcasting is a process that involves preparation, recording, editing, publishing, and even possibly responding to comments and reactions.** There's a tendency to think of podcasting as a brief activity where someone sits down with a recording device and randomly records a short audio snippet. But it encompasses a variety of skills and can be a compelling educational activity for any group of students.

✓ **Podcasting is fun.** Have some fun and distribute student work as a podcast every now and again. You can incorporate some of the content or skills required in a mini lesson before giving them their work.

✓ **Podcasting is a great tool for any type of language lesson.** Whether students are learning English or English speakers are learning a foreign language, having them practice speech is the most difficult part to incorporate in class. We're all naturally shy to speak in a language until we're comfortable using it. Podcasting is an excellent opportunity to have students practice their speaking skills, and it can incorporate learning new vocabulary, writing skills, and more.

Preparing for Your Podcast

Start by defining what you're preparing. You want students to research, plan, and script an audio broadcast that can be published in a location where it becomes available for others to hear at any time. You may allow others to subscribe to future podcasts in the series as appropriate. The teacher will define the private or public extent of the audience. Although I focus on audio-based podcasting, there's also the option to incorporate images and video.

Looking for opportunities

Start by looking for opportunities to augment familiar old written projects with podcasting. Consider broadcasting activities either within or outside your standard curriculum. The following list offers some ideas:

✓ **Archives:** Many colleges and schools are using video podcasts as a way of archiving lessons or snippets of lessons for future reference.

✓ **Oral histories:** Podcasting can be used for interviewing family members and creating oral histories.

✓ **Special projects:** Use podcasts for special projects such as "This Week in History." Incorporate research and mock interviews.

Another idea for a special project is to have students create a modern version of the old broadcast radio dramas. Find some episodes of old dramas on the Internet and play them for students. Websites such as www.archive.org and www.radiolovers.com have libraries of old radio shows you can listen to for free. Discuss how they were produced. Afterward, your students can write, produce, and publish their own episodes.

> ✔ **Professional development:** Podcasting and its close cousin, screencasting, can be used for professional development. Have teachers record tutorials and examples of technology use and then share them.
>
> ✔ **Communication:** Use podcasts to communicate within the community and with parents. Students can manage and produce their own podcasts such as "What We Learned This Week," "Upcoming Events," "News around School," and so on.

Allowing a degree of creative license

Technology empowers students to be creative. Don't make the mistake of giving them the technology and then mandating how it's to be used ("Submit a three-minute recording of the main achievements of Abraham Lincoln"). Children can do amazing things with technology when you give them the trust and autonomy to be creative. California schools have a unit on the missions in California every year. They have a field trip to a mission, and then they research the missions and submit a written assignment. In 2012, the teachers allowed students to take their iPads. Students recorded the bells, conducted interviews, snapped pictures, shot video, and more. They were given the opportunity and incentive to actually listen when they visited the mission and really look at structures they would normally ignore. Now they were searching for fine details that would make interesting photo opportunities. They were talking and asking questions of people at the mission. Giving students the freedom to use media creatively allowed them to experience the mission on a deeper level.

Clarifying the planning process

Podcasting isn't just about the actual recording. The most effective learning may come in the preparatory stages, during which students research, collaborate, script, interview, and contact outside experts. Podcasting encompasses valuable skills above and beyond the simple act of recording, and I guarantee students will be enthusiastic and immersed in planning a production.

Make sure that you clarify what you expect of them in these planning stages. If you are evaluating their work, the most important part of the evaluation may occur before the actual podcast. Create and share a rubric and any required deliverables.

Collaborating

Podcasts are generally done in groups, and you might think that all you need to do is throw students together and the ingredients will magically cook themselves into a great collaborative assignment. You know that isn't the case. There are always the students who dominate the discussions and others who remain quiet. Some will do the tasks they enjoy but avoid more mundane duties. And of course, there are those who leave the work to others, members of that latter group who get angry and resentful at having to complete most of the project themselves. Plan collaboration carefully. Some teachers have been successful defining roles for team members and then drawing numbers to decide which roles are assigned to each member. Others create groups that combine students with different skills.

Considering technical issues

Where and how will they record? How do you minimize background noise? What apps will be used for recording, editing, and publishing? Do you need external props such as microphones or stands? The Internet is a wonderful resource, and many educators have gone down this road. Reach out to other teachers in online educational communities or sites such as Twitter. There's a wealth of knowledge and experienced teachers willing to help you get started.

Publishing a podcast

The practice of podcasting has traditionally meant uploading a series of recordings to iTunes, where listeners can subscribe and listen to them at any time . . . and isn't it funny how anything that lasts even a few years in technology becomes "tradition"!

There are now a variety of sites and services to create and store recordings. Some even enable live online broadcasts in both audio and video format. The criteria for defining a podcast in this chapter are very simple: It should require some planning, recording, publishing to a private or public audience, and (obviously) have educational value. Technologies change way too rapidly for any of us to remain purists when it comes to defining practices.

Producing and Publishing Your Podcast

The planning is complete, and the students are ready to start recording on their iPads. As part of your planning process, you've probably looked at some options for recording. You may want to consider more than simple audio recording. Do you want the students to be able to produce a short musical theme for their podcast? Do you want to publish it with an image?

Just as important is how you will distribute the final product. Who will have access and how? If you plan on making podcasts a regular event, you want to consider allowing listeners to subscribe and be notified every time a new podcast is published.

In this section, I review some of the mort popular alternatives on the iPad.

GarageBand

GarageBand (shown in Figure 16-2) has been around for a few years on the Mac and is known as a powerful tool for making music. However, it has a voice feature that can be used for adding vocals to music . . . or just as easily for recording your voice on a podcast. Even better, you can use the same tool for creating a musical opening or background soundtrack.

Figure 16-2: GarageBand has Smart Instruments that make it easy to produce theme music.

With the range of options offered for music and voice along with the capability to export and publish your final product, GarageBand has become the popular choice for many people producing simple podcasts on iPads.

Going into a full tutorial on using GarageBand to create music is outside the scope of this book. Many GarageBand tutorials exist in abundance on the Internet, and you can always take a look at the *Macs All-in-One For Dummies,* 3rd Edition, by Joe Hutsko and Barbara Boyd (John Wiley & Sons, Inc.), for additional information. The following step list, however, gives you a quick-and-dirty introduction to using GarageBand for podcasting:

1. **Create a new song with a few simple tracks, as shown in Figure 16-3, to use as a themed intro.**

Figure 16-3: A musical theme can be as little as a few simple instruments tracks.

2. **Save your theme by tapping the My Songs button in the top right of the display.**

   That will return you to the My Songs browser display.

   You'll use it each time you create a new podcast.

   Of course, you may also consider adding some royalty-free music.

3. **Make a copy of your theme music by tapping and holding your Theme in the My Songs browser and then tapping the + copy icon.**

4. **Tap Done and then select your copy to use for your podcast.**

   You'll find yourself back in TrackView, where you can tap the Instruments button on the top toolbar.

5. **Tap the Audio Recorder (shown in Figure 16-4) to begin recording the podcast.**

6. **Tap the Record button, and speak clearly and directly into the iPad microphone.**

   The iPad mic is located in the top-left corner when the iPad is facing you (with the Home button at the bottom). You could also use an external microphone attached to the iPad. I discuss external mics a little later.

7. **Press the record button at any time to stop. Listen and re-record as often as needed.**

8. **Tap and hold the podcast in your My Songs view and then tap the Share icon above it to select how you want to share it.**

   Your options include uploading to a SoundCloud account (which I discuss in the next section), taking it into iMovie if you want to add images or video, or sharing it via iTunes or e-mail.

You can publish your GarageBand podcast via iTunes. Tap iTunes from the Share menu, and save your podcast as an iTunes file or as a GarageBand file for editing on a different computer. To publish, select iTunes. Now start iTunes on your computer with your iPad connected wirelessly or by cable. Click your iPad in the source list and select your iPad's Apps pane on the top tabs. Scroll to the File Sharing options at the bottom of the window and select GarageBand. Your podcast should be listed, and you can drag it to your desktop or any folder. At that point you're ready to submit to iTunes.

Figure 16-4: Select the Audio Recorder to record the spoken portion of your podcast.

Go to www.apple.com/itunes/podcasts/specs.html for all the details of podcast submission.

You can also publish your podcast by uploading to a blog-based website such as Posterous or WordPress. Apple also provides Podcast Producer as part of its Mac OS X Server installations; you may want to look into it as an option for publishing your podcasts.

Keep things moving if you want to maintain interest. Try to keep topic segments around seven minutes or less. Using guests or recorded interviews is a great way to mix the conversation flow and tone. You should also consider incorporating musical backgrounds and little jingles as a way to transition between topics in a longer podcast.

SoundCloud

SoundCloud (http://soundcloud.com) describes itself as "a social sound platform" where registered users share original music, spoken word, comedy, radio shows, and any other audio recordings. Use SoundCloud directly over the web at the website or from the SoundCloud app on your device.

The recording process is simple. Just open an account, start recording (by tapping the Rec button, shown in Figure 16-5), and decide how you want to share the audio. You can upload it to your account and share it with the world, or keep it completely private.

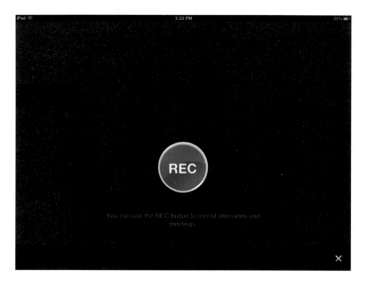

Figure 16-5: Tap Rec to start a SoundCloud recording.

Every account has a public page, but you can elect to keep recordings private. Your options include the following:

✔ **Complete privacy:** It's secure and will not be listed or appear in search listings.

✔ **Selected access:** You can give people access to a recording in four ways:

- *Add their e-mails addresses or SoundCloud usernames.*

- *Add a previously created Contact List.*

- *Create a secret link (requires a premium account).* When you set a recording to private, only users with the URL of the recording can hear it. You can send and share that URL with anyone you please.

> • *Create a group:* Groups have moderators that determine access rights and contributors that upload and share recordings with the group.

Audioboo

As is the case with SoundCloud, Audioboo (see Figure 16-6) works both over the web at `http://audioboo.fm` or via a downloadable app on your device. Record your "boo" and then publish it to your account. The free account limits your recordings to 3 minutes each, but you can upgrade your account and get up to 30 minutes recording time. You can add titles, tags, geolocation info, and a photo to the recording before you upload it, and it's all saved with the recording.

Figure 16-6: Use Audioboo for simple recordings of up to three minutes.

iPadio

I've discussed podcasting — but how about phonecasting? iPadio (www. ipadio.com) allows you to broadcast live to the web from any cellphone, or record and publish from the iPadio app. Download the iPadio app and sign up for an account on the iPadio website. You'll be given a phone number to use for live phonecasts and an account to upload your published recordings.

iPadio will record and share high-quality audio of up to 60 minutes. When you create and upload a recording (a *phlog*) to your account, it's given a unique URL that you can include on any website to share with others. You can also create a channel for your class phlogs and designate yourself as the moderator.

Using Microphones

The single most important accessory is a good-quality microphone. The microphone will give you higher-quality audio and minimize background noise. Remember that you need only a few microphones because you won't have all students recording simultaneously. You can choose expensive, high-end mics to more reasonably priced ones. Here are two microphone options to consider:

- **Apogee MiC Studio:** MiC is a high-quality microphone that connects to an iPad, iPhone, or a Mac or Windows computer. MiC is about the size of an iPhone and can record vocals, voiceovers, instruments, interviews, and everything in between, and build a track right on GarageBand. The quality is great, and if you're recording music or producing more professional podcasts, it's a great choice. The bad news: It's fairly expensive at around $200.

- **iRig MIC Cast Ultra-Compact Microphone:** The iRig connects via the iPad headset jack and is moderately priced at around $40. It's an ultra-compact, portable voice-recording microphone designed specifically for recording podcasts, interviews, lectures, voice memos, speeches, and more.

17

Directing Your Own Screencasts

In This Chapter

▶ Exploring the role of screencasting in education

▶ Creating simple screencasts with ScreenChomp

▶ Designing more elaborate screencasts with Explain Everything

▶ Recording your iPad screen directly with Display Recorder

A screencast is basically a recording of the interactions you see on a computer screen. For example, you might create a software tutorial by recording menu selections and button clicks on your laptop as you narrate the process. You may want to critique a piece of art by displaying it onscreen and commenting as you zoom and point at sections of the painting. Screencasting is a simple process that has many educational applications, some of which I discuss in this chapter.

Screencasting on the iPad differs slightly from traditional screencasting on computers. If technical discussions bore you to tears, feel free to put your fingers in your ears and jump quickly to the next paragraph. Screencasting software runs in the background, recording everything you do on a computer; by contrast, apps can run in the foreground or in a background state on an iPad or iOS device. An app that runs in the foreground fills the screen, and you have access to all its features. Some apps are designed to offer functionality that runs in the background. For example, an alarm app may run in the background, checking the time until it arrives at a designated time to wake you while you hurl abuse at it. Apps have limited functionality when they run in the background. The operating system on iPads doesn't allow you to run two apps at the same time and have them share the full functionality of the iPad. For example, only one app can access the audio output at a time. Instead, most screencasting apps on the iPad use a single screencast app where you can dynamically add and change content and record interactions within the app itself. Getting dizzy yet?

Screencasting across the Curriculum

Screencasting on desktops and laptops has been around for a number of years. Screencast software records whatever is displayed on your screen and enables you to add a voiceover narration during the recording — or edit and add to it after the fact.

Most screencast apps on the iPad give you a blank whiteboard interface and a set of tools to use during your recording. You can use these programs to create imaginative tutorials for just about anything that you can illustrate visually and explain.

What are some of the ways you might use screencasts? You can certainly use them to create tutorials for students who require additional help. You can easily upload these movies to the Internet or a classroom website where students can access them at any time. Whether you're explaining an algebraic equation or illustrating a concept in science, a screencast is an effective way to get your point across.

Here's another thought . . . *"The best way to learn anything is to teach it to someone else."* Isn't that what you've always been told? It's also a great philosophy to apply in school. The iPad enables students of all ages to learn through creating their own tutorials. Here are some benefits from doing so:

✔ **Students can teach you.** Take math as an example. You can always have students work out a problem and return the answer to you. Instead, try having students record a tutorial explaining the concept behind the solution to a particular problem.

Imagine the following situation: Your students have become proficient in single-digit addition, and now you'd like to progress to double-digit addition. You could take the traditional route of demonstrating a rule in front of the class, writing examples on the board, showing the students your method for solving the problem, and then sending them off to solve reams of problems using the rule you just taught them. That's certainly the method most often used. Consider an alternative approach. Send students off with a double-digit problem and ask them to record a screencast detailing any approach — right or wrong — of solving it. No instruction. Encourage them to learn math by thinking like mathematicians. This gives students an opportunity to develop logic by expanding on their existing knowledge of single-digit addition. Also, using a screencast instead of a paper-based response allows them to explain and verbalize their logic and thoughts.

✔ **Students can teach each other.** Students can create screencasts to help each other with homework or problems. Compile the best screencast tutorials that students build into a curated library that all students can access — now and into the future.

✓ **Students can actually teach anyone if given the opportunity.** Display student tutorials on a blog or website and make them publicly available over the Internet to anyone requiring assistance. If privacy is a concern, you can always leave omit any personal information.

Outsmarting iOS by mirroring your iPad

iOS doesn't allow both a foreground and background app to run simultaneously or interact with each other with full functionality. You can't make a screencast from the iPad that records all the workings of another program running on the same iPad. Of course, as is often the case with technology, you can often find a way to work around limitations.

One way to record a screencast of an iPad app is to *mirror* your iPad, which means to display the iPad screen on the monitor of a laptop or desktop computer. If you download and install software called AirServer from the AirServerApp website (`www.airserverapp.com`), you can turn your laptop or desktop into an AirPlay receiver for your iPad screen. You then can record the iPad's screen interactions on that

computer using software such as QuickTime! Pretty smart, no?

One thing that I love about technology is the way it both feeds off innovation and also encourages it. Every time you chisel out a technological rule in stone, it challenges someone to quickly come along and rewrite it. The programmers at BUGUN software have done a remarkable job with an app called Display Recorder. It comes pretty close to the type of computer screencast software that runs in the background, recording everything on your desktop or laptop computer screen. In other words, it does exactly what I just said an app couldn't do on the iPad . . . well, almost! I take a look at the app and its limitations later in this chapter.

Creating Simple Screencasts with ScreenChomp

Creating screencasts with ScreenChomp couldn't be easier. Start the ScreenChomp app by tapping its icon; then tap the large Draw and Record arrow in the top right of the opening menu screen to start a ScreenChomp. You'll be presented with a screen that looks very much like a whiteboard or, as the app publisher calls it, a *doodleboard,* as seen in Figure 17-1.

Return to Main menu   ScreenChomp files   Doodleboard

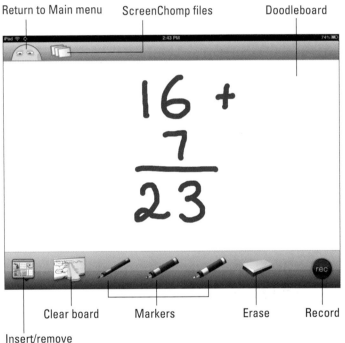

Insert/remove
background image

Clear board   Markers   Erase   Record

Figure 17-1: ScreenChomp gives you a doodleboard with tools to record your screencast.

We tend to break down school into nice, neatly packaged academic courses. In reality, however, learning always tends to span varieties of skills and traditional academic disciplines. You may be teaching mathematics, but any screencast or presentation is an opportunity to stress the importance of skills such as preparation, organization, rehearsal, and enunciation. Learning should never be one-dimensional.

Setting your stage

You can start recording your ScreenChomp with the default empty board, or you can prepare it ahead of your recording. Have you ever been to a stage play? The players could conceivably start with an empty stage, turn down the lights, and then bring out all the props while you sit there in your seat, but it would destroy the magic of the opening scene. There are also times when good teaching parallels theatrics, especially when you want to capture someone's attention and draw him into your presentation.

If you want to create a tutorial on Impressionist art, for example, you could load images while recording, or you could preload a background image, such as the one shown in Figure 17-2, so that it's ready onscreen when you tap the button to start recording. I show you how to use all the tools to load images and more in the next section, but for now, just decide how you want your opening set to look.

Figure 17-2: Prepare your screen with objects you'll need when you start recording.

Using the ScreenChomp tools

The row under your ScreenChomp board includes a set of tools to use before and during your recording. I describe them here, starting from the left:

- **Background image:** Background images sit behind anything you draw onscreen. You can select your image from the library on your iPad or from a Dropbox account if you have one, or tap the button to take a photo with the iPad camera and have that inserted as your background. To clear your background image, tap the Background icon on the left of the bottom toolbar and select Remove Background.

- **Clear board:** Tap and hold this icon to erase everything on your board.

- **Markers:** There are three markers. Use the markers to draw on the board, whether you're writing numbers and working on a math problem, writing some text, highlighting a part of an image, or doodling a picture of your own. Tap and hold any of the marker icons to change their color and thickness.

- **Eraser:** Tap the eraser, and drag your finger over anything you've drawn on the board to erase it. Note that the eraser doesn't erase any part of your background image. You need to use the Remove Background option on the Background Image tool to do that.

And you're on air

After you've set the stage and prepared your narration, you're ready to go live. Follow these steps:

1. **Tap the Record button.**

   ScreenChomp displays a short sequence of countdown numbers, as shown in Figure 17-3.

2. **Clear your throat and start recording when the count gets down to zero.**

   You don't have to record everything in one session.

3. **Use the Pause button to stop the recording at any point.**

   Take time to collect your thoughts, change or erase anything onscreen, and then tap to resume recording when you're ready.

4. **When you're done, tap the Stop button.**

5. **On the screen that appears, name your screencast and save it or tap the large Trash icon to throw the screencast away and start over.**

6. **Upload your recording to the ScreenChomp website by tapping the ScreenChomp icon in the lower-right corner.**

   You don't need to create an account, and you'll get a link to your video that you can share or paste anywhere. ScreenChomp also enables you to post directly to your Facebook account.

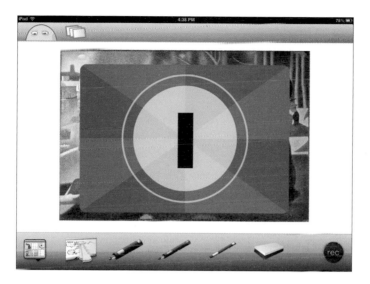

Figure 17-3: Tap the Record button, wait for the countdown, and start recording.

Creating Tutorials with Explain Everything

One of the most full-featured options for screencasting on the iPad is an app called Explain Everything. As the name indicates, it's a great app for creating all sorts of tutorials. This app enables you to add images, websites, and more to your tutorial. Explain Everything also does a wonderful job of linking to the cloud-based accounts you use, so you can import files from a wide variety of sources such as Facebook, Dropbox, Evernote, YouTube, and more. You can then draw the viewer's attention with tools for pointing and annotating your content during your narration.

As shown in Figure 17-4, a column of tools appears on the left of the screen, and on the bottom of the screen are the slide selection arrows (on the left), the recording buttons (in the middle), and the Export and Save icons (on the right).

The Recording screen has a terrific assortment of tools for creating any project you might want. Use them before recording to design the slides for your screencast or wow your audience as you use them during the screencast itself. In descending order from the top of the left column, your design tools include the following:

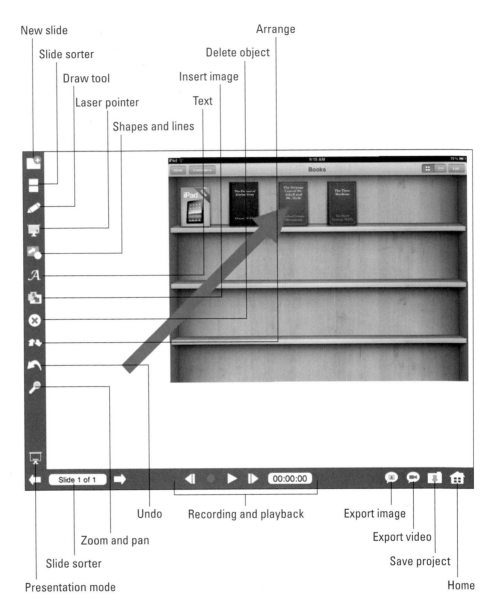

New slide
Slide sorter
Draw tool
Laser pointer
Shapes and lines

Arrange
Delete object
Insert image
Text

Undo
Recording and playback
Export image

Zoom and pan

Export video

Slide sorter

Save project

Presentation mode

Home

Slide 1 of 1
00:00:00

Figure 17-4: Explain Everything has several tools for creating screencasts.

✔ **New Slide:** Your screencast can have multiple slides. Add slides to your project by tapping the + icon in the top left of your screen. Adding slides is especially helpful if you want to prearrange content on different slides and move between them while recording your screencast.

✔ **Slide Sorter:** This tool displays thumbnails of all your slides. Tap and drag any one to a new location to change their order.

✔ **Draw:** Tap and hold the pen to change options such as color, thickness, transparency, and even the type of pen tip. Use it for anything from scrawling some numbers to doodling a Picasso!

✔ **Pointer:** Use the Pointer during your screencast to highlight anything onscreen without marking it. Tap and hold it to choose the style of Pointer.

✔ **Shapes and Lines:** Tap to select a shape such as a circle, square, line, star, or arrow. You can also change its color, transparency, and border. Once you've selected your shape, tap and drag in the slide editor to draw it.

✔ **Text:** The text tool is indispensable for people like me who couldn't write anything legible onscreen with his finger even if his life depended on it. Again, tap and hold to change text options such as size, font, and color.

✔ **Insert Image or Web Browser:** Add images from your iPad photo library or from any of your linked cloud accounts. You can also tap the From Camera option (iPad 2 and higher) to take a photo with the iPad camera and insert it directly. When you select an image to insert, you'll be presented with a screen with options to crop and rotate the image before insertion.

The Insert tool even has an option to insert a fully functioning web browser on your slide. Edit the top line of the browser to type the address of the website you want. Use the browser window to demonstrate and highlight content on any web page during your screencast. For example, if you want to create a tutorial about how to navigate the school website, you can insert a browser window into your Explain Everything project, type the web address of the school website, and demonstrate how to use it. Use the Pointer to highlight items and the Draw tool to mark up and annotate them.

✔ **Delete:** Select any object by tapping it and then tap the Delete icon to remove it from your slide.

✔ **Arrange:** Select any object by tapping it and then tap the Arrange icon to move it behind or in front of other objects.

✔ **Undo:** Don't you wish everything in life had an Undo tool? Well, Explain Everything does.

✔ **Zoom and Pan:** When you tap this icon, you can use the standard two-finger pinch and reverse-pinch gestures to zoom in and out of your slide.

✔ **Presentation Mode:** This tool hides most of the toolbar icons. Use it to present in full-screen mode, and tap it again to return to your normal screen with toolbars.

✔ **Slide Sorter:** Tap the arrows to move between the different slides.

Create your screencast in Explain Everything by following these steps:

1. **Tap the Explain Everything icon on the iPad to start the app.**

   The Explain Everything app opens and displays the home page, where you can select options to start a new project or edit an existing one.

2. **Tap the New Project button in the upper-left corner of your screen to get started.**

   You'll be prompted to start with either a blank project or by importing content such as documents or images you have stored in your iPad photo library or in one of many popular cloud services.

3. **Tap New Project to start a blank project or to import content from your cloud accounts.**

   You'll need to link to your cloud account first by tapping the Preferences button on the top right and linking any of the accounts offered to Explain Everything.

   Explain Everything will import images, documents, and even presentations and spreadsheets. When imported, each document page, presentation slide, or photo is placed on a separate slide in Explain Everything.

   Once you select one of the options for starting your project, Explain Everything displays the editing window, shown in Figure 17-5. Time to roll up your sleeves and get to work!

4. **Add a slide by tapping the New Slide icon (refer to Figure 17-4).**

5. **Use the tools to add drawings, images, shapes, and text to the slide.**

   Draw, type, annotate, use the laser pointer, and more. The best screencasts capture the viewer's attention by being entertaining and easy to understand. Make your screencast interesting and use the tools to help illustrate your points.

6. **Repeat Steps 4 and 5 to add and edit more slides.**

   Remember that you can delete and arrange objects, sort slides, and undo anything you don't like (or did accidentally).

7. **Prepare and rehearse your narration.**

8. **Tap the red Record button on the bottom of the screen, and start recording.**

The timer will indicate time elapsed as you record, and a Pause button will appear. Tap the Pause button to stop while you adjust content, change the slides, or simply collect your thoughts. Tap Record to continue when you're ready.

Start over by tapping the Rewind button and starting your recording again.

Figure 17-5: Insert a fully functioning web browser in your Explain Everything screencast.

9. **Complete and save your screencast by tapping the folder icon with a downward arrow at the bottom-right corner of your screen (refer to Figure 17-4).**

10. **Tap either the Export Image or Export Movie icon in the bottom-right corner of the display.**

    The Export dialog (shown in Figure 17-6) appears. You can choose to export your screencast as a video, image, or even a PDF document; send it directly via e-mail; or export it to the iPad's Photo gallery, YouTube, Dropbox, and more.

Figure 17-6: Export your Explain Everything project as a movie.

Partnering with students

If you're teaching in an environment with lots of iPads, it's guaranteed that there will be times someone needs to explain how to use apps. Sure, you could spend your evenings and weekends trying to catch up and learn how to use the technology, but I can literally feel the level of tension rise as you think about it. Of course, you can ask your tech guy to help, but you know he's already running around helping 20 other people turn on projectors, fix their e-mail, and get their documents to print. Let me remind you that you probably already have direct access to an amazing talent pool of technology experts who would be highly motivated if given the opportunity to help. Yes, your students!

Let your students create tutorials. Allow them to help other students who are having problems using technology. Need help using iMovie? Your iMovie expert is probably seated somewhere in your classroom and would love the opportunity to show what he or she can do: Just ask! Recognizing that you don't always have to be the expert and allowing students to become partners in the educational process will increase student motivation and result in a rich learning environment for everyone — including you. Try it!

18

Releasing Your Inner Artist

In This Chapter

▶ Teaching younger students how to draw

▶ Creating "Doodlecast" narrated illustrations

▶ Producing stop-motion animation

▶ Taking simple time lapse photography

▶ Using Brushes to produce more complex art

*T*he iPad and tablet computing in general progressed rapidly from simple media consumption devices to devices that enable content creation and sharing. One of the areas where that's most evident is in the development of apps for producing different forms of art and media.

Several sections in the book are devoted to the topic of digital storytelling. In this chapter, you're going to break out your virtual painting smocks and get your fingers dirty creating art. Also, don't assume that art is limited to that hour or two a week that kids go to their art lesson. Most traditional academic disciplines have artificial boundaries. They cross over and have relevance in other subject areas as well. Art can be used effectively in English literature, history, and most other subjects. Can you find or create music or art that represents the theme of a book? Some students who have difficulty expressing themselves verbally and in text would excel if given the opportunity to use their artistic abilities.

In recognition of the need to bolster STEM subjects (science, technology, engineering, and mathematics), educators often sacrifice the teaching and use of art in education. That is changing, however. Many now advocate for the teaching of STEAM: science, technology, engineering, art, and mathematics. The outside world is multifaceted. Apple, one of the world's most successful technology companies, would not be where it is today without Steve Jobs's strict emphasis on the art and design of Apple's products, packaging, and marketing. Just as important, our children are not one-dimensional. They have different strengths and talents, and it's essential that you provide them ample opportunity to exercise all of them.

Fortunately, whether you're a professional artist or a kindergarten student, you have at your fingertips many iPad apps that you can use to tap into your creative potential and produce beautiful works. This chapter looks at one app that teaches younger children how to draw from the "bottom" up — a terrible pun that will become apparent when you read the next section. Another app records your narration as you draw and offers tremendous potential for use across the curriculum. You'll have a lot of fun learning how to create stop motion animation. Finally, I look at one of the most popular drawing apps for those who want to unleash their inner van Gogh — and you'll never even have to clean a paintbrush.

Narrating and Illustrating a Doodlecast

Doodlecast for Kids, a unique app for younger iPad users, turns the typical doodled illustration into a narrated video. It takes a novel approach to the typical drawing app by recording your voice while you draw so that you can see and hear your artwork come to life. It's easy to use; just draw and talk at the same time. Tap the Play button when you're done, sit back, and watch and listen as the drawing unfolds in front of you. Kids love watching, and parents or teachers can save the movies and share them.

Doodlecast for Kids is a fun and creative activity. It's also a compelling educational tool. It can be a useful method for children to practice their letters, spelling, and numbers, or even to get children to discuss their feelings. Doodlecast can help children explore their imagination by telling stories while drawing elements in them . . . or, alternatively, practice their drawing skills while explaining the illustration.

The interface is simple and easy to navigate. It comes with more than 20 drawing prompts, which are simple questions designed to give children a starting point in creating a story. It could be a topic like "clothing" or an adjective such as "messy." Budding artists take their inspiration from there. Frankly, I could go on talking about "messy clothing" for hours — just ask my kids! These prerecorded prompts are played at the beginning of the video.

The following steps take you through the process of creating a Doodlecast:

1. **To begin creating your own Doodlecast, tap the Start prompt on the opening screen.**

2. **Select a theme from 12 drawing templates that contain an object or location.**

   Your choices include a sky, park, or boots (among others), or select among 12 word bubbles that contain adjectives, such as *loud, happy,* or *stinky.*

Depending on the theme you chose, the app then asks you a question such as "Who is wearing the boots?" or "What tastes yucky?" You can also elect to skip the themes and start with a blank page.

3. **Select the Brush tool to start your drawing.**

   A brush menu appears with nine color options and three brush sizes.

4. **Tap your selection and start your Doodlecast.**

   The recording will start automatically when you enter the following screen. While you're drawing, the app records the audio. You have up to three minutes, and a time meter at the top of the screen (see Figure 18-1) keeps track of the time remaining.

   You can pause the recording at any point by tapping the large dot on the lower left of the display.

Watch your time here

Figure 18-1: Doodlecast records your narration as you draw your picture.

5. **Tap the Record button, and tap Pause.**

   The button will change from red to black. To resume, tap the button again. Use the break to change or clear your drawing or to collect your thoughts.

6. **When you're finished, tap the triangular Play arrow, and tap Done on the pop-out menu.**

Doodlecast prepares your movie, and you can tap the Play arrow to see your completed movie. You can also tap Save (see Figure 18-2) to export the video to the camera roll or upload it to YouTube if you have an account.

Figure 18-2: Doodlecast turns your drawing into a movie with your narrated soundtrack.

Drawing from the "Bottom" Up with Everything Butt Art

Sometimes when you want to capture someone's attention, you resort to using little gimmicks. This small app has one that seems to resonate with younger children. Everything Butt Art is an iPad drawing app that teaches kids how to draw zoo animals . . . with a twist. It shows you step by step how to create the drawing, and it starts with a butt shape. It's really just a rounded lowercase *w,* and of course, it isn't really about derrieres. That's just the hook the app uses to engage children to learn how to draw. And it works.

When you first open the app, you have the option of creating a profile that will give you certain benefits, including saving and sharing, earning badges for drawing accomplishments, and getting e-mail notifications — or using a guest profile. Tap your selection and proceed to the next screen.

The home page of Everything Butt Art, shown in Figure 18-3, presents a menu of four choices — Draw, Read, Butt Hunt, and Gallery — and I explain each in the following sections.

Figure 18-3: Everything Butt Art has a main menu of four choices.

Everything Butt Art is an engaging way for kids to learn how to draw simple animals, and younger kids are sure to get a giggle out of the whole butt gimmick. It's quite simple and easy to master, and although it has limited use, it's still a nice start to developing the skill of drawing. True, your child may never become a Picasso by using this app . . . but then again, how many butts do you think Picasso would have found in the illustrations?

Draw

When you tap Draw, you see a screen full of animals. Choose any one that you'd like to draw by tapping it and following the step-by-step instructions. You can also tap the Freestyle button at the top-right corner, which takes you to an empty page where you can use drawing tools and draw anything yourself.

To draw an animal, follow these steps:

1. **Tap Draw.**

   You will see a selection of animals and animal packs to choose among. Three animals come free with the app, and two add-on packs of six animals each can be purchased separately. (Each comes with step-by-step drawing, book pages, and shape search game.)

2. **Tap an animal to select it.**

   The next screen displays your animal and step-by-step directions for the final drawing on the bottom. You are presented with two choices: Show Me and Draw.

   Tap the Show Me button to see an animated demonstration as the animal is drawn onscreen for you. The Draw button starts the step-by-step drawing process.

3. **Tap the Draw button.**

   You'll see the steps numbered in a row under the drawing. Your notebook page will be blank except for the outline of the starting butt shape.

4. **Select the Pencil tool and a color, and trace the outline.**

5. **When you're done, tap the next step to display the next set of outlines.**

6. **Continue until you have completed the drawing.**

   Note that as you tap any of the tools, such as Pencil or Paintbrush, you get a pop-up slider that enables you to set the width of the strokes.

7. **To color in your drawing, tap the Paintbrush icon, and select a paintbrush color.**

   This generally is the last step. The paintbrush layer is underneath the pencil layer so that when you color it in, you don't cover the drawing lines.

   A completed drawing is shown in Figure 18-4.

Once you have tried it a few times and feel like you're getting the hang of it, try a more challenging task and draw the animal without tapping each step to add the tracing outlines.

Maybe I'm just a klutz, but my fingers weren't made for drawing on a touchscreen. If you're anything like me, invest in a stylus, and use it for writing and drawing. Also, I recommend paying a few extra dollars to get one that's responsive and accurate.

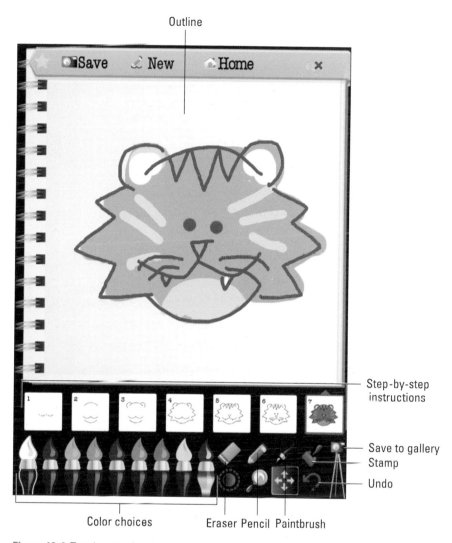

Figure 18-4: Tap the step-by-step instructions and trace the outline of your animal.

Read

Tapping the Read option on the main menu takes you to an illustrated page with fun facts about one of the animals. This page includes an illustration of the completed animal plus the step-by-step drawing Instructions — this time including the body (see Figure 18-5).

Tap the speech bubble icon at the top-left of the screen to have the facts read out loud using the voice of a child. The facts are usually informative and entertaining. Did you know how many pounds of bananas a gorilla eats every day? I didn't think so.

Tap the arrows in the bottom corners to turn the page. Each animal has an illustrated page. Tap the star button on the top right to pop up the Home Menu option.

Figure 18-5: Each animal in the Read section has an illustrated page with fun facts.

Butt Hunt

The Butt Hunt option leads you to an illustrated page where you can search for hidden butt shapes. Take a tip from me: Have your children turn down the volume before they start this activity. The background jungle noises aren't quite as cute when they all go off at full volume.

Ready for your butt hunt? Tap the Start button to begin as the child narrator challenges you with that question for the ages: "How many butts can you find?"

Tap the butt shapes in the illustration as you find them, and they highlight while a scoreboard keeps track of your finds. I have to confess that it's actually pretty difficult to find them all. (I found only 2 out of 17 butts, but that jungle soundtrack was making me crazy!)

Gallery

If you signed up for an account, the drawings are saved to an online gallery that can be set to public or private. If you elected to remain a Guest, the Gallery remains in the app.

Creating Stop-Motion Animation

Mix an iPad camera, some art supplies, the Animate It! app, and a healthy dose of imagination, and you can create some amazing stop-motion animation videos. Aardman Animations Studios, the creator of the *Wallace and Gromit* series, has created Animate It!, a wonderful app that lets you create your own stop-motion animations.

Traditionally, creating stop-motion animation was a cumbersome and time-consuming process. You'd have to physically arrange objects, walk back behind a camera, and snap a photo; then move the objects and repeat the process. Of course, if your objects weren't moved in exactly the right alignment and spacing, you'd have to shoot the frames again.

Animate It! lets you snap a series of images on your own portable device. Take it anywhere, create a scene, and animate on the go. You can create your scene and objects out of anything that's available. Plasticene (you've probably heard of claymation) is great. Use LEGO pieces, paper, puppets . . . anything. You can even draw or write something on paper and take images of the message/illustration developing and moving. Considering the quality of the output you can produce, using the app is relatively simple. And I can guarantee it's a boatload of fun.

Animate It! (see Figure 18-6) includes features and tools that bring any subject to life, including a time-lapse feature, variable frame rates (to ensure that your animation is smooth and consistent), as well as copy, paste, reorder, and frame deletion functions. You can export your creation in several formats, including HD.

Figure 18-6: Create amazing stop-motion animation videos with Animate It!

Why use stop-motion animation? I'm glad you asked:

- **It makes you break down, analyze, and re-create an event in small, bite-sized pieces.** Consider using it in a science class, for example, to have students demonstrate the evolution of a process. It could be the water cycle showing the stages of transpiration, precipitation, and so forth. Maybe it's the life cycle of a butterfly.

- **Re-create events.** Use it in a social science class to get students to re-create a famous scene from history, such as the Battle of Little Big Horn or the American soldiers raising the flag on Iwo Jima in World War II. One motivated group of students did a stop-motion movie of U.S. history from the Native Americans to the moon landing! Okay, I admit, it was an abridged version of American history, but it was wonderfully entertaining nonetheless. Imagine the planning, research, and teamwork that went into that project.

- Have students create a short animation to illustrate an event or scene from the book they're reading in literature. It's a great alternative to dioramas.

Students can use action figures, plastic figurines, LEGO pieces, Kinex, paper cutouts, drawings, plasticene, or Play-Doh to create scenes. Kids will have a blast creating movies. Your biggest problem might be dragging them out of their chairs at the end of the lesson.

To create a stop-motion project, follow these steps:

1. **Develop an idea, and build your scene complete with props and objects that move.**

   Be creative! Use a variety of props and materials. Paper, LEGOs, plants, plasticene . . . whatever is available to set up your scene, like the one shown in Figure 18-7.

   - Plan how your objects will move, and make sure you've built your objects out of material that can move in the way you've intended.

   - If you need objects to move through the air, think of a way to move them with string or wire.

   - To add titles and comments, just take photos of colorful, handwritten pieces of paper. You can have titles appear a letter at a time by taking photos of the message as it develops.

   - Set your scene in a spot with even lighting. The camera has a hard time dealing with shadows and glare.

Figure 18-7: Set up your scene in advance by using creative materials and props.

2. **Start a new project by tapping the + icon on the top-right corner of the opening screen.**

3. **Set up your camera and take a picture by tapping the camera button (see Figure 18-8) on the right side of the toolbar.**

Your picture will appear as a frame on a filmstrip along the bottom of the screen.

Animate It! shows you a ghosted copy of your previous photo onscreen to help you adjust your objects for the next photo. This helpful feature gives you a precise idea of where your last frame is and guides you in placing your objects.

Export　Undo　Copy　Play　Review　Take photo

Figure 18-8: Tap the photo icon to snap an image and then move your objects.

4. **Continue moving your objects and taking lots of pictures that tell your story.**

   Most users underestimate the number of images needed. Remember, you're taking every frame as a photo. Even at a fairly slow rate, you'll display between four and eight images per second. Move your objects in reasonably small increments.

5. **Review and edit your stop-motion movie:**

   • To delete and move frames, touch and hold a frame to move it to a different position, or move it out of the timeline to see it "vaporized."

   • Tap the Undo button to erase your last action.

   • Review the last five frames by tapping the Review button.

- Adjust the camera's exposure, white balance, and focus settings, and switch between front and rear cameras if your device supports these features. Tap the Review button and then tap the editing screen. The menu buttons will appear onscreen.

6. **Tap the Play button to see your animation.**

7. **Tap the Settings icon on the top-right corner of your screen and select Project Settings; on the Project Settings menu, use the sliding bar to adjust your playback speed.**

Even at the slowest playback speeds, your animation may sometimes move too quickly. In the middle of the toolbar, you'll see a button with two frames and an arrow. Highlight any frame and tap that button to duplicate the frame. Creating copies of your frames is a simple way to slow down the animation in areas where it moves too quickly.

8. **Tap the Export button on the toolbar and select an export size.**

Animate It! will create the final video and place it in your photo gallery.

One of the features sorely missing in Animate It! is the capability to add a soundtrack. Take your final video to a movie editing app such as iMovie, and you can add a soundtrack there. Note that another stop-motion animation app, Stop Motion Studio, does allow you to add music or record your own sound. It doesn't, however, have the ghosting feature which is so helpful in building your animations.

Time-lapse photography is when you set up a camera to take a series of photos over a period of time and then turn them into a video. It effectively allows you to accelerate a slowly changing scene and watch it in a fraction of the time.

Animate It! includes a time-lapse feature that allows you to set the capture time (for example, every 30 seconds), the duration in minutes, and the number of frames that you want to capture. The time lapse will automatically stop once the required number of frames has been captured. Time lapse can be a wonderful way of documenting a changing scene. (Think sunset.) You could set up the iPad and take photos of the actions of a turtle or lizard in your classroom overnight. You just need to set up your iPad in a safe spot to record the action taking place.

Painting a Masterpiece with Brushes

The brilliant thing about the Brushes app (see Figure 18-9) is that it's used by artists all over the world, yet it's still simple enough for beginners. It's a powerful tool for creating original artwork on the iPad, and paintings created with Brushes have been shown on the web and in galleries, and have illustrated the cover of *New Yorker* magazine. Even iconic pop artist David Hockney uses Brushes. The app features an advanced color picker, several realistic brushes, layers, and zooming to 32x — all in an uncomplicated but comprehensive interface. And your class of fourth-graders will love it just as much as David Hockney does.

Brushes has multiple layers that you can work on separately and that can be used with or without a stylus, which is a bonus in an educational setting. Another unique feature is that it has a Playback function that allows you to see any art redrawn onscreen. Its quick results certainly make it a hit with kids.

Copyright 2012, Debbie Azar

Figure 18-9: The Brushes iPad app can be used by beginners and professional artists alike.

Getting started in the Gallery

The first thing that you see when you open the app is the gallery, shown in Figure 18-10. It displays your paintings and allows you to navigate between them. Simply swipe your finger to switch from one painting to the next and tap a painting to select it.

The gallery is really a digital sketchbook and can be used as such. Why not create a series of paintings to create a storyboard for a video, a presentation, or to tell a story?

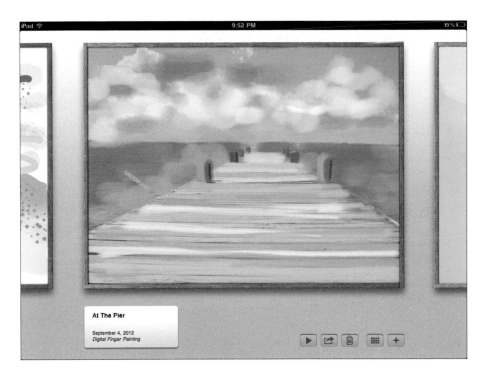

Figure 18-10: Swipe left and right to browse the paintings in your Brushes Gallery.

The main steps in using the Brushes app are as follows:

1. **Tap the + button on the Gallery page to create a new blank painting.**

2. **Choose your color, brush size and shape, and begin painting with your finger or stylus.**

   Paint by moving your finger across the screen. It's as simple as that. If you want more detail, you can pinch to zoom in up to 32x. I discuss the tools in more detail later in this chapter.

   Brushes creates a painting on multiple layers. Each layer is independent of the others so you can work on a layer without disturbing the contents of the other layers.

   A navigation bar runs along the top of the screen, and a toolbar runs along the bottom. If you want more screen space, tap and hold the bars anywhere on the screen to turn them off.

3. **To name your masterpiece, tap the Settings icon on the top right and select Properties; type the name of your painting in the first line.**

The name of the artist (yes, that would be you) goes on the second line.

4. When you're finished, tap the Gallery button to return to Gallery.

Your painting will automatically be saved. Brushes also allows you to share and export your paintings.

The painting interface offers the following set of tools (along the bottom toolbar, as shown in Figure 18-11):

✔ **Color palette:** Tap the white rectangle in the lower-left corner to bring up an RGB color wheel, as shown in Figure 18-12. Select a color from the boxes on the right, or mix your own individualized palette by using the hue/saturation color wheel on the left. Note that you can also change the darkness and opacity by using the two sliders underneath the wheel.

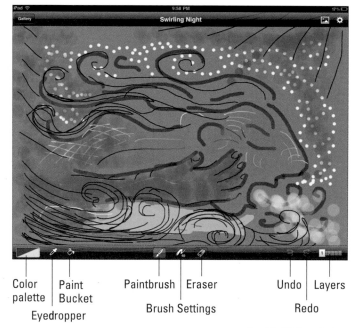

Color palette | Paint Bucket | Paintbrush | Eraser | Undo | Layers
Eyedropper | | Brush Settings | | Redo

Copyright 2012, Benny Ferdman

Figure 18-11: The painting interface has a set of tools along the bottom toolbar.

Sometimes you'll want to blend colors in your painting. Use the transparency slider to make any color more transparent and easier to blend.

✔ **Eyedropper:** Tap the Eyedropper tool or tap and hold anywhere onscreen to activate it. It reads the color under your touch, and makes it the active color. Note that after you use the Eyedropper, the active tool automatically reverts to the Paintbrush.

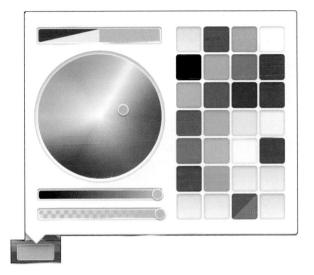

Figure 18-12: Select your painting color from the color palette.

✔ **Paint Bucket:** Use this tool to fill an entire layer with color.

✔ **Paintbrush.** Select this tool to start painting.

✔ **Brush Settings:** Tap the brush icon to bring up the Settings menu, shown in Figure 18-13. There's a sliding selection of brush shapes in a row toward the top. Swipe through and tap to select a brush type. You can control brush spacing, size, and opacity with the sliders underneath.

Although the iPad is not pressure-sensitive, you can make lines with varying thickness that will give you the tapered look of a natural paintbrush stroke. Tap the Brush Settings icon and turn on the options Vary Size with Speed and Vary Opacity with Speed. This enables you to create a truly organic-looking line.

✔ **Eraser:** This tool uses the same features as the Paintbrush except that it removes color instead of adding it. Use the Brush settings to control the quality of the eraser. Just make sure you're on the right layer when you're using it.

✔ **Undo:** Use the Undo tool to step back through the actions you've taken. This feature is for all your "Ugh!" moments.

✔ **Redo:** It looked better before, didn't it? Press Redo to reverse your Undo.

Layers: Layers is a cool feature that artists and designers use all the time in programs like Adobe Photoshop. Brushes allows you to create up to six individual layers that can be separately manipulated and worked on. Work on any one layer without disturbing the contents of other layers. This feature gives you a lot more control over the final result, and layers can be duplicated or discarded as needed.

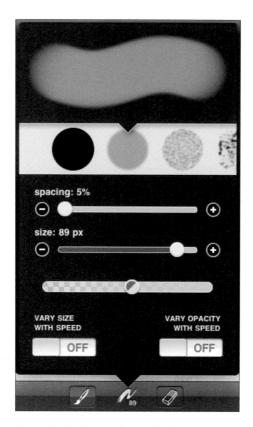

Figure 18-13: Use the Brush Settings to select the brush type, spacing, size, and more.

Layers can be rearranged, deleted, merged, and copied between paintings. You can also adjust the opacity of each layer. How would you use layers? You could have a colored layer as a background, do your drawing in a dark outline on the top layer, and color it in on the middle layer. You can change the background at any time without altering any other layer.

Tap the Layers icon to display the layers menu, shown in Figure 18-14. Your layers will appear as thumbnails with the base layer to the far left. Some things you can do with layers include the following:

- To add a new layer, tap the + icon on the top right.

- To delete a layer, select it by tapping, then tap the Trash icon.

- Use the slider on the bottom-right corner to change the opacity/transparency of a layer.

- Tap any layer to make it the active layer. The selected layer will have a blue highlight around it.

- Change the order of your layers by dragging and dropping them.

Figure 18-14: Work on any one layer without disturbing the contents of other layers.

Layers has many other cool features, and I encourage you to experiment with them. Half the fun is playing with all the different features and seeing how they affect your image.

Paint a little blob of your favorite colors on a separate layer of your painting. That way, using the Eyedropper tool, you can quickly select colors from your palette by tapping and holding the blobs.

Painting over a photograph

An important feature of Brushes is the capability to use photos as the basis for your artwork. In fact, this is the method used for creating the *New Yorker* magazine illustrations. Here are the steps:

1. **Tap the photo icon on the top navigation bar, and pick a photo from your Camera Roll.**

2. **Drag and pinch to position your photo, and tap Accept (or Cancel).**

3. **Add a layer for painting by tapping the Layer icon and then tapping +.**

4. **Select a paintbrush, sample a color from your photo with the Eyedropper tool (or pick an entirely different color), set your brush settings, and paint.**

Note: It's particularly effective to play with the opacity when painting over a photograph if you want to keep some original detail. Do you want to create an impressionist painting? Sample the colors of the photo with your

Eyedropper tool, and choose a large brush to trace the lines and colors of the scene. By getting rid of the detail and just highlighting colors and shapes, you can create an Impressionistic effect. Make sure to work on separate layers so that you can always undo or erase your steps while leaving the photo intact.

Those annoying telephone wires? Just paint them out. You can get different effects by playing with the blending modes in the Layers menu to have your layers interact in different ways, as shown in Figure 18-15. The best way to learn is by experimenting.

Figure 18-15: Brushes enables you to insert photos and use layers to paint over them.

Watching a masterpiece evolve

Brushes records all the actions taken in a painting. You can then watch a "video" of your painting as it took place, revealing all the steps you took in creating your art. It's kind of magical — like those time-lapse movies of flowers blooming that you used to love as a kid. Just tap the Play button in Gallery to watch an exact replay of your painting process.

You can also open your paintings in Brushes Viewer, a free application for Mac OS X. Brushes Viewer allows you to replay your paintings stroke for stroke, export them at very high resolutions (up to 1920x2880 pixels), and even export them as QuickTime movies.

19

Creating Multimedia Conversations

. . . .

In This Chapter

▶ Examining the educational role of multimedia conversations

▶ Creating a VoiceThread project

▶ Commenting on shared VoiceThreads

▶ Managing student accounts and sharing options

. . . .

You've probably used presentations at some point at school or work. They can be an effective way to deliver information visually, but one of their drawbacks is that the information flows in one direction. They tend to become lectures. It's always ironic to sit in a presentation that calls for more communication and collaboration in education . . . yet the presenter spends the entire session giving a frontal lecture. Education thrives in an atmosphere of interaction and dialogue.

VoiceThread (www.voicethread.com) is a unique site that enables you to create web-based multimedia slide shows that encourage conversation among the audience. It has been used successfully in many schools for several years and can be accessed by logging into the site — and now there's even an app that enables you to create and contribute to VoiceThread conversations directly on your iPad.

Designing Multimedia Conversations

You start your VoiceThread conversation by creating an online slide show comprised of any combination of media, such as images, video, audio, and text. When you're done with that part, you share your VoiceThread by inviting friends, students, and colleagues to view and comment on it, as shown in Figure 19-1. They leave comments using text, audio, or a webcam. The end result is a vibrant, multimedia conversation that gives everyone a voice — even those students who may not normally participate in your regular classroom discussions.

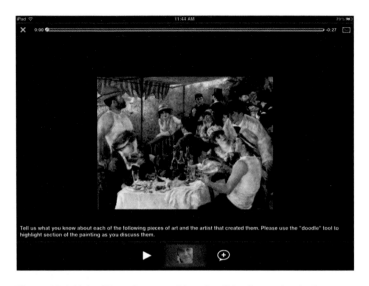

Figure 19-1: VoiceThreads are multimedia slide shows that invite conversations.

There are many reasons to use VoiceThread as an educational tool:

- ✓ Communicating with different media is an important component of a modern education. VoiceThread is a simple method for integrating multimedia into any curriculum. Instead of reading a textbook about learning French, you can have your students use their language skills by creating and narrating a virtual tour through Paris.

- ✓ VoiceThreads give students feedback from an audience. That can be an empowering experience. Sharing options enable you to set the parameters of your audience to a single teacher, classmates or group, the school community, or the public. You also have the option to moderate comments so that they require approval before appearing online.

- ✓ VoiceThreads can be the work of an individual or the product of group collaboration. People can work together and contribute individual slides into a single VoiceThread.

- ✓ VoiceThreads can be a unique way for a student to deliver a portfolio of work in the format of a slide show with narration and reflection upon the objectives and results of each piece of work.

- ✓ Giving meaningful feedback on a VoiceThread is a critical part of the process and an important skill in itself. Allowing students to contribute comments on VoiceThreads develops their ability to critically evaluate the work of others and offer constructive feedback.

- ✓ Multimedia slide shows are extremely effective tools for expressing knowledge of a concept, delivering compelling stories, creating tutorials, relating historical events and biographies, practicing use of a foreign language, and much more. Some sample projects might include

- Explaining a concept in science with images, video and narration. You can also use a doodle tool to highlight parts of an image as you discuss them.

- Using VoiceThread with K–2 students who may not be ready to write but are perfectly able and willing to tell stories with audio. VoiceThread comments can be left as text, audio, or video. (See Figure 19-2.)

- Creating groups that allow conversations with classes in different cities or countries.

- Learning about basic mathematical concepts such as parabolas or right angles by finding or taking images of real-world examples and explaining them in a VoiceThread.

- Using webcam commenting to enable conversations between people in sign language.

- Adding new dimensions to the art of writing a story by having students find or create images that express their story themes and then writing and narrating their stories while displaying the images.

- Researching and creating a narrated family history that includes photos and video interviews of family members.

- Distributing visuals to students as a VoiceThread and having students respond with comments. For example, use a series of related photos and have students write a story to explain the images. Find a public-domain clip from a famous movie or create a short video. Strip the sound out, and ask the students to write and narrate a screenplay with dialogue for each character.

Figure 19-2: Leave comments as text, audio, or video.

Creating a VoiceThread

To use VoiceThread, you must create a VoiceThread account. To register, go to www.voicethread.com and tap the Register link in the top-right corner of the screen. Sign up for a free account with your e-mail address and password.

Once you have a VoiceThread account, you can create VoiceThread slide shows by logging in on the website or by using the VoiceThread app on the iPad.

To create a VoiceThread slide show on your iPad, follow these steps:

1. **Tap the VoiceThread icon on your iPad to start the app.**

2. **Tap the Create icon on the bottom toolbar.**

   You'll get a screen with a large green + symbol.

3. **Tap the symbol.**

   You'll be prompted with a Library icon to add content from your iPad photo library, and a Camera icon, which will activate the iPad camera so you can take a photo that is added directly to your VoiceThread.

   The version of the VoiceThread app at the time of publishing was somewhat limited in its handling of video and commenting on slides that contained video. To work with a VoiceThread with video, use a laptop or desktop computer and log into the VoiceThread website. Open your project and add your video there.

4. **Add as many images as you want; each one becomes a slide in your VoiceThread.**

5. **Add comments by tapping the + balloon on the bottom toolbar.**

   You have several options to add comments to any slide in your VoiceThread. Add comments using your preferred media:

   - Tap the ABC icon and type text comments.
   - Tap the microphone icon and add audio narration.
   - Tap. the camera icon, primp your hair, and talk to the iPad's webcam

   Leave your comments on any slide by swiping the screen to the left or right to navigate between slides in your VoiceThread, and then tapping the + comment icon.

   If you're adding an audio or video comment, you can also "doodle" by tapping the circle icon in the bottom-right corner and drawing on the screen with your finger or a stylus. Doodling is a great way to highlight parts of the slide as you talk.

6. **Share.**

   If you are using the VoiceThread Educator account (available through the VoiceThread website), each time a student in your class group shares her VoiceThread with you, it automatically appears in the My Groups section on the home page of the VoiceThread app. At this point, the iPad app only allows sharing via e-mail. For more advanced sharing options, I recommend logging into your VoiceThread account in the browser on a computer.

The basic VoiceThread account is free. You also have the option of upgrading to an Educator account that enables you to add and manage student accounts. Upgrade to a Single Educator account and you can manage up to 50 student accounts. You can also get a School or District subscription. With this upgrade, a central administrator can create teacher and student accounts for everyone in the school. You can then create VoiceThread groups for each class or grade level for easy sharing among groups.

To comment on a shared VoiceThread, tap the Home icon on the bottom row (see Figure 19-3) for your menu of options and then tap the Shared with Me category. These are all the VoiceThreads that others have shared with you. If commenting has been enabled, you will be able to open the VoiceThread and add your comments to it.

If you're a teacher with an Educator account, all VoiceThreads created by the students in your group are automatically shared with you.

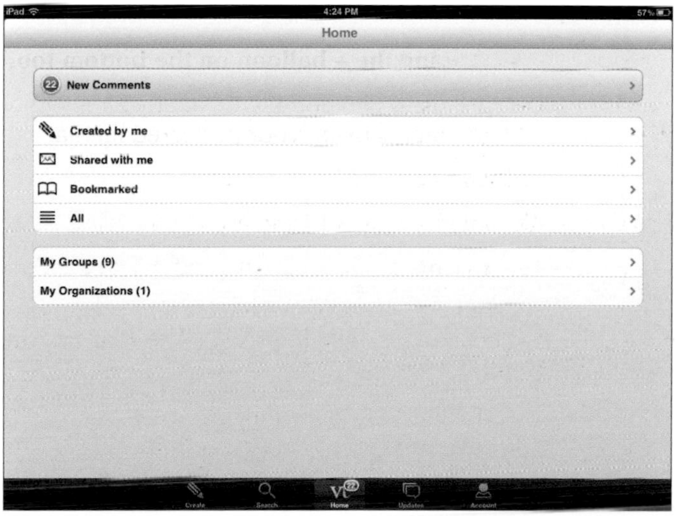

Figure 19-3: The main menu gives you access to the VoiceThread projects.

Managing Accounts and Sharing Options

The VoiceThread iPad app is a great tool for students to create quick and simple multimedia slide shows and add comments. When it comes to your more administrative functions such as managing student accounts and sharing their VoiceThreads, I recommend using a laptop or desktop computer and signing into the VoiceThread website at www.voicethread.com. At this writing, you can add and manage student accounts and groups only through the website, as shown in Figure 19-4. That function is not available in the iPad app. Similarly, you'll also have a greater range of sharing options using the VoiceThread website.

All the VoiceThreads created by students in your class group will be listed under the My Voice tab. You can keep any VoiceThread completely private, share it with any group such as your class, or make it completely public. When sharing, you can also specify whether the user can only view or is also permitted to leave comments. The iPad app is limited to sharing via e-mail in the current version.

Many students may be using an iPad at school but not at home. VoiceThread is web-based, which means it works on any web browser as well as the app on your iPad. If you don't have your iPad, simply go to www.voicethread.com on any laptop or desktop to access your VoiceThread account. All the projects you started on your iPad will be available in the My Voice tab, where you can continue to edit and share them.

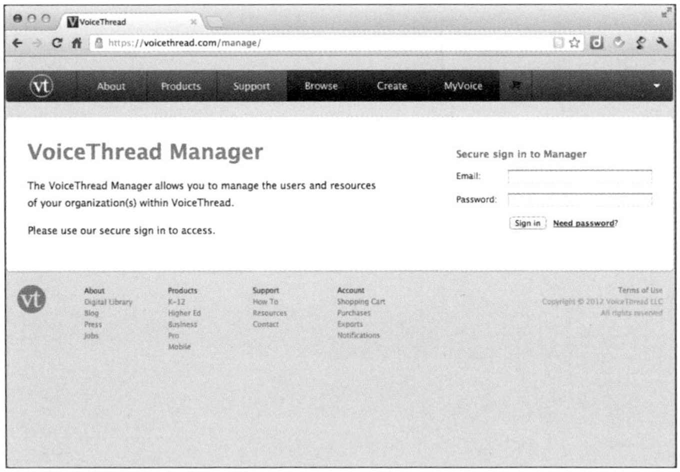

Figure 19-4: Use the VoiceThread website to administer accounts and manage sharing.

Part VI
The iPad Classroom

The 5th Wave — By Rich Tennant

"I understand you've found a system to reduce the number of complaints we receive by 50 percent."

In this part . . .

Printing, photocopying, presenting, using your whiteboard . . . you know there's a better way. I show you some exciting digital alternatives you can start using immediately! Create a digital whiteboard and share it with others. Record snippets of your lessons for later review. A range of options awaits you.

20

Printing and Scanning

*A*ny new technology, iPad or otherwise, takes time to develop and mature. We find new ways to use the technology and discover features we'd love to see included. Printing is a perfect case in point. Initially, Apple didn't feel that the iPad needed a print function. Content was becoming digital, and the prevailing opinion was the less paper used, the better. Then users started clamoring for a way to print the content they consumed and created on iPads. That was certainly the case in schools. Teachers have traditionally required students to create and hand in paper-based work. When schools jumped to buy iPads, teachers struggled with the problem of how to collect work from students. Frankly, many still do.

In this chapter, I look at how Apple added a new AirPrint capability to allow users to print to certain printers wirelessly. I discuss some of those solutions and how they can enable anyone to print. Some popular solutions allow for *virtual printing* — the delivery of files to a common location where you can store and browse them in digital format or print them on paper. There's an incredible wealth of options when setting up virtual printers to handle all different storage and file handling needs.

Paper-based workflows aren't the requirement they've been in the past, and this chapter is about more than just printing. It's about options for delivering content from an iPad to other computers, people, and applications. There are some wonderfully innovative solutions in this chapter. Go grab a cup of tea, sit back, and have fun reading about them.

Printing with AirPrint

The iPad was meant to be part of a paperless environment, but it is still (perhaps reluctantly) designed for printing, which means the good news is yes, printing is built into your iPad. More good news: You can print from your iPad without the help of that expensive IT guy. AirPrint is a wireless technology that creates a connection between AirPrint-enabled applications on your iOS device and any printer that supports AirPrint technology. So, in short, you can print from your iPad . . . but only from iPad apps that include AirPrint support and only to printers that are AirPrint enabled. Sounds complicated, but I break it down for you in this section.

To check whether a printer is AirPrint enabled, go to the Apple support website (`http://support.apple.com/kb/HT4356`), where a list is constantly being updated.

Apple apps such as Pages, Keynote, Mail, Photos, and Safari all support AirPrint. There are also many third-party apps from the App Store that support AirPrint. If you have an AirPrint-enabled printer, the process is easy: You simply tap Print from within your app, select an AirPrint-enabled printer, and print. Follow these steps:

1. **Tap the curved-arrow action icon shown in Figure 20-1.**

Tap this icon to see printer options.

Figure 20-1: Print directly to AirPrint-enabled printers from apps that have AirPrint support.

2. Tap Print.

You see a list where (ideally) you can select your printer. If you can't find any printers listed, there are several possible reasons:

- Your printer isn't turned on, has an error such as an empty paper tray, or needs a firmware update.

- Your printer isn't connected to the same Wi-Fi network as your iPad. AirPrint works only if the two are on the same Wi-Fi network.

- Your printer doesn't support AirPrint printing.

3. If your printer is listed, configure the printer options and tap Print.

At this point, you're either elated to see your print job coming out of the printer or cursing and wondering how you're going to print. Relax — there are plenty of options for those with and without AirPrint-enabled printers.

Connecting to Physical and Virtual Printers

So your printer didn't show up as an option on the AirPrint list when you went to print? Join the club. The list of AirPrint-enabled printers is growing, but many of us still don't have one. Several app developers jumped in to fill that void and, in doing so, offer features way above and beyond simple printing from your iPad. Options include enabling you to print to any physical printer, as well as creating *virtual printers* that use the iPad print function to send content from iPad apps to a folder on any computer on your network.

Printopia

Download and install Printopia on your Mac computer and share its printers with any iOS device on the same wireless network. Any physical printers available to your Mac will show up as an AirPrint-enabled print option for iPads. Printopia also offers compelling workflow options other than printing. You download the Printopia utility directly to your Mac laptop or desktop, not your iPad. (Printopia works only on Mac computers, but I look at a comparable solution for Windows users in the next section.)

Printopia turns your computer into an AirPrint server, allowing you to share any or all of the shared or networked printers on your network. Whether you have an inkjet printer, a laser printer plugged into your router, or a network printer — whatever type of printer you have — if your Mac can print to it, Printopia will share it with your iOS devices.

Once Printopia is installed on your computer, go to any iOS app that supports printing and tap the Print button, and all of a sudden, all the printers connected to your computer will show up as options — whether they support AirPrint or not!

To get started, follow these steps:

1. **Download and install the Printopia software on your Mac computer.**

   It's available from the publisher's website at www.ecamm.com/mac/printopia.

2. **Double-click Install Printopia.**

   After installation, the Printopia dialog (see Figure 20-2) displays the list of printers connected to your computer. All of your available printers and the Printopia virtual printers are automatically enabled for sharing via AirPrint. (I explain how to use the virtual printers in the next section.)

Figure 20-2: Select printers to share, and Printopia connects them to your iOS devices.

3. **Select the ones you want to make available for sharing by clicking the check box to the left of the printer name.**

4. **Close the dialog when you're done.**

   Checked printers will appear as available printing options for iPads on the network.

5. **Select the Print option in an app on your iPad.**

   The printers you shared in Printopia appear as print options. Easy.

Using virtual printers

Physical printing isn't the only function Printopia offers. Its *virtual printers* (which send your iPad content to a folder on a Mac) are great solutions for digital workflows as well. Click the + button at the bottom of your printer list in Printopia on your Mac for additional options. You'll see the following options:

- **Send directly to a folder on your Mac.** Create a Send to Mac virtual printer to save/print a PDF copy of a document, or a JPEG or PNG version of an image, to a folder on your Mac.

  Add unlimited Send to Mac virtual printers. This lets you deliver a file directly to your Mac. Let's say that you want to collect some Pages documents from student iPads. Open Printopia and create a folder on your Mac — let's call it Pages Assignments. Click the + symbol under the printers in your Printopia dialog on your Mac and select the virtual printer Save to Folder on Mac. Select the Pages Assignments folder you just created. Now students can send their documents right on to your Mac in a folder ready for your review. Printing from Pages is shown in Figure 20-3.

  Keep your files organized by configuring multiple virtual printers with different save destinations. For example, set up one folder as a virtual printer on your Mac to collect the history project students are submitting. Set up another folder and virtual printer for the science assignment, and so on. In that way, student submissions will be neatly organized in separate folders on your Mac.

- **Send directly to an application on your Mac.** A feature in Printopia sends a copy of any content file on your iPad to your Mac and then opens it within a designated application.

Figure 20-3: The Send to Mac virtual printer sends files to any folder on your computer.

For example, I'm constantly taking screen shots and pictures on my iPad. Given my less-than-stellar photographic skills, I always end up needing to touch them up in a photo editor. Using Printopia, I can create a virtual printer that sends a file directly into Adobe Photoshop on my Mac.

Tap the + sign in under the printer list in the Printopia dialog, and select Send to Application. Select Adobe Photoshop as the application, and that's it. You now have a virtual printer that will send an image to your Mac and open it automatically in Photoshop! Figure 20-4 shows you the process. It's so incredibly convenient!

✔ **Send files directly to your Dropbox or Evernote account.** Add a virtual printer to send content to your Dropbox folder. You can even designate which folder in Dropbox to use. Once sent to your Mac's Dropbox folder, the content is synced to your online account and all your other devices that use Dropbox.

Do you need to save expense receipts? Take a quick picture and send it to an Expenses folder you created on Dropbox. Having a special day at your child's soccer game? Create a folder and send the photos directly to it for easy organization and archiving.

✔ **Password-protect your folders:** Worried about junk? Every physical and virtual printer you share in Printopia can be configured with password security. Even if someone has access to your wireless network and can therefore see your shared printers, he or she can't print or save files to your Mac without knowing and using a specific password.

Printopia has done a wonderful job of satisfying users who still require some amount of paper printing while also offering a host of virtual printer options for organizing and working with digital content. It's one of my indispensable tools.

Figure 20-4: Send to Application sends iPad content directly to an application on your Mac.

Other printing solutions

If only everything in life could be perfect . . . but it isn't. There are two potential problems for some users looking to purchase Printopia: It doesn't work in Windows, and it shares printers with users on the same wireless network. Collobos Software offers a product called Fingerprint that's close in functionality to Printopia and works on both Windows and Mac platforms. Setup and use are remarkably similar, and you can download the software from www.collobos.com. Remember that just as with Printopia, the software is installed on your computer, not your iPad. It will then share your physical and virtual printers so that they can be accessed from the Print function on any iOS device.

Epson iPrint

The Epson iPrint app, shown in Figure 20-5, is one example of how printer manufacturers have jumped to create printer-specific apps that address users needing to print directly from their iPad. It's published by Epson and a great solution for those who already own a wireless Epson printer. Here's what you get with the free Epson iPrint app:

Figure 20-5: Control your Epson printer and scanner with the Epson iPrint app.

- ✔ You can arrange and print the photos on your iPad.
- ✔ Use the built-in web browser to print web pages.
- ✔ iPrint will print a variety of files, including Microsoft Word, Excel, and PowerPoint files, and PDF documents. Print stored files or e-mail attachments.

✔ iPrint allows you to connect to cloud services such as Google Docs, Dropbox, Box, and Evernote, and print files you have in your account.

✔ If you have an Epson multifunction printer, you can connect to the scan function and preview any document you've placed in the printer. Set the scan resolution, crop, and then scan the document. Save the scan to your iPad; then e-mail or print it. The entire interface is controlled wonderfully from your iPad without the need to use your laptop or desktop.

✔ Configure your print options, including paper size and type, number of copies, and one- or two-sided printing.

✔ Check your printer's status and ink levels.

iPrint does have one rather annoying flaw: Everything has to be managed and printed from within the iPrint app itself. It isn't a very convenient interface because you usually want to print something from within the app you're using as you're creating and editing it. Instead, you have to save your file somewhere that iPrint can get it and download it into the iPrint app, and only then can you print. That can be a little frustrating. If and when iPrint can function as a print service that's available from within all apps, it will be a killer app for owners of Epson printers.

Hewlett-Packard also offers its own app, called HP ePrint, that's available through the App Store. ePrint will print to your HP printer over a Wi-Fi network or over the Internet.

21

Presenting

As I discuss in Chapter 1, I'm not an advocate for frontal lecturing in school. The use of technology should focus on empowering students to research, explore, discover, and create. Having said that, it doesn't mean that there's isn't any need for teachers to lecture and demonstrate on occasion. Teachers still need to teach core skills, present important information, facilitate classroom discussions, and more.

In this chapter, I look at a couple of ways to deliver presentations on an iPad:

✔ Creating and delivering the presentation with Keynote on an IPad

✔ Creating presentations on a computer and then displaying them on an iPad

Either way works, and you can create your presentation in whatever method seems more convenient to you. I also give you a sneak peek of a new presentation platform — SlideShark — that allows you to deliver a presentation complete with interactive components that check and report on student comprehension.

Creating a Keynote Presentation

The iPad version of Keynote does an admirable job of encapsulating many of the basic functions of its more full-featured version for Macs. You can easily integrate media on your iPad and present it on your iPad. Here is a quick look at some of the many features you can use to build a stunning presentation:

1. **Tap the Keynote icon on your Home screen to open the app and then tap the + icon to start a new presentation.**

   The screen that first appears when you open Keynote is the Document Manager.

2. **Tap the Create Presentation option.**

   You get a selection of 12 designs. Each theme comes with a selection of predesigned slide formats that contain placeholders for titles, text, images, and more.

3. **Select the theme of your choice.**

   You enter the presentation editor.

4. **Add slides by tapping the Add Slide icon at the bottom of the column to add a new slide.**

   When you add a slide, you'll be presented with a range of slide layouts that are included with the theme.

5. **Select a layout by tapping it.**

6. **Organize and edit your slides.**

   The Navigator (see Figure 21-1) displays your slides in the column on the left of the editor. From there, organize slides:

   • Tap any slide to select it.

   • Move a slide by simply tapping it in the Navigator and dragging it to a new location in your presentation.

   • Move multiple slides by tapping and holding one and then tapping additional slides with another finger.

7. **Add and edit text and objects such as images, charts, shapes, and tables.**

   You can manipulate text and objects in these ways:

   • *Edit text.* Double-tap text to edit and replace it with your own. Select any text and tap the Format icon on the top toolbar to change the font and style of the text.

   • *Edit objects.* Tap and edit any object in your slides. When you select an object, handles appear around the selection. Drag a corner to resize the object or twist and rotate it. Drag the object to move it to a new location. Guidelines automatically appear to make it easy to align the object with other objects in your slide.

Tap to return to
Document Manager

Tap to undo

Insert Tools

Format

Play

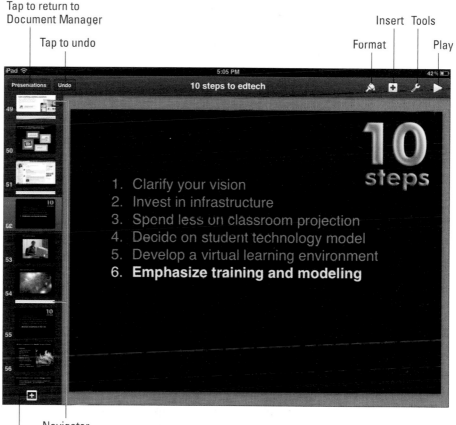

Navigator

Tap to add a slide

Figure 21-1: Organize and edit your slide in the Keynote editor.

- *Add text and objects.* Tap the + Insert button on the top toolbar to add text, charts, tables, shapes, or any images from your Photo galleries.

- *Change object styles.* Select an object in your slide and tap the Format paintbrush button on the top toolbar; a menu pops up (see Figure 21-2) that enables you to change the appearance of your object. Change colors, font, and styles of text. Add shadows, reflections, and frames to images and shapes. Play with the design of your objects to add maximum visual impact to your slides.

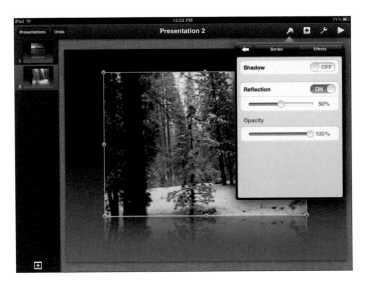

Figure 21-2: Use styles to add shadows, reflections, and frames to images.

- *Use charts to present data visually.* Tap any chart that you added, and select the Edit Data option on the pop-up menus to add your data to a spreadsheet. The chart will update to reflect your data.

- *Add object animations.* You can make objects appear dynamically on your slide by adding animation effects. Tap an object and select Animate from the pop-up menu. Experiment with the Build In options to alter how the object first appears on your slide. Build Out animations add a transition effect to the way the object disappears. Keynote will demonstrate the animation for you when you apply it. Click the Done button on the top left of your screen when you're Tap.

8. **Add slide transition effects**.

   Slide transitions are effects applied to the way one slide leads into the next during your presentation. Tap a slide in the Navigator to select it and then tap it a second time to pop up a menu of options (see Figure 21-3). Select Transition and experiment with the different transition effects. Keynote will demonstrate the transition as you tap and select it. Tap the Done button on the top left of your screen when you're finished.

9. **Tap the Play button on the right of your top toolbar.**

   The presentation plays in full screen from the current slide. Tap once or swipe left to move to the next slide, and slide right to go backward. When you're done presenting, pinch anywhere on your slide to go back into editing mode.

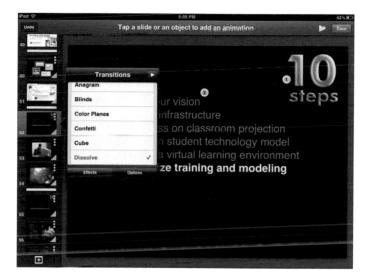

Figure 21-3: Add transitions between the slides in your presentation.

10. **Tap the Tools button on the top toolbar to print or share your presentation via e-mail.**

    You can also copy your presentation to iTunes and then access it on your computer in Keynote, PDF, or PowerPoint format. If you have an iCloud account, you can have it backed up and synced to your other devices automatically.

    Saving is the easiest part because your presentation is automatically saved for you — in the Document Manager — as you work.

11. **In the editor, tap the Presentations button in the top-left corner to return to the Document Manager to rename your presentation.**

12. **To rename a file, tap its name and replace it with a new name.**

13. **(Optional) Drag one presentation over another (see Figure 21-4) to organize them into folders.**

Figure 21-4: Drag one presentation over another to organize presentations into folders.

You can create your Keynote on a Mac or on your iPad. As much as I love Keynote for the iPad, if you're more comfortable on your laptop or desktop it may be easier to create your presentation there. Be aware, however, that the versions of Keynote for Mac and Keynote for iPad are not the same, and you'll need to be careful to avoid potential pitfalls (such as your formatting getting all messed up) when displaying your Mac Keynote on an iPad.

Winning presentations aren't the result of dazzling slide transitions and animations. It helps to keep some simple rules in mind when creating your presentation:

- ✔ **Less is more.** Keep your slide text to a minimum. Your audience will become bored very quickly if you just read text from your slides.

- ✔ **Use imaginative visuals that capture people's attention and represent a point you're trying to make.**

- ✔ **Challenge your audience to think.** Pose questions and encourage participation.

- ✔ **Prepare and rehearse.** The most convincing presentations occur when the speaker is well prepared and rehearsed.

Showing PowerPoint Presentations on an iPad

My more Mac-centric friends — and there are a lot of them in the education community — may get upset when I say that Keynote is a great program, but it's traditionally been regarded as the little cousin of PowerPoint. Most of us who have been giving presentations for years have been using PowerPoint and looking for ways to migrate those presentations over to Macs and iPads. Luckily, if you're in that same position, you have several options.

PowerPoint to Keynote

If you have a simple PowerPoint file, you can often open it directly in Keynote. Let me stress, however, that it needs to be a pretty simple PowerPoint presentation. Some functions won't translate — including complicated animations, embedded fonts, branching and linking within the presentation, image editing done in PowerPoint, embedded video, and more — and if your presentation contains those functions, you'll see an error similar to what's shown in Figure 21-5. If you aren't using any of those functions, this may be the easiest way for you to display your PowerPoint presentations on the iPad.

Upload the presentation to a cloud storage service such as Dropbox, e-mail it to yourself, or sync it via iTunes to move the content over to your iPad. Whatever app you're using to open it should have an Open In option that offers Keynote as an option.

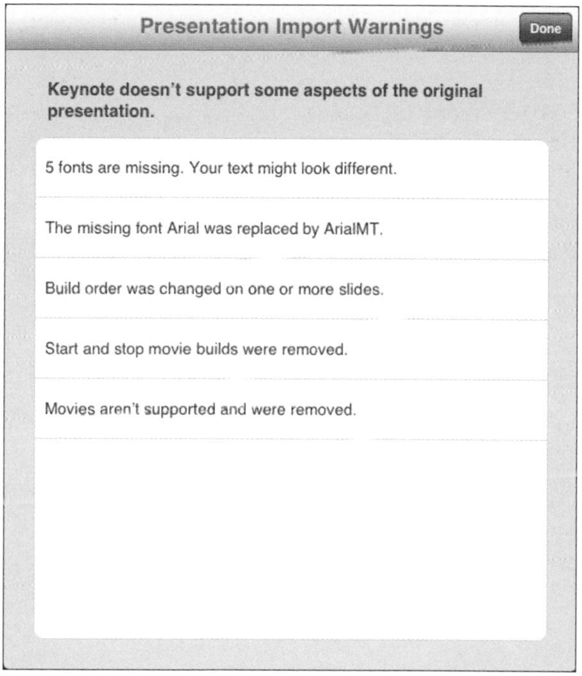

Presentation Import Warnings	Done

Keynote doesn't support some aspects of the original presentation.

5 fonts are missing. Your text might look different.

The missing font Arial was replaced by ArialMT.

Build order was changed on one or more slides.

Start and stop movie builds were removed.

Movies aren't supported and were removed.

Figure 21-5: Opening PowerPoint presentations in Keynote can result in errors.

Exporting as a PDF file

Another option for you to consider is to use the export function in PowerPoint and export your presentation as a PDF. If you're familiar with PDF files, you know they are static documents, which means you lose any animations, transitions, and video in your presentations. If that's not an issue for you, the PDF export function might work well as a solution.

You can use any PDF reader on the iPad. My personal favorite happens to be GoodReader (see Figure 21-6). It will actually also open your PowerPoint file directly, but there are some advantages to converting your presentation to a PDF:

✏ PowerPoint creates a PDF file with single pages for each slide in the presentation. GoodReader then presents each page/slide of your presentation as a full-screen image, and you can flick through slides one at a time as you would in a regular presentation.

✏ GoodReader allows you to annotate PDF files; you can select the Pen tool and draw on a slide with your finger or a stylus as you are presenting.

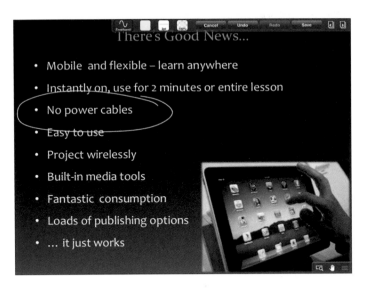

Figure 21-6: You can annotate PDF slides in GoodReader as you present.

Using SlideShark

If you don't want to convert your PowerPoint files or want to present them as closely as possible to their original version, consider using the SlideShark app and web service. SlideShark allows you to upload your PowerPoint file to a web-based account and then use the SlideShark app to present it on your iPad. Here's how it works:

1. **Go to the App Store, and download the SlideShark app on your iPad.**

2. **To sign up for the SlideShark web service, tap the Register button on the opening screen of the SlideShark app and sign up for a free account.**

3. **Upload your presentations.**

   After you sign up for an account at www.slideshark.com, you can tap the Upload button on your account page to upload your PowerPoint presentations to the SlideShark website. You can then download and present them on the SlideShark iPad app at any time. You can upload up to 100MB of files to your account.

   Note also that the newest releases of SlideShark now link to cloud services so you can retrieve PowerPoint presentations from your accounts at Box.net and Dropbox.

4. **To download and show your presentation, open the SlideShark app and sign in to your account.**

5. Download any presentation.

SlideShark does a fairly good job of preserving PowerPoint's animations, fonts, graphics, and colors; a release coming shortly promises to also play embedded video and allow slide annotation.

6. To show your presentation on your iPad as a PowerPoint file, tap or swipe up in the SlideShark viewer to progress through slides and animations; swipe left to go back.

One additional nifty feature is that when you swipe up, you get a thumbnail of each slide in your presentation and can jump to any slide or sort and change the order of slides (see Figure 21-7). You can even set it to loop and autoplay while you go out for lunch.

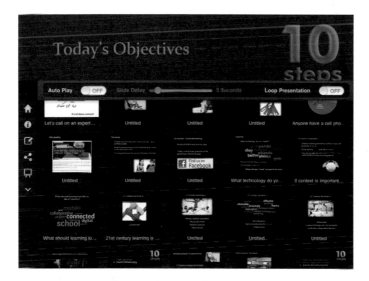

Figure 21-7: Swipe up in SlideShark and jump to any slide or reorder slides.

SlideShark recently introduced a wonderful new feature for those of you lucky enough to have an iPhone or iPod as well as an iPad. You can use your iPhone/iPod as a remote control device to manipulate the presentation on your iPad:

1. Tap the Remote Control icon on the left menu bar, as shown in Figure 21-8.

You're given a PIN number for remote control.

2. If you don't already have it, download the free SlideShark app on your iPhone/iPod.

3. **Tap to select the Remote Control option in the menus and enter your PIN number.**

4. **Swipe left or right on your iPhone/iPod to move forward and back and swipe upward to reveal all slides and jump to a particular one.**

Make sure you have Bluetooth turned on in Settings for both devices.

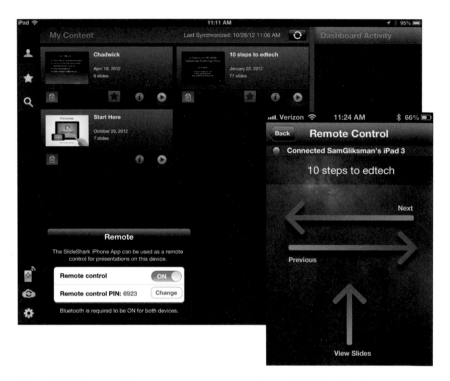

Figure 21-8: Use your iPhone as a remote to control your SlideShark iPad presentation.

22

Digitizing the Whiteboard

*I*f you've read a significant portion of the 21 chapters that precede this one, you know I'm not a fan of the "sage on the stage," frontal content delivery approach to education. It's unfortunate that large chunks of school technology budgets are used to invest in technology such as interactive whiteboards that primarily reinforce frontal teaching pedagogies.

Most of this book focuses on putting technology into the hands of students and empowering them to use it as a learning tool. Having said that, even the most student centric educational environments still need some amount of instruction. It can, however, be done relatively easily and inexpensively without the need to use large amounts of budget money for expensive digital equipment and projection systems.

In this chapter, I take a brief look at some options you have for projection. I also break down digital whiteboard apps into different categories:

✔ Apps that enable you to create content on your iPad and then project it on the whiteboard

✔ Apps that share whiteboard space so that students can contribute and collaborate on material being presented

✔ Apps that connect to and control a computer, enabling you to project the screen and giving you the option to mark up and interact with the content

In addition, I examine ways to record your presentation material in advance and also ways to record and archive whiteboard content for students to review at a later time.

Defining Your Projection Needs

"Defining your needs" is really stating the obvious, isn't it? It's what we should do before setting out on any important venture. It's also what so many people rarely do when it comes to purchasing and using technology. The basic question really is "What do you want to project and why?" Following are some typical responses:

- ✔ I'm teaching content that I want my students to remember so I want them to copy it from the board (biting my tongue).

- ✔ I want to have a way of facing and talking with the class while material is presented on the board.

- ✔ I want to review some text with the class so we need to look at it together.

- ✔ I want students to discuss and critique text while I annotate it.

- ✔ I want to show images and/or video during class.

- ✔ We need to browse and display the Internet.

- ✔ I want to display important information during class and record it for review later.

- ✔ I want to prepare and/or record materials ahead of class and then present it during class.

Determining your objectives will help decide what projection, hardware, and software you need. I've seen way too many schools rush out and invest heavily in expensive interactive whiteboard systems before really asking these basic questions and determining whether the whiteboards met their objectives.

Understanding Projection Options

You definitely need some form of projection. Your options include the following:

- ✔ **A portable projector that's rolled into a room on a cart:** It's inexpensive because one projector can service multiple rooms; however, it's cumbersome, not always available when you need it, and time-consuming to locate and start up. Sharing a cart isn't ideal, but if that's what your budget allows, you can make it work.

- ✔ **Ceiling-mounted projectors:** They can be controlled by remote and usually sit somewhere toward the front and center of the ceiling. The main problem with ceiling-mounted projectors is that you must make sure you are out of the projected area when you're at the front of the class.

✏ **Short throw projectors:** These are mounted right on top of the board that they project upon. They are a little more expensive than regular projectors, but you don't have the concern of blocking the projection and casting a shadow.

✏ **HDTV sets:** Becoming popular options, HDTV sets are easily cabled to a computer, and you can connect to them wirelessly with an iPad. The cost has come down and will continue to fall, and they tend to be more durable than projectors. They also don't have any bulbs to replace. You do need to be careful to purchase one that is large enough for the room in which it will be used. Also, check it out from the sides and corners of the rooms because those areas tend to have the worst vantage points, especially if students need to read from it.

Examine all your options and consult with an expert. Whether you just want to show the occasional video or really want a full-blown, expensive interactive whiteboard, you need to find projection that works well in your physical space and fits cozily into your budget.

Presenting on the board doesn't mean you have to be anchored to the front of the room. With the help of a relatively inexpensive Apple TV (around $100 and the size of a hockey puck), an HDMI cable, and possibly a cheap converter if the projector doesn't have an HDMI interface, teachers can roam around the class and wirelessly mirror their iPad displays at the front of the room. The coolest part about iPad mirroring is that you can have students project their own iPads to the AppleTV as well. That's a real bonus for collaborative activities and when you want students to share their work with the rest of the class. Consult the Apple website for more information about Apple TV: www.apple.com/appletv.

Creating Your Whiteboard on an iPad

Let me make one thing clear: We all have things we're good at doing and then there are skills that we . . . well, let's say we're more "challenged" when it comes to those skills. For example, when I try to write in small, delicate handwriting on an iPad screen, it looks like somebody spilled her lunch on it. If I had to project handwritten iPad notes to save my life, the best I might manage is to scratch out a large "SOS" onscreen.

Yet there are people who can happily write notes on the iPad and project something legible enough for a class to read. With the use of an iPad stylus and some inexpensive apps, you can write on your iPad while walking around the room — and even save your notes for posterity.

Your simplest app choices for simple digital whiteboards are probably the ones I discuss in Chapter 17 on screencasting:

- ✔ **ScreenChomp or ShowMe:** These apps are simple without a lot of frills. In both cases, you start the app and you get a whiteboard, writing tools, an eraser, and an image insertion tool. If you choose to, you can use the screencast feature to record the whiteboard interactions as you create them.

  I don't recommend using it for more than simple illustrations, maybe to demonstrate a principle in math, as shown in Figure 22-1. It's great, however, for anything that doesn't require too much space or complexity. If that's what you need, it will do the trick.

- ✔ **Educreations:** If you want the simple interface of drawing on a whiteboard but need a couple of more robust, additional features, Educreations — shown in Figure 22-2 — is one app to consider. It adds Undo and Redo features as well as a handy Text tool for typing text on the whiteboard instead of having to write with your finger or a stylus.

Not all iPad styluses are created equal. Some are best for drawing, some are best for writing, and others may be multifunctional. When you buy an iPad stylus that you intend to use for writing, make sure it has a small nib, is well balanced, and can produce sharp changes in directions and curves that typify writing.

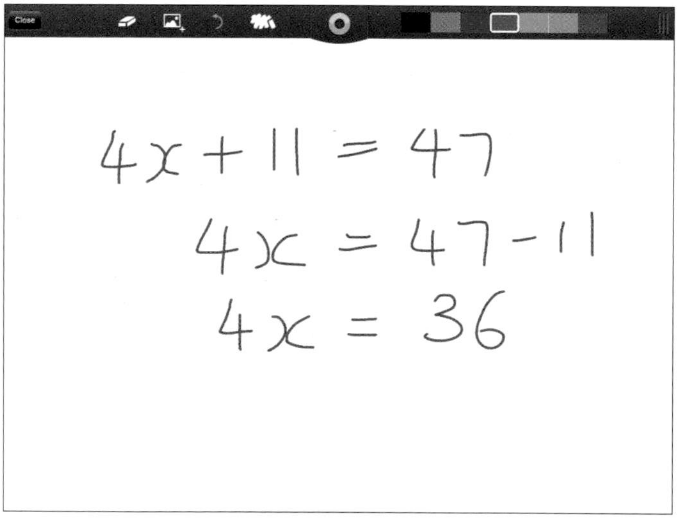

$$4x + 11 = 47$$
$$4x = 47 - 11$$
$$4x = 36$$

Figure 22-1: Create and record simple handwritten whiteboards with ShowMe.

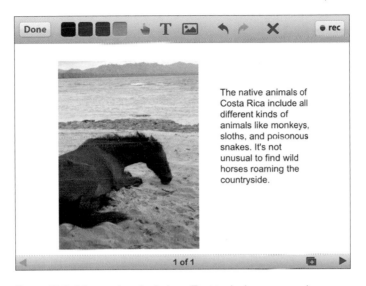

The native animals of Costa Rica include all different kinds of animals like monkeys, sloths, and poisonous snakes. It's not unusual to find wild horses roaming the countryside.

Figure 22-2: Educreations includes a Text tool when you need more precision and clarity.

Collaborating on the Jot! Whiteboard

Over the past few decades, classroom boards have gone from being blackboards to whiteboards and even interactive whiteboards. No matter what color or substance you use to make or write on them, they've become symbolic of pedagogy that emphasizes frontal teaching and content delivery. What if you could instead turn that whiteboard into a hive of collaborative activity? Some apps enable you to share your whiteboard with others in the classroom or even in remote locations over the Internet. For a few dollars, you can have an app that turns your classroom whiteboard into a space for collaboration and knowledge construction. Now that's a new type of whiteboard.

Jot!, shown in Figure 22-3, is a simple and fast whiteboard app that's available through the App Store. Jot! lets you start a whiteboard and share it in real time. In much the same manner as the iPad apps discussed in the preceding section, Jot! enables you to draw and show media.

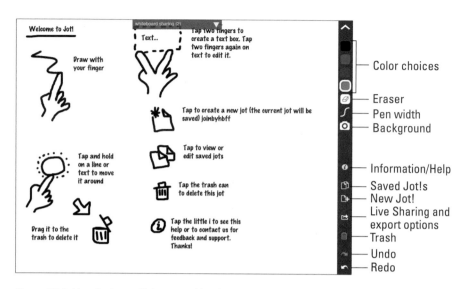

Figure 22-3: Use Jot! to collaborate with others on a common whiteboard.

Exploring Jot! features

The makers of Jot! kept the app simple to use without a lot of complicated menus to navigate. It enables you to

- ✔ **Draw or write.** Use your fingers or, if you prefer, a stylus.

- ✔ **Add text.** Add text boxes for typed notes — great for those of us with ten thumbs when it comes to writing on the iPad.

- ✔ **Add images.** Import photos or take a picture from your iPad camera.

- ✔ **Move items.** Select and move individual or groups of text boxes and pictures.

- ✔ **Use a Clipboard.** Cut, copy, paste, and duplicate.

- ✔ **Get creative.** Choose among 16 colors, 4 line widths, and 5 fonts.

- ✔ **Save when you're done.** Save your Jot! page to your photo library, e-mail it, or print it. Share it any way you want.

- ✔ **Share through Live Sharing.** Jot! is simple to use and looks great on the iPad. The standout feature that makes Jot! stick out from the crowd is a feature called Live Sharing. It gives you the capability to collaborate with other users locally or remotely in real time. Jot! works over the Internet so that users can share the whiteboard without the need to be on the same local Wi-Fi network. Share your whiteboard with the students in your class or students in another school or country. Imagine inviting an expert in another location to chat to your students via Skype while sharing the whiteboard in the front of the room with them. Help a student with homework after school by sketching on a common whiteboard or have students help each other. What an age we live in!

Using Jot!

To create a Jot! whiteboard session, follow these steps:

1. **Tap the Jot! icon to open the app.**

   If this is the first time you're using the app, it opens to the Jot! whiteboard tutorial.

2. **Open a blank whiteboard by tapping the + sign in the right menu; then start writing and drawing.**

   If you've used Jot! before, just tap the New Jot! icon on the top-left corner of the screen.

   Your whiteboard has a toolbar on the right side of the screen with tools and options you use to do the following things:

   • **Write, sketch:** To start writing or drawing, select a color and line width by tapping their icons in the menus. Use your finger or a stylus. Tap and hold a color to change it.

   • **Add typed text:** Tap with two fingers to create a text box. Your keyboard will automatically appear and you can start typing. Change font sizes in the pop-up menu above the text box and select colors in the menus on the side of the display. Tap anywhere outside the text box to close the editing tool, and tap it at any time with two fingers again to edit the text.

   • **Erase freehand drawings:** Use the eraser tool to get rid of anything you've drawn.

   • **Add images:** Tap the camera icon and select any image from your photo library, or take one with the iPad camera directly.

   • **Change Background:** Background options include plain, lined, and grid, which would be a great asset for graphing anything.

   • **Move, delete, copy:** Select any object by tapping and holding it for a second. An edit panel will pop up with options to move, drag it to the trash, copy it, change colors, and more.

3. **To complete your whiteboard page, tap the Saved Jots! (double page) icon to return to your list of Jots!.**

   The completed whiteboard is automatically saved within the app.

4. **Tap any Jot! in the list of Saved Jots! to open it for editing.**

To export a whiteboard, tap the curve- arrow icon and choose an option:

- ✔ E-mail as an image, PDF, or Jot! file
- ✔ Save to the iPad Photos app
- ✔ Print
- ✔ Through Live Sharing: At any point you can choose to share your white-board with anyone else who has web access. When you're ready to share, tap the curved arrow toward the bottom of the toolbar and select the Live Sharing option on top. You will be prompted for your name and a name for the session. Anyone with the Jot! app can enter the session name to join. You can also join through any web browser (see Figure 22-4) by going to http://jotwithme.com and entering the session name.

  Anyone can create or join a Live Sharing session for free, but to host a session, or collaborate during a session you must be a paid subscriber to the service.

An alternative to Jot! Whiteboard is ZigZag. It's designed a little more for business meetings and has excellent controls for monitoring participants, view options, whiteboard size, and more. It lacks tools for inserting typed text and images, making it a touch less adaptable for classroom use.

Figure 22-4: You can access and join a whiteboard session with any web browser.

Using the iPad as an Interactive Whiteboard with Doceri

You've probably heard the complaints 1,000 times over: The iPad is just for consuming media. The iPad doesn't display Adobe Flash or run Java. I can't highlight and annotate web pages or text like I can with the software for my interactive whiteboard.

As opposed to an interactive whiteboard that costs several thousand dollars, there's a small selection of iPad apps — such as Doceri (http://doceri.com), which I focus on in this section — that duplicate a lot of the functionality for $30 or less. Stop rubbing your eyes. That isn't a typo. Take a look at a couple of apps that can do the things you've been told an iPad can't ever do. They enable you to play Flash or run Java on your iPad, and they also duplicate many of the functions of an interactive whiteboard that other people have paid several thousands of dollars to purchase. Magic? Well, sit back while I pull a rabbit out of my hat.

My only complaint with Doceri is that it has so many functions, I can't cover them all in this one small section. (What a complaint, huh?) It's a remote desktop app, which mimics the functionality of an interactive whiteboard, and is also a screencast app.

Exploring Doceri's features

Download Doceri from the App Store on your iPad. If you plan on using Doceri in conjunction with a computer, you should open a browser on your computer, go to http://doceri.com, and download Doceri Desktop on your computer or laptop. Once the installation is complete on both your iPad and your computer, the two devices will find and recognize each other, enabling your iPad to control your computer.

Doceri connects you to a computer desktop from your iPad and enables you to control that computer as though you were using a mouse and keyboard. Open a document, web page (see Figure 22-5), or application — anything you have on your computer.

Figure 22-5: Doceri enables you to display and interact with your computer from your iPad.

Anything you can do sitting in front of your computer, you can now do remotely via the iPad as you wander around the room, including these tasks:

- ✒ **Drawing over presentations, web pages, applications, and more:** Doceri displays what's on your computer, and you can switch to Drawing mode and anything on your computer — whether a PowerPoint, Keynote, an Internet browser, or any other desktop application — can easily be annotated. Switch to Drawing mode during any presentation, and Doceri gives you a complete selection of tools to paint, mark up, highlight, insert images, and more. What's more, it records any actions you take while in Drawing mode on a timeline that you play back and edit.

- ✒ **Connecting to a computer or creating content directly on the iPad:** Doceri also lets you write and edit projects without being connected to a computer. Instead of displaying a computer, you can select a custom background for a whiteboard. Select different colors, types of graph paper, maps, and more. You can even create your own custom background. Now go ahead and use Doceri's authoring tools to create your presentation as shown in Figure 22-6. Your interactions in Drawing mode will be saved on a timeline that you can edit and play back.

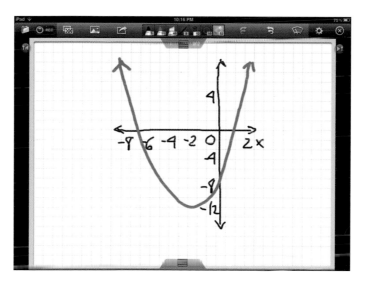

Figure 22-6: Use Doceri on its own as a whiteboard with any custom background.

In addition, you can prepare your lesson presentation in advance or present it live in front of the class. Using Doceri's timeline-based authoring platform, you can prepare your presentation in advance, edit, save, and replay it for your class at any speed. You can go back and work with your annotations, refine them, rearrange, clean up, and improve the overall quality of your screencast. Doceri also has a separate Record function that can capture and record all screen video and voice; you can also save your project as a movie to be shared.

Most apps enable mirroring of what you see on the iPad screen. Doceri shows only the actual drawing content; it doesn't display the onscreen controls (which can be extremely distracting). Also, Doceri's AirPlay output is always in landscape mode, and iPad rotations do not result in a rotated image on the AirPlay output.

As you can see, it could take several chapters to cover all the intricacies of Doceri. Given that this chapter is on digital whiteboards, I focus primarily on using Doceri as a live in-class presentation tool, either connecting it to a computer or running it on its own.

When you tap Doceri to open it, the opening screen, shown in Figure 22-7, offers you two choices:

- **From My iPad Alone:** Choose this option if
    - You are editing or playing a saved presentation.
    - You plan on using the built-in whiteboard and creating your own content.
- **Through a Computer:** Choose this option if you want to control, display, and annotate presentations, websites, applications, and more on a computer.

Figure 22-7: Doceri's opening screen asks whether you want to display from your iPad or through a computer.

If you connect to a computer, the next screen presents a list of computers it finds that are running Doceri Desktop. Note that Doceri Desktop must be started and running on the computer. Tap a computer in the list, and that computer screen should display on your iPad.

At this point, Doceri is controlling your computer. Use your finger to open applications, search the web, make annotations, and more, as shown in Figure 22-8.

Projects folder | Drawing mode | Resume last project | Disconnect from desktop

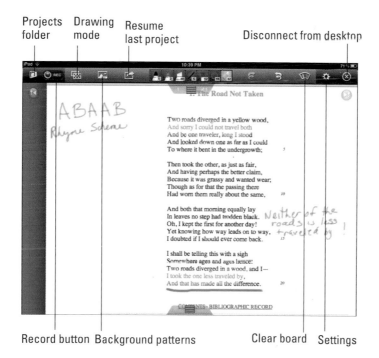

Record button | Background patterns | Clear board | Settings

Figure 22-8: Doceri connects and controls a computer that has Doceri Desktop running.

Connecting to a computer

When using Doceri through a computer running Doceri Desktop, you can open files, display web pages, open and use applications, and more. Additional features include these:

- ✓ Tap the keyboard icon whenever you need to type, and a full QWERTY keyboard pops up onscreen.

- ✓ Use the Record button to record your screen presentation into a movie. Doceri records the iPad display while also capturing your narration on audio.

- ✓ The QuickLaunch button lets you open any document on your computer with a single touch: images, website links, slide shows, movies, or any other material you want to access quickly and easily for your presentation or lesson. To add files to QuickLaunch, paste a shortcut to your file (document, image, movie, presentation, spreadsheet, PDF, and so on) directly into the Doceri directory on your computer's home directory.

- Tap the Drawing Mode button to switch to editing and annotating the content on your computer. You can use a highlighter, select a pen, and write on the screen to add shapes.

- The Background Patterns button switches you to authoring a whiteboard with the background that you selected.

Using Doceri with PowerPoint or Keynote

Doceri is often used to deliver PowerPoint and Keynote presentations. Save a shortcut to any file in the Doceri Home folder, and it will be available within QuickLaunch in Doceri. Switch to Drawing mode to modify and mark up presentations as you deliver them. It's sometimes a great idea to deliberately leave gaps in your presentation and then fill in the missing information interactively with your audience during the delivery of the presentation. By the way, Doceri has little arrows on the left and right that will advance your presentation when you tap on them.

Creating your own content with Doceri

Chapter 17 covers screencasting; when you create a project with Doceri, it becomes a full-featured screencasting app as it automatically records your presentation. You have two ways to create your own content (as opposed to presenting and drawing over your computer desktop):

- On the opening screen, select the From My iPad Alone option. Tap the + sign in the bottom-left corner to start a new project. You'll start with a blank whiteboard and a set of tools.

- If you are connected to a computer, you can tap the Background pattern icon on the top toolbar to open a new blank board.

Tap the Background Pattern icon to select a background for your board. It can be a simple color, texture, map, graphing paper, or something else. Use the tools along the top toolbar to write, illustrate, insert images, add shapes, and so on. Unleash your creativity!

Doceri includes a Wrist Guard feature, as shown in Figure 22-9. When you slide up the Wrist Guard, it enables you to rest your wrist at the bottom of the screen without the app interpreting the touch as a drawing stroke.

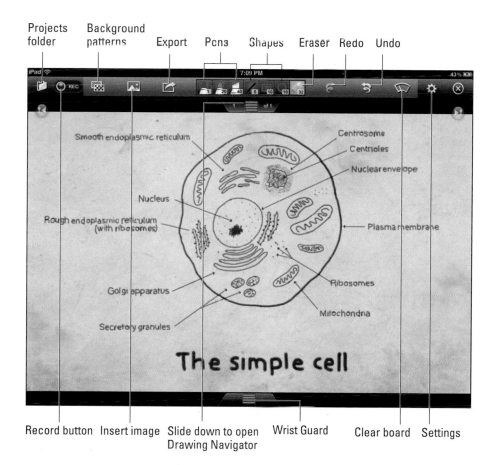

Projects folder   Background patterns   Export   Pens   Shapes   Eraser   Redo   Undo

Record button   Insert image   Slide down to open Drawing Navigator   Wrist Guard   Clear board   Settings

Figure 22-9: Doceri has a range of editing tools for creating content on your whiteboard.

Traveling through time with the Timeline

When you create a project in Doceri, it records each action you create in your drawing and it can be played back later as a presentation. You can replay all your annotations as they were written or reveal a section at a time by adding stops along the timeline. The following list explains the items shown in Figure 22-10:

- ✓ Tap and drag the Drawing Navigator slider down to reveal the timeline and other Drawing Navigator controls.
- ✓ The timeline enables you to see and access any point in your drawing.
- ✓ Drag the slider to traverse the timeline.

✔ Stop at any point in the timeline and make changes with the drawing tools.

✔ Tap the pushpin icons to add a stop in your presentation.

✔ The Playback Speed Control slider enables you to control the playback speed.

Splashtop Whiteboard is another wonderful app and certainly worth checking out.

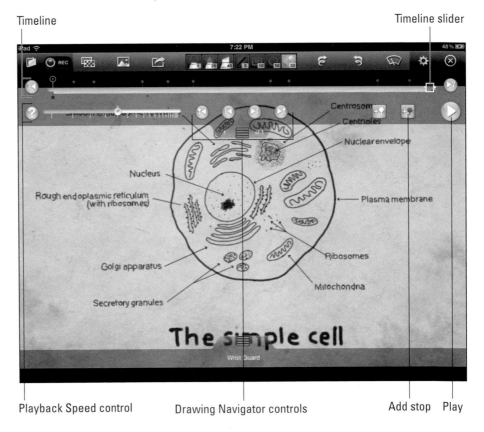

Figure 22-10: Edit your presentation and control playback speed with the timeline.

Part VII
The Part of Tens

In this part . . .

I save the best for last. Part VII begins with a chapter of essential apps for any educator. You won't want to miss it. Any iPad implementation requires some fundamental building blocks, so I give you ten key elements that are required for any successful iPad program.

Finally as an added bonus, the Appendix takes you into some actual classrooms where I have invited some creative educators to contribute their most innovative lesson plans using iPads.

23

Ten Essential Apps for the Educator's Toolkit

*W*hat's necessary — or essential — for someone living in the Arctic is different from what's needed by someone living on the beach in Tahiti. Okay, they're both likely to eat a lot of fish, but that's about as similar as it gets. The same principle applies when selecting a list of "essential" apps. Not the fish — the fact that a high-school algebra teacher is likely to have very different academic needs than a second-grade teacher. So before you shoot off that "Why on Earth would I need that app?" e-mail, let me explain that I'm listing apps that have widespread general usage and enable you to accomplish tasks that might otherwise be more difficult.

In this chapter I list and summarize helpful apps according to their category of usage: productivity, reference, professional development, utilities, content creation and handling, and news. The list isn't exhaustive by any means, and of course, everyone has his own individual preferences. It will, however, provide a good starting point for anyone wanting to expand his use of the iPad.

Keep in mind also that apps frequently come and go. Today's essential app becomes outdated very quickly, and the indispensable utilities one year from now may not even have been conceived yet. To that end, you'll find an updated list on my website — http://iPadEducators.ning.com — where new and essential items will constantly be added to the list of apps you might want to consider (whether you live in the Arctic or Tahiti).

More essential apps

The following is a list of essential apps that I discuss elsewhere in the book, with the chapter where you can find more about each:

- ✔ **Diigo:** Diigo is a social bookmarking tool that gives you the tools to collect content, highlight and annotate it, archive . . . and share it. See Chapter 6.

- ✔ **Evernote:** The dominant filing resource for anything and everything digital, Evernote lets you take notes, capture photos, create to-do lists, and record voice reminders. See Chapter 6.

- ✔ **Flipboard:** Offering a unique and beautifully designed alternative to browsing the web for news, Flipboard aggregates news into a personalized magazine based on publications you're interested in reading. See Chapter 6.

- ✔ **GoodReader:** GoodReader for iPad will link to your Dropbox account, your Google Docs, Box.net, SkyDrive, SugarSync, a FTP server, and a WebDAV server, and can even pull up all the attachments in your e-mail accounts! See Chapter 8.

- ✔ **iMovie:** Widely regarded as the premiere video-editing tool for the iPad, the version on your iPad 2 or higher isn't as robust as the version available for the Mac, but it's a very capable movie editor. See Chapter 14.

- ✔ **Notability:** A note-taking app for the iPad, Notability gives you the power to integrate handwritten notes, drawings, typing, audio, pictures, and PDF annotation all into one document. See Chapter 9.

- ✔ **Pages:** If you're even thinking of creating any document that rises above a simple text file, Pages is the app to purchase. See Chapter 9.

- ✔ **Printopia:** Install Printopia on any laptop or desktop computer, and your iPad will print anywhere it can. See Chapter 20.

- ✔ **Twitter:** Twitter gives you access to the latest content and opinions on any subject. Don't forget to drop me a tweet when you join: @samgliksman. See Chapters 6 and 8.

Pocket Informant Pro

We're all inundated with so much data and so many tasks, meetings, and general responsibilities that life can seem a little overwhelming at times. Pocket Informant Pro, or PI Pro, as it's known, is not the cheapest personal organizer in the App Store, but it's definitely one of the best. This productivity app is an all-in-one organizer that combines a full-featured calendar, task manager, notes, and contact management. It really shines in task management, where it enables you to define folders, tasks, subtasks, deadlines, tags, reminders, and more. Views are easily customized so that you can view tasks and calendar items however you need.

PI Pro, shown in Figure 23-1, will sync with services such as Google Calendar and Tasks, Toodledo, and more so that you can create and access your data from multiple sources. If you share a common sync source such as Google, you can share or assign tasks with other team members, friends, or family. You'll probably have about as much luck as I did when you're trying to assign tasks to your spouse.

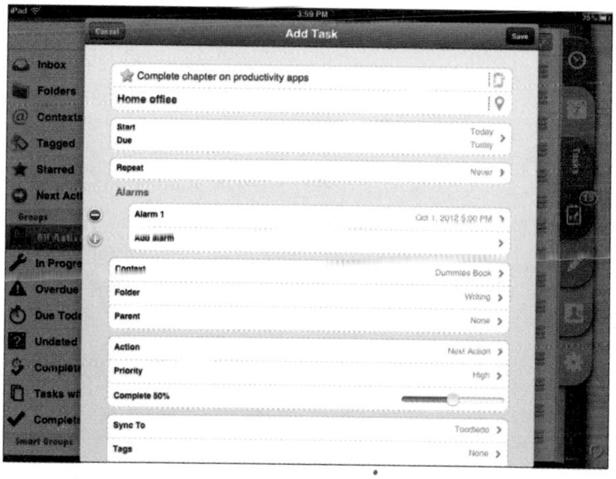

Figure 23-1: Pocket Informant Pro has a very robust task management system.

Pocket

There's so much information to read on the Internet that it's a full-time job just trying to keep up. You constantly run across pages and articles that you may need at some later time. Wouldn't it be great if you had an easy way to file and sort them? Pocket could be your solution (see Figure 23-2). The latest release of Pocket has certainly put it at least on par with Instapaper (I discuss Instapaper in Chapter 6) in terms of functionality, and it's extremely well designed and easy to use.

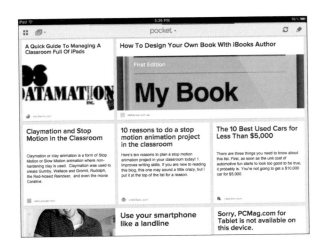

Figure 23-2: Pocket presents your archived content in an easy-to-navigate visual grid.

Add a button to your browser toolbar, and whenever you find something on the web that you want to view later, tap the button, tag the content, and put it in Pocket. Pocket automatically syncs content to all your devices and computers so you can view it any time — and you can even read it without an Internet connection.

Access your Pocket account directly over the web or through the various apps it offers for different mobile devices. The iPad app presents your content archive in a beautifully designed and easy-to-navigate visual grid. Tag and archive articles, videos, web pages, and more. Pocket also works with hundreds of other apps so that you can easily pocket items referenced in apps such as Twitter and Flipboard. You also get a personal e-mail address for your Pocket account so that you can send content via e-mail.

Google Search

Google is the web tool that has become so ingrained in our daily life experience that it's actually become part of our language. We no longer search for information on a topic — we Google it.

The Google Search app is a reference app that gives you that same easy access to the information on the web. In addition, the iPad Google Search app, shown in Figure 23-3, enables you to see search results and websites side by side to quickly browse pages and results. Swipe left and right to easily switch between the two. You can search by voice as well as typing, compare search results as web page snapshots in Instant Previews mode, use the Visual Search History to see past search results, and more.

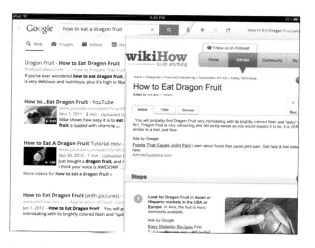

Figure 23-3: Swipe between side-by-side Google Search results and websites.

Dictionary.com

No longer those thick volumes you used to pull off a shelf, today's digital dictionaries provide access to millions of words and will even pronounce them for you. The app from Dictionary.com (see Figure 23-4) offers a complete English dictionary and thesaurus with more than two million definitions, synonyms, and antonyms.

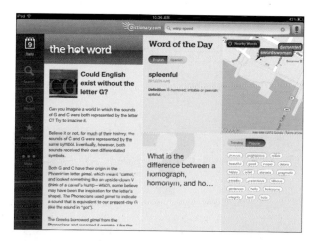

Figure 23-4: The Dictionary.com app provides both a dictionary and a thesaurus.

This reference app gives you offline access so that you can access most of the content even when you don't have an Internet connection. It uses the iPad's microphone and audio by offering search by voice and audio pronunciation of words. Standard dictionary features are included, such as sample sentences, spelling alternatives, and word origins. Expand your vocabulary with the Word of the Day, and shake your iPad to receive a random, surprise word at any time. My only criticism of the app is that it tends to nag you with all sorts of unexpected in-app purchases for additional functionality.

If you're fortunate enough to have a third-generation iPad or higher, you can also use Siri to help you spell and find synonyms. Just activate Siri by holding down the Home button and saying aloud, "How do you spell Mississippi?" I have to admit that Siri's not only pretty good at spelling, but she can recommend some pretty good restaurants for dinner as well!

Calculator Pro

Calculator Pro for iPad can be used as a standard calculator for basic operations (see the left image in Figure 23-5) or extended into a scientific calculator for more complex requirements, as shown on the right in Figure 23-5. Hold your iPad in portrait mode, and Calculator Pro for iPad is simple to use, with large, clear buttons for standard functions. A simple flip of your iPad from portrait to landscape mode turns the app into a scientific calculator, adding all those little funky keys for people who know how to use them — something I clearly haven't needed in a long time.

Figure 23-5: Calculator Pro becomes a scientific calculator when you flip your iPad to landscape mode.

Dropbox

There are many cloud storage services, and Apple has now entered the market with iCloud. Dropbox (see Figure 23-6) is the market leader and a great service for syncing documents and content across multiple devices. Just save or drop files into your Dropbox folder on a PC, Mac, or any other device. Take your iPad to class or a business meeting, or pull up a chair in the backyard, and open the Dropbox app. All your documents are synced across all devices and can be opened with a simple tap. Add any content to your Favorites list, and it will download for offline reading when you aren't connected.

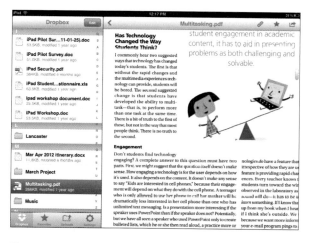

Figure 23-6: Use Dropbox to store and synchronize content among all your devices.

Dropbox is available as a share or export option in many popular apps and can be used to upload your photos, video, and other content. You can also share any of your Dropbox folders, making Dropbox an ideal tool for collaboration and communication. Use Dropbox folders to share work resources, project files, and photo albums with friends, coworkers, and family. Oh, and those little USB thumb drives you used for storing and moving files? They make great little building blocks when playing with the kids.

PhotoSync

We've all struggled with transferring files on or off an iPad at one time or another. When it comes to moving photos and video wirelessly, you can't beat PhotoSync. PhotoSync makes it simple to transfer your photos and videos to and from computers and other iOS devices. No cables, no e-mails, no file size limits, and no fuss. Open PhotoSync, select the photos and videos you want to transfer along with a destination device and computer (that also needs to have PhotoSync), and choose where you want to transfer your photos to (see Figure 23-7).

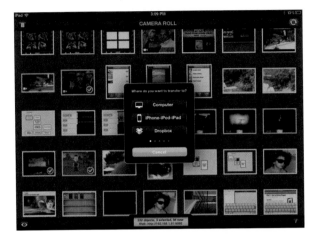

Figure 23-7: PhotoSync wirelessly transfers photos and video to any device or computer.

Pastefire

Essential? Maybe Pastefire isn't one of those "I can't live without it" apps, but this utility app, shown in Figure 23-8, is a real timesaver, and sometimes being very cool does count for something. So you found a really cool website on your desktop but you have to leave in two minutes. Sure, you could e-mail the address of the website and get it later on your iPad. Boring. Click the Pastefire icon on your browser, and the website address is sent immediately to your iPad or iPhone. What's more, Pastefire doesn't just copy content: It knows what to do with it. Pastefire knows it's a web address, so it opens the site in your mobile browser.

Find a phone number on a website, and you want to call it? Pastefire sends it to your iPhone and calls the number. That shirt you saw and really liked on the shopping website? Copy the image, and Pastefire puts it into your iPad's photo gallery so you have it when you go to the mall. Copy text, and Pastefire will automatically SMS or e-mail it.

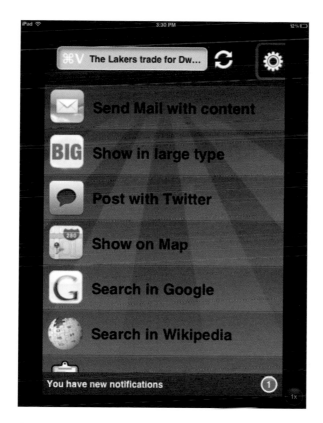

Figure 23-8: Pastefire copies content from a computer to iOS device and then acts on it.

Splashtop Remote Desktop

You're out there in the digital wilderness and realize that the file you really need is still on your computer desktop. The meeting starts in five minutes, and you could lose your job if this presentation doesn't go well. Okay, so I have a tendency toward the overdramatic, but there are lots of times you need your iPad to connect to your desktop and find files, use applications, or even just show something. Splashtop Remote to the rescue. Install the Splashtop utility app (see Figure 23-9) on your iPad and download the Splashtop Streamer on your desktop, and then you can access all your content from any device — anywhere, at any time. View and edit your files remotely, use software, watch movies, show a presentation, play music, and more. If your iPad doesn't play that Flash video you really needed to watch or show the class, use Splashtop to connect to your computer and show it that way!

Figure 23-9: Splashtop Remote connects and controls your computer from your iPad.

TED

The motto of the TED not-for-profit organization is "Ideas worth spreading," and it's certainly true. The acronym TED comes from Technology, Education, and Design, although the organization has now spread beyond those themes. I categorize the TED app under the professional development heading, and TED delivers on that: offering international conferences several times a year where innovators (see Figure 23-10) present unique and thought-provoking presentations. TED talks are captured on video and shared across the world via the Internet. Download the TED app to access the wide variety of incredibly fascinating and stimulating talks available on video.

Figure 23-10: TED presents videos of talks by fascinating and innovative people.

iTunes U

iTunes U gives you access to complete courses from leading universities and other schools — plus the world's largest digital catalog of free education content. Visit the iTunes U Library and subscribe to a course or just download content as needed into the iTunes app.

Whether you're a college student interested in political science, a high school student taking algebra, or an adult interested in learning how to program apps for the iPad, iTunes U (see Figure 23-11) is a valuable tool to help you learn any time, anywhere. Choose among more than 500,000 free lectures, videos, books, and other resources on thousands of subjects.

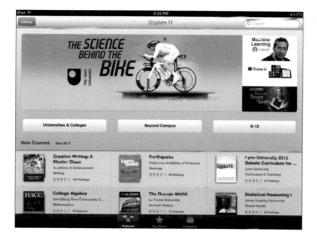

Figure 23-11: iTunes U is the world's largest digital catalog of free education content.

24

Ten Keys to Successful iPad Implementation

. . . .

In This Chapter

▶ Are you ready?

▶ Asking why you want iPads

▶ Identifying learning goals

▶ Learning management strategies

▶ Understanding that iPads aren't laptops

▶ Moving beyond "There's an app for that"

▶ Knowing when sharing doesn't work

▶ Planning for training and support

▶ Making connections

▶ Enabling the unpredictable

. . . .

*I*t seems that every school is considering purchasing iPads these days, and Apple has reported that iPad sales to schools are currently outselling MacBook sales by a very large margin. However, the rush to purchase iPads often precedes the careful planning and preparation that's so crucial to their success as educational tools. Technology alone is never the answer. Instead, iPad use needs to be integrated within a holistic approach to 21st-century education that encompasses a thorough and ongoing review of the skills and competencies required in our rapidly changing society and the educational processes that best help students acquire them.

Well-planned technology deployments can be tremendously successful and transformative for schools and students. In this chapter, I list ten vital components of a successful iPad implementation.

Determining Whether You're Ready

There's no point in purchasing iPads if you don't have the technical infrastructure to manage and deploy them. Consider the following questions before going down that road:

- Do you have adequate incoming Internet bandwidth to connect all the devices and use them at the same time? Remember that you may also need significant upload bandwidth as students start to create and deliver large media files.
- Is your wireless network robust enough to manage and distribute a strong, reliable wireless signal all around campus?
- Do your classrooms have safe, secure locations to store iPads?

Understanding and Communicating Why You Want iPads

This is the elephant in the room — the most critical question that is rarely discussed and evaluated from an educational perspective. It's imperative that the entire organization be on the same page. That requires a clearly communicated explanation of how iPad use complements your educational mission, which then needs to be clearly communicated to all the various constituent groups, including teachers, students, parents, directors, and administrators.

Targeting 21st-Century Learning Objectives

There's a natural inclination to stay in your comfort zone. Many teachers, especially older ones, prefer to stick to the methods they have always used in the classroom. An iPad program should take full advantage of the educational potential of the technology and be designed to address 21st-century learning objectives. That means integrating multimedia, communication, collaboration, project-based learning, and more. What point is there in purchasing expensive technology and then using it to reinforce outdated pedagogical practices such as frontal lecturing, content delivery, and drill and practice?

Developing Simple iPad Management Strategies

Research and document your plans for the following:

- Which responsibilities and processes are in place for buying and deploying apps? How will you decide what apps to buy, and who will be responsible for the purchasing?

- How will you manage user profiles? What restrictions will you enforce? Will you have one common student profile or vary them by class or group?

- What are your processes for system and app updates and data synchronization? How often will they be done and by whom?

- Would you consider allowing your older students to manage their own iPads? Have you considered the risks versus benefits of such a policy?

- Where and how students will store and submit work? Will you use cloud services such as Evernote or Dropbox? Will you create and/or use a WebDAV server? How will you students submit digital work to teachers?

- How will you deal with instances of damage and theft? Will you buy insurance? Under what circumstances, if any, will students be held accountable? Has this been clearly communicated to parents through a Responsible Use policy?

- How do you plan to create and use e-mail accounts? Will students be given e-mail, and if so, at what age? If not, will the iPads have generic e-mail accounts to enable outgoing e-mail of content from students to teachers?

Understanding That iPads Aren't Laptops

Many laptop programs use network servers and domain logins that also set permissions. Laptops are controlled and administrators can often view screen activity. It's important to remember that iPads are not laptops. There's no login, and the ability to secure and control them is minimal. If you're using iPads, utilize their unique assets. Look for ways to take advantage of their mobility, built-in camera, microphone, video, and so on. If monitoring and controlling activities are important criteria to you, it may be advisable to consider staying with laptops.

Overcoming "There's an App for That" Syndrome

You hear it all the time: "There's an app for that." One of the biggest mistakes teachers make is to constantly search for apps that directly address specific curriculum content — everything from 20th-century American history to the geography of California. Many great apps exist, but the real benefit comes from viewing iPads as tools that can be used as part of the learning process. Encourage students to create mock interviews with famous historic figures, explain scientific phenomenon with stop-motion animation, create podcasts for the school community, practice and record speech in a foreign language, create a screencast to explain a principle in algebra, and more. Given the opportunity, students will naturally gravitate toward creative and innovative iPad use if allowed to use it as a learning tool.

Knowing That Share and Share Alike Doesn't Work with iPads

You learned the value of sharing all the way back in preschool. Although it may be an important life guideline, you need to forget all about sharing when it comes to using iPads in school. iPads are designed to be personal devices; you need to protect your user login and all your personal data and files. Sharing them will create huge privacy and security issues. I generally push for 1:1 deployment of iPads from 4th grade upward. If that causes financial concerns, you need to discuss those concerns and either scale down your deployment or consider an alternative approach, such as allowing children to bring their own devices to school — which comes with its own set of problems, especially for families that cannot afford them. Sharing at upper grade levels, however, is not the solution.

Building an Ongoing Training and Support Structure

Deploying iPads is (I hope) a major step toward addressing the learning needs of 21st-century students. It also involves a major change in school culture. We're all naturally resistant to change. Organizational change requires adequate training and support. It's also important to stress that "training" doesn't mean that one day at the start of the year when you bring someone into school for a half-day workshop. Schedule time for ongoing training sessions throughout the year. Develop teacher support groups within your school and with other schools, where teachers can exchange experiences, share their successes, and learn from each other.

Connecting

The web has many helpful resources. You can easily connect and benefit from the knowledge and experience of other teachers. Join Twitter (www.twitter.com) or sites such as the iPads in Education network (http://iPadEducators.ning.com).

Enabling the Unpredictable

In other words, let them fly. Technology is most effective when used as a tool for student empowerment. Don't expect to control every aspect of students' learning. And you don't always need to be the expert. Technology is their canvas. Give them the freedom to paint their own masterpieces.

Just in case you have any doubt regarding my stance on the issue, I want to stress that I don't believe that all education should revolve around technology use. This book is all about appropriate technology integration. Sometimes that means not forcing the issue. There's no doubting the importance of using crayons and paints. Getting your hands dirty planting in a garden is an extremely valuable educational experience, and how can you ever replace the experience of having a teacher or parent read to a child? It's crucial to use technology wisely and creatively. Sometimes that also means knowing when to put it away.

Appendix

Modeling the iPad Classroom

· ·

Education is not the filling of a pail but the lighting of a fire.

— William Butler Yeats

*T*eachers around the world are starting to recognize the potential of technology to innovate and reform our educational systems. This is their chapter. It isn't easy when you have to deal with ever-increasing class sizes and work within the constraints of compulsory testing procedures. Slowly but surely, however, teachers are recognizing the transformative potential of technology to empower students and change the ways in which they learn. It's the recognition that education in the 21st century is about developing lifelong learning habits.

Chapter 11 takes a close look at a series of sample math and science lessons. This appendix presents a small additional sampling from teachers across all disciplines who are striving to use technology in unique and innovative ways. I'm extremely grateful for their participation in the book and for the work they do with children every day.

Learning Geography with Virtual Trips

Submitted by	Jenny Ashby, Epsom Primary, Victoria, Australia
Grade level	4th- to 6th-grade geography
Objectives	Learn about the geography of an area by creating the narrative of a virtual trip.
Apps/tools	iPad 2 and iOS 5.1 (minimum), Google Earth, Google Maps, iMovie

Geography is always best learned when you travel and experience locations firsthand. That usually isn't a practical possibility. However, with the aid of an iPad and an app such as Google Maps, students can travel the world without leaving their seats.

Students are given the challenge to travel from one major city to another while crossing at least three states along the way. Students are then required to create an oral narrative of their virtual trip.

Students use the Maps app to navigate from one city to another while taking screen shots along the way, including screen shots from street-view level. They research landmarks, geographical features, and land uses along the way. They then collate the various images they have collected into iMovie, adding visual effects and informative audio narrative. Last, a music track is added to enhance the atmosphere and mood of the production.

This project also could be used for creating virtual trips through a period in history or set in the future, where travel may be to a different planet!

Image courtesy Jenny Ashby

Designing the Next Space Vehicle

Submitted by	Leah LaCrosse, science teacher, Huron City School, Ohio
Grade level	5th-grade science
Objectives	Learn about a planet in our solar system by paying attention to specific planet characteristics, such as size, composition, orbiting moons, rotation speed, and presence of rings.
	Learn about NASA's previous exploratory vehicles, including rovers, satellites, probes, and bases.
	Design, build, and make a visual presentation for the next NASA exploratory vehicle for the students' planet.
Apps/tools	General apps: NASA, BrainPop, The Solar System, Planets, Dropbox, DrawingPad, iMovie, Keynote, StripDesigner, Blocks! Camera, Edmodo
	Websites: http://solarsystem.nasa.gov/planets/index.cfm
	www.nasa.gov/mission_pages/station/main/index.html
	http://marsrover.nasa.gov/home
	www.nasa.gov/mission_pages/hubble/main/index.html
	Numerous LEGO pieces, random motors, wires and wire strippers, light bulbs and holders, random wheels, various recycled bottles, boxes, egg cartons, electrical tape, and so on

The students were given the challenge to design and present NASA's next exploration vehicle. The time frame was one week, and students were required to use iPads, building tools, teamwork, and presentation techniques.

The Design to Explore lesson had three overall stages:

⟋ **Research.** The students used a variety of iPad apps and recommended sites to research the planet for which they would be designing a vehicle. Although students had previous knowledge of the planets, they needed to review specific planet characteristics such as size, composition, orbiting moons, rotation speed, and the presence of rings. These characteristics would help them design the vehicle (rover, satellite, probe, or base).

In addition, to get ideas of exploratory vehicles, they researched NASA's previous vehicles.

⌐ **Design/build.** After the preliminary research, students worked in groups to design their vehicle using the LEGOs and recycled materials. Students could use the app Blocks! to aid in the design process or just work hands-on with the materials. The groups designed a mission patch incorporating their vehicles, initials, and planet. For this, they used the DrawingPad app.

⌐ **Present.** In creating their presentations, students chose whether to use Keynote, iMovie, or StripDesigner apps. The presentations included information about the planet, the LEGO vehicle, and the mission patch; students were encouraged to add pictures or videos of their vehicles. Students presented their projects to the class as though they were NASA officials, deciding whether to adopt their ideas.

This LEGO project extended into a Skype call with astrophysicist Dr. Neil DeGrasse Tyson. During that call, the class sent samples of students' work and discussed their ideas for exploration.

Understanding Culture through Stories

Submitted by	Linda Buturian, senior teaching specialist, College of Education and Human Development, University of Minnesota
Grade level	3rd to 5th grade
Objectives	Understand culture and tradition.
	Foster pride in one's own culture and respect for others' cultures.
	Develop storytelling.
Apps/tools	iPad 2 and iOS 5.1, StoryRobe, StoryKit, iMovie

Digital stories are academically rich. Students go through processes similar to the development of a formal paper: brainstorming, incorporating research, narrowing focus, creating an outline (or storyboard), peer review, revision, and sharing the final project. In creating a digital story, students build knowledge about their topic and skills in media production, research, and communication. They make connections between their course work and the world around them.

Students are asked to create digital stories that are two to six minutes long — a short video that combines image, audio, and text to convey a narrative or concept. The culture in a story assignment asks students to create digital stories capturing a conversation with a family member or friend about a tradition or event related to a specific culture. Students integrate the digital story into a presentation they give to their classmates — a presentation that includes a culturally relevant artifact or object.

Creating a Digital Artifact with Real World Patterns

Submitted by	Lisa Johnson, TechChef4u LLC, Texas
Grade level	Kindergarten math
Objectives	Locate and recognize real-world examples of patterns.
Apps/tools	iPad 2 (with camera), iOS 5.1, Skitch, Strip Designer

Math and patterns are all around us. This activity captures patterns in the home using the iPad camera. The images are opened in Skitch and annotated to highlight the shape that created the pattern. Students then record their favorite pattern on a sheet of paper by drawing and labeling it. A photo is taken of the hand-drawn work. All images are imported into the Strip Designer app to showcase the pattern scavenger hunt in a comic form. Finally, the comic is e-mailed to the teacher as a PDF, and all student PDFs can be assembled in a class pattern book.

A lesson of this nature could be altered and achieved in a multiday station in which each part of the activity (for example, locating objects, annotating patterns, and creating a comic) could be completed separately.

Image courtesy Lisa Johnson

Broadening the Storytelling Experience

Submitted by	Julie Hersch, Temple Israel of Hollywood Day School, Los Angeles
Grade level	4th to 5th grades
Objectives	Develop a story as a thoughtful interpretation of a visual image.
	Broaden the traditional written story experience by combining it with a rehearsed oral reading.
	Develop students' ability to speak in front of an audience and present themselves confidently.
Apps/tools	iPad 2 (with camera), iOS 5.1, VoiceThread

A series of 15 images was hung on the wall, and students were not given any explanation for their presence (even though the display obviously piqued the curiosity of many of them). After two weeks, the students were asked to select one image that had some meaning to them and write a story about it.

VoiceThread is a multimedia presentation tool that enables users to share their final product with others and opt to allow comments on it. Students were asked to start their project by drawing an image on paper that represented why they had chosen a particular photo for their story. They scanned the image into a VoiceThread presentation and added a narration explaining the image to the teacher.

The next step was to write the story; students then were asked to rehearse the reading of the story. Students selected from a number of recording apps on the iPad and read the story out loud; students listened to the recording, noting which parts sounded good or needed improvement. Once they were ready, students scanned the photo they had chosen into a VoiceThread and then read their story.

Teachers often require students to write, and that remains an important basic skill. It's difficult, however, to allow them to develop speaking skills in class; that's why VoiceThread was an effective tool for this class. Next time, students might benefit from the process of providing feedback in a VoiceThread comment; others in the immediate school community could also listen to the stories and comment.

Image courtesy Julie Hersch

Documenting a Lab Experiment

Submitted by	Lisa Johnson, TechChef4u LLC, Texas
Grade level	6th- to 8th-grade science
Objectives	Document and review lab procedures.
Apps/tools	iPad 2 (with camera), iOS 5.1, Keynote, Pic Collage, Stop Motion, Snapguide, Coach's Eye

This lab showcased how you use the iPad throughout the scientific process to document learning and discovery. The teacher created an ePub or PDF file with directions and materials (and hyperlinks for all the apps used or sites needed) and shared the link with students to access and open in iBooks.

This particular lab focused on estimating the number of water drops that would fit on the head of a coin, but truly, any lab could be achieved using this process. Students used the Chart Data Editor in Keynote to create a table to make their observations and document their hypothesis for each coin. Students then worked in collaborative pairs to execute the water drop activity. One student dropped the water while the other student counted and captured photos and video. Students returned to Keynote to create another table of their results. To discuss their findings, analyze their hypothesis, and reflect on the lab, students recorded themselves using the iPad video camera. All these elements were then included in the Keynote presentation.

Creating a Music Video

Submitted by	Elizabeth Driskell, band director, Cedar Rapids Community School, Cedar Rapids, Iowa
Grade level	High school
Objectives	Create a music video that exercises skills in creativity, photography and filming, editing, lighting, sound, and more. Practice comprehensive planning and execution of a plan. Organize and complete a complex project within the allocated time frame. Foster teamwork.
Apps/tools	iPad 2 (with camera), iOS 5.1, Camera app, iMovie

Students were divided into groups of four or five students. They chose an appropriate song and concept and decided on which roles each of them would play: director, editor, cameraman, and actors.

Next, the group created a storyboard of their music video to guide their shooting. They shot and edited the video, and added opening title and credits. The project took about ten days to complete, ending with a screening party.

The students' work was evaluated using a rubric that included the following elements: creativity and style, film treatment, lyric sheet/shot list/script, sound quality, composition and framing, camera angles and moves, special effects, lighting, editing, and time management.

Stop-Motion Animation Storytelling

Submitted by	Rosamar Garcia, teacher consultant, Richmond, British Columbia, Canada
Grade level	4th to 12th grade
Objectives	Generate and communicate ideas, learn the fundamentals of storytelling, and develop a personal voice.
Apps/tools	NFB Pix Stop; generic storyboard templates; story-map template; chart paper; class-generated brainstorm chart on what makes a good story; plasticine or clay; figurines for creating characters; cardboard; paint; felts, pastel crayons, and colored papers; critic's evaluation form

Start by brainstorming with the class on the topic: "What makes a good story?" Look for stories that have interesting problems; characters the audience can care about; and a plot (beginning, middle, end) where a problem is presented, action developed, and issues resolved. Ask the students to provide examples of these elements from classic or familiar stories.

Divide the students into pairs or small groups to create a story map, and ask them to draw out the scenes they will be filming using a storyboard template. When the storyboard is complete, have the students use the art supplies (paint, pastels, felts, cardboard, plasticine, clay, paper, and so on) to create the characters and the scenery.

Before filming begins, explain the concept of stop-motion animation, in which objects are moved in small increments between shots and the shots are shown in fast sequence to create an animated movie.

TIP

Watch *La Boite,* an animated film by Coe Hoedeman, at www.nfb.ca/film/boite. Have students look at the film with a filmmaker's eye to collect ideas about creating special effects, camera angles, close-ups, and pans. Discuss how they might create one or two of these special effects in their own animations.

Start filming. Assign roles: iPad camera operator, someone to move the characters between the still shots, others to add scenery changes as necessary, and so on. Rotate roles so everyone gets an opportunity to perform the various roles.

When the films are completed, celebrate with a film festival, serving popcorn and asking the students to fill out a critic's evaluation form to critique the animations. Criteria could include each critic noting what he or she considers the best thing about the film; his or her favorite part, and mentioning a specific element that the film's creators did an especially good job on.

Encouraging Student Involvement in a Large Lecture

Submitted by	Florence Newberger, professor, Department of Mathematics and Statistics, California State University, Long Beach
Grade level	high school or college calculus
Objectives	Encourage student involvement and opinion in the lecture.
Apps/tools	iPad 2 (with camera), iOS 5.1 (or higher)

Writes Florence, "I teach a precalculus class of 270 students, meeting twice per week in an auditorium. I use my computer to project slides consisting of unsolved examples, and with the Doceri software and my iPad, I write on the slides, solving the problems.

Often, I ask students to solve an exercise from the notes at their desks. I walk up the aisles and look at some of the students' work as they engage in the exercises. I take my iPad with me on these expeditions, and using the camera feature in Doceri, take pictures of student work, and immediately project it up to the screen. With Doceri, I can then annotate and commend good work."

Index